COMPLETELY REVISED AND UPDATED

Nothing Down for the 2000s

DYNAMIC NEW WEALTH STRATEGIES IN REAL ESTATE

Robert G. Allen

FREE PRESS
New York   London   Toronto   Sydney

*f*P

FREE PRESS
A Division of Simon & Schuster, Inc.
1230 Avenue of the Americas
New York, NY 10020

First Free Press Edition 2004

FREE PRESS and colophon are trademarks
of Simon & Schuster, Inc.

The poem "The Reluctant Investor" reprinted from *The Reluctant Investor and Other
Light Verse* by Donald M. Weill, copyright © 1977 The Eldon Press.

For information about special discounts for bulk purchases,
please contact Simon & Schuster Special Sales:
1-800-456-6798 or business@simonandschuster.com.

Manufactured in the United States of America

1   3   5   7   9   10   8   6   4   2

Library of Congress Cataloging-in-Publication Data

Allen, Robert G.
    Nothing down for the 2000s : dynamic new wealth strategies in
real estate / Robert G. Allen.
        p. cm.
    Rev. ed. of: Nothing down for the 90's. c1990.
    Includes index.
    1. Real estate investment.   I. Allen, Robert G. Nothing down
for the 90's.   II. Title.
HD1382.5.A38.   2004
332.63'24—dc20   2004053680

ISBN 0-7432-6155-0

To my father, John L. Allen,
the greatest man I have ever known

Contents

Contents

CONTENTS

Nothing Down
for the 2000s

Second Chance

Thank you for reading the latest edition of *Nothing Down*. I was thirty-one years old when Simon & Schuster published the first edition of *Nothing Down*. Little did I know at the time that it would go on to become the all-time bestselling real estate investment book. It has sold well over a million copies and helped untold thousands buy their first home or investment property . . . and for hundreds, perhaps even thousands, earn their first million. (If you're one of those, please go to www.millionairehalloffame.com and log in your success story.) Although I've updated the book to reflect current laws and tactics, the principles in this book are timeless. The following phrase is still as true:

> Don't wait to buy real estate. Buy real estate and wait.

Real estate is the simplest, easiest, safest, shortest route to financial freedom. This is also as true today as it will be twenty-five years from now. If you want financial freedom, real estate will be a large part of your portfolio.

Although these principles are timeless, you and I are not. If you'll indulge me, just before you launch into this book, let me tell you about a lesson I learned recently that has caused me to be even more intent on getting this timeless message out to as many people as possible.

Time moves rapidly for all of us. For me, it almost came to a dead stop on March 15, 2003. On that day I was driving home after giving a speech to about a thousand beginning real estate investors at the Anaheim Convention Center (near Disneyland). It was a very rainy night and there were numerous accidents on Southern California's freeways that evening. At about nine P.M., just north of San Diego, my Lexus skidded off the freeway at full speed and smashed directly into a large tree. Miraculously, another motorist witnessed everything and called 911. It took the rescue crew over half an hour to extract me from the wreckage using the "jaws of life."

I was transported to the Scripps Trauma center in La Jolla where I spent six days in intensive care with my multiple injuries. Even though the airbags had deployed, I broke my left wrist, blew out a quadracep tendon in my right knee, had my scalp peeled back (probably by the rearview mirror) leaving a nasty scar on my forehead, suffered cracked vertebrae, a broken big toe, multiple bruises, cuts, and a serious concussion. They tell me that amnesia is common for someone who has had a close encounter with a tree at high speed. Mercifully, I have no recollection of the accident, the ambulance ride, the operations, and most of the first three days of the hospital stay.

In addition to the physical trauma, there were emotional issues to deal with. What goes through your mind when you realize that you were seconds away from death? It's all pretty heavy stuff. I have come through all of this and am healing nicely both physically, spiritually, and emotionally, although I'll probably have lingering pains and limps and other issues to deal with for the rest of my life.

So why bring all of this up at the beginning of a book on real estate?

When I look at the photos of my demolished car, I wonder how I could have escaped alive . . . or more important, why I was able to escape alive. (After serious consideration, I've decided to post the photos of my crashed car at www.robertallenrealestate.com.)

I feel as if this has given me a new lease on life—my second chance. The "old" Bob was too focused on unimportant things. The "new" Bob is more connected to heart and soul and love and people. I have so much love for Daryl, my amazing wife of twenty-six years, as she stood by me through such a frightening ordeal. When I became fully conscious again, it was wonderful to see my two older children, Aimee and Aaron, standing at the foot of my hospital bed, and then to receive a phone call from my youngest son, Hunter, who was at the time serving as a missionary in Brazil. I have so much love and respect for my business partners and associates for letting me take this extra time for "research." Thanks a million.

Finally, I thank God for this "accidental" wake-up call. I wouldn't wish the same experience on anyone else, but I pray that each of us can wake up to the new life that is possible—to leave behind the parts of our old selves that don't serve us and embrace the attitudes and feelings that lead to a new life and a brighter future.

I hope that you allow this book to be your mentor to a new life. As you read this book, I hope you'll be inspired to believe that you, too, deserve a second chance—a life of financial freedom and prosperity. I hope you'll read this book and be empowered to learn techniques and strategies that will move you more quickly toward what you want. I hope you'll find yourself saying, "I can do this."

I've intentionally written *Nothing Down* in layman's terms (because that's who I was when I made my first million). Yes, you can find more technical investment books—and I encourage you to read them—but this book is designed to reach the part of you that has always known you were destined to be financially successful. There is so much you can accomplish in life, you don't have to be held back by a lack of finances. Besides, real estate investing can be a lot of fun (mixed with a modicum of frustration to keep you humble).

The mere fact that you picked up this book tells me that you are blessed (or perhaps afflicted) with an entrepreneurial spirit. While in Hawaii a few years ago, as I sat at the breakfast table on the outdoor patio, a swarm of little tropical birds flitted anxiously around my table chirping and begging me to share some of the crumbs from my breakfast muffin. I flicked a few crumbs off the table and they attacked the crumbs as a flock. I wondered if there was an entrepreneurial bird among them, so I placed a large chunk of juicy muffin on the edge of my table. The flock flitted about, chirping and screeching, but not one dared land to enjoy the moist morsel. For several minutes nothing happened, and then finally one of them landed on the farthest edge of my table. He glanced out of one eye at me . . . very leery, skeptical, skittish . . . and out of the other eye at the prized muffin. He moved his way, ever so carefully, toward the muffin and finally began to pick at it, retreating from time to time to enjoy his luscious treat and then returning for more. And then he did something unexpected. He purposefully dragged the muffin off the table so the other birds could enjoy it. This was apparently an enlightened bird, willing to share his plenty with his feathered friends.

I hope you will become like that little bird, and dare to do things the other birds won't do. If you do, you will eat well all of your days. Just remember to share some of your well-deserved excess. Moreover, teach other birds how to do the same. There's plenty for all of us . . . if we're just courageous enough to go get it.

As long as I continue to breathe, I'll continue to teach as many people as I can that we are all destined for greatness. Regardless of what other people may have told you, I know you can become financially successful.

I wish you well. I hope that someday we can meet and that you can tell me, "You know that little bird? Well, that's me."

Have a great life.

CHAPTER 1

You Can Still Make a Fortune in Real Estate

"I am twenty-three years old with zero experience and less credit. After applying Bob Allen's techniques, I was able to buy $915,000 worth of properties with no cash out of my pocket and achieved a cash flow of over $85,000 in my first year of investing!"

—JOSEPH BELMONTE

Back in 1492, Christopher Columbus launched the greatest real estate venture the world has ever seen. Using money borrowed from Spain's rulers, King Ferdinand and Queen Isabella, Columbus discovered the vast undeveloped lands of the New World and claimed them for Spain. Within a few short decades, Spain became the richest nation in Europe and Columbus achieved undying fame. Not bad for a once-penniless Italian seaman.

Today, real estate is still the most powerful wealth-producing tool in the world, with countless opportunities for you to build your personal fortune. And just like Columbus, you can use money from other people to help you do it. Do you want to retire at age fifty? Or forty? Or even thirty? How about paying for your child's college education, taking a luxurious trip around the world, or supporting your favorite charity.

Whatever your financial goals, this book can help you discover the fabulous "New World" of real estate; it will guide you along the path to building your personal fortune. For more than twenty-five years, my Nothing Down program has produced one millionaire after another. Each winter, they go skiing in the Swiss Alps or relax on the beaches in Barbados. Maybe next year you can join them!

I can tell you from personal experience that it doesn't matter whether you've saved $1,000 or $10,000 or $100,000—or if you're still trying to balance your household budget each month. My Nothing Down program has been proven to work over and over again. Best of all, it works whether the real estate market is going up, down, or sideways.

So, if investing in real estate is the ideal way to achieve the American dream, why are there still so many Americans who are trapped in dead-end jobs, worried about the next round of corporate layoffs, or struggling to pay their monthly bills?

Studies show that about two thirds of Americans will live from paycheck to paycheck until the day they die. Many of them earn a nice living because both spouses work. But that's not financial freedom. Only about 10 percent of us achieve a true measure of financial security. And only 3 percent break into the blue sky of true financial freedom.

In my seminars and talks around the country, I've found that there are three reasons why more Americans haven't achieved their financial dreams:

1. Most people don't believe it's possible to become wealthy.
2. Most people don't have a specific plan for building a personal fortune.
3. Most people aren't willing to do something *now* to make their dreams come true.

Too many people are simply unaware of the incredible opportunities all around us. Some are saddled with outdated beliefs. Others find it hard to change their spending and saving habits—even if it's clearly a change for the better. But unless you change your outdated beliefs, create a specific plan for your finances, and take action now, you will never take true control of your life. If you drift through life, others will make your decisions for you.

I once saw a television commercial portraying an elderly gentleman standing on the docks in New York City. Behind him, in the harbor, a beautiful ocean liner is putting out to sea filled with rejoicing vacationers. The old gentleman looks directly into the camera and says: "When I had the money, I didn't have the time. Now, I have all the time in the world, and I don't have the money."

You don't have to live from paycheck to paycheck for the rest of your life. You don't have to retire broke. You don't have to believe that "it takes money to make money" or that "the rich get richer and the poor get poorer" or even that "money talks." You can create your own wealth—and use it for whatever you want. This I know for certain.

Are you substantially better off today than you were ten years ago? If you are, it's because you looked at your beliefs, made a plan, and acted on it.

But let's face something right now. In order to make it financially, you're going to have to become a lifelong investor. There just isn't any other way. The lottery isn't going to bail you out. Forget about winning a million in a game of chance and concentrate on making it the good old-fashioned way.

So, let's get right to the basics. I call it the "Spend or Save" theory.

Spend or Save

In simple terms, the theory states that each of us has a limited amount of income (in case you hadn't noticed). We may spend our precious dollars on consumer goods—fancy cars, home theater systems, and other disposable items that depreciate and lose value over time. Or we put money aside for the future—investing in stocks, bonds, precious gems, gold, land, or real estate, all of which we hope will grow in value.

As you know, the more you spend, the less you are able to save. And if you decide to become an investor, every day you will face tough decisions about spending. But remember, it takes "saved" money to make "spending" money. In this world, the savers get richer and the spenders get poorer.

Not too long ago, a couple came to me with a tough decision. They had received a $100,000 windfall and were agonizing about how to spend it. They wanted to buy new furniture for their home, a new car, and a few little luxuries for their children. I convinced them to hold off for a bit longer and to invest the windfall dollars in a small apartment building a few miles from their home. Three years later they had more than doubled their money. It was a small sacrifice, but it paid off big.

To be financially independent, you will probably need to change your current spending habits and think more about where you want to be ten years from now. While there are few guarantees in the world of investments—which can go up or down in value—unless you get into the investment game, you'll never have a chance to achieve a life free of financial worries.

And when it comes to investments, real estate is clearly the safest way for the beginner to get started on the road to financial freedom. The journey to financial freedom begins with buying your own home—undoubtedly, the best investment that millions of us have ever made. Take a look at home prices in your neighborhood today, then look back to the past. In 2000, the median U.S. home price was about $150,000; in 1990, the median home price was about $100,000; in 1970, the median price was about $23,000. That's a truly remarkable long-term performance. A little later in this book, I'll talk more about buying your first home and how private mortgage lenders and the U.S. government will help you buy it for virtually nothing down!

But for now, I want to focus on real estate investing in general. Before you consider buying an apartment building, a shopping center, or a vacation condominium, you need to know how to maximize your potential profit. You need to know the rules of the game so you can make smart decisions about your purchases. You need to know how to use money from other sources to buy real estate with nothing down. And you need to know when to sell your properties and move on to something better.

Although I introduced the concept of Nothing Down back in the early 1980s, I remain firmly convinced that real estate is the right investment for those of us who have long-range financial goals like a comfortable or luxurious retirement. Even though real estate prices have climbed considerably in the past decade, I'm convinced that real estate is still one of the true bargains on this planet. Sure, there will be ups and downs in the market from year to year, but there is still incredible potential for long-term growth.

That's because:

1. People like to sleep with a roof over their heads.
2. Young families keep making "tricycle motors." (Think about it.)
3. No one has found a way to manufacture vast quantities of vacant land near major cities.

Seriously, can you envision a time when people won't be buying and selling real estate? Can you envision a time when people won't want to be financially independent? Of course not. That's why I am so confident about the bright future of real estate. As long as people need roofs and families grow kids, real estate of all kinds will be in demand. Even in an economic depression, people still need shelter and families will still be raising children. And there's only a limited amount of land to go around.

It is *completely* plausible for you to retire wealthy from your real estate investments. Thousands upon thousands of my seminar graduates have done so over the years. For example, a retired couple in Arizona earned more from real estate in three years than they had earned in an entire lifetime. A young woman in California left a job that paid a high salary because she was earning too much money (and having too much fun!) investing in real estate. Starting from almost nothing, a man in Florida made a million dollars from real estate in less than three years. Like thousands of courageous investors from coast to coast, you can take matters into your own hands by buying your first piece of investment property. My system works!

As you read these words, thousands of people just like you are investing in choice investment properties using the principles outlined in this book. It's time you joined them in the real estate game!

CHAPTER 2

Creative Solutions to
the Money Problem

"Sometimes, you don't believe that you can buy real estate with no money down. I was one of those people until after taking Bob Allen's seminar. As a real estate student, I found an investor who was willing to hold the financing for me. I bought a property from him and received money at the closing. I'm now working on a second property!"

—MICHAEL DI CARLI

Why would anyone want to buy real estate with little or no money down?

First, the smaller the investment in terms of your down payment, the larger the return you will enjoy because of the power of leverage.

Second, most of us don't have much money, if any money at all, for making investments. And this is the most compelling reason behind the nothing-down philosophy: We have no other choice.

So, regardless of the state of your bank account, it's time to get started on your journey to financial independence. The real estate investment world is still open to you if you understand money and if you know how to make money (or the lack of it) work for you.

Consider a building that is selling for $200,000. The seller wants $20,000 down.

The property is a great investment as it stands, but there is one glaring problem: You don't have $20,000 sitting around waiting for the right deal to come along. The majority of us barely have enough money in savings (if we have any savings at all) to buy a new television or lawn mower. Obviously, we'll have to come up with some rather creative solutions.

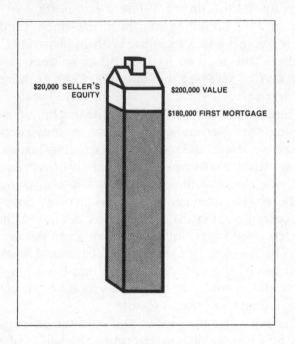

After many years of success in the investment world, I have found there are only a few basic sources for creative down payments:

1. Cash saved up by sticking to a tight household budget (the hard way).
2. Mortgages used with all parties involved, including the seller.
3. The use of rent and deposits involving the subject property.
4. Short-term borrowings from banks, mortgage companies, or other lenders.
5. Long-term borrowings from banks, mortgage companies, or other lenders.
6. The equity in other properties you own.
7. Partners who have the cash or the credit rating necessary to provide you with funds in exchange for a share of the profits.

8. Options that let you tie up the land until you can raise funds for the down payment.

The first source is up to you. You must begin to save money. Limit your current consumption of those little luxuries of daily life—a cappuccino, a new pair of shoes, an expensive bottle of wine—in favor of saving for the future. While it's important to live within your means and start building your own investment fund, you can't wait years for your savings to grow. With today's rates, that could take decades! You need to look at other sources to obtain the $20,000 needed to purchase that building. Let's examine the other areas open to you.

Meanwhile, you must realize that the nothing-down concept involves using borrowed money. This money may come from the seller himself or from banks or from partners—just as long as it doesn't come from your own pocket. This process requires a creative mind, one that is willing to try any solution. Basically, it is a process of borrowing yourself to wealth using other people's money.

The process of creativity is a mysterious and interesting one. It is brilliantly described in the following story, from Alexander Calandra's book *The Teaching of Elementary Science and Mathematics*. A student refused to parrot back what he had been taught in class. When the student protested, Calandra was asked to act as arbiter between the student and his professor.

"I went to my colleague's office and read the examination question: 'Show how it is possible to determine the height of a tall building with the aid of a barometer.'

"The student had answered: 'Take the barometer to the top of the building, attach a long rope to it, lower the barometer to the street, and then bring it up, measuring the length of the rope. The length of the rope is the height of the building.'

"A high grade is supposed to certify competence in physics, but the answer did not confirm this. I suggested that the student have another try at answering the question. I gave the student six minutes, with the warning that his answer should show some knowledge of physics. In the next minute he dashed off his answer, which read:

"'Take the barometer to the top of the building and lean over the edge of the roof. Drop the barometer, timing its fall with a stopwatch. Then, using the formula $S = \frac{1}{2}at^2$, calculate the height of the building.'

"At this point, I asked my colleague if he would give up. He conceded, and I gave the student almost full credit.

"In leaving my colleague's office, I recalled that the student had said he had other answers to the problem, so I asked him what they were.

"'Oh, yes,' said the student. 'There are many ways of getting the height of a tall building with the aid of a barometer. For example, you could take the barometer out on a sunny day and measure the height of the barometer, the length of its shadow, and the length of the shadow of the building, and by the use of a simple proportion, determine the height of the building.'

"'Fine,' I said. 'And the others?'

"'Yes,' said the student. 'Take the barometer and begin to walk up the stairs. As you climb the stairs, mark off the length of the barometer along the wall. You then count the number of marks, and this will give you the height of the building in barometer units. A very direct method.

"'Finally,' he concluded, 'there are many other ways of solving the problem. Probably the best,' he said, 'is to take the barometer to the basement and knock on the superintendent's door. When the superintendent answers, you speak to him as follows: "Mr. Superintendent, here I have a fine barometer. If you will tell me the height of this building, I will give you this barometer." ' "

Creativity is born when you have a problem to solve. And as you can see from this story, there are many ways of solving a problem. Creativity is the art of looking for solutions that are out of the ordinary, different, unorthodox.

Most of us spend countless hours trying to solve ordinary problems in the same old ways. We enter school at age five and exit some years later with hardly the bare essentials we need to solve problems. We have usually been drilled to see only the *obvious* solutions; we haven't learned to dig just a little bit deeper for fresh ideas. We haven't learned to devise creative solutions to both ordinary and complex problems.

Consider, for instance, the most common problem of every real estate investor: lack of investment capital. Some of us don't even have enough cash to make an initial investment. To make matters worse, most of us have been trained to believe that it is impossible to buy real estate unless we have cash down payments bursting our bank accounts wide open. So most of us, lacking that kind of bank account, never even *try* to invest.

There are other solutions to the cash problem. These solutions require creative thinking. Some of the solutions presented in this book will appear ridiculously contrived. That kind of thinking, though, is a trap. Don't let it muddle your creativity. Be concerned only with whether or not the solution will work.

Stretch your mind to new dimensions. Begin to be creative. To do these things, you will have to make a firm commitment to the following:

Positive thinking. Positive thinking solutions require positive thoughts. If you continually tell yourself "It can't be done," you will find exactly that. It can't be done. Creativity is born and nurtured in an environment of "can do" thoughts. It *is* possible for you to buy hundreds of thousands of dollars' worth of real estate in your own area. I have done it with little or none of my own money. Each year the graduates of my seminars buy hundreds of millions of dollars' worth of real estate. You can, too.

Broadmindedness. Regard the obvious real estate solutions, such as large cash down payments, as only a small percentage of the solutions that will ultimately work. Look for these solutions as a prospector looks for gold. They are just as precious as gold to you, because they will enable you to buy real estate without having to invest the cash you either don't have or don't want to spend. Whenever someone says, "I must have cash," dig deeper for a better solution. This book will show you how.

Disdain of the ordinary solution. Develop a healthy disdain for the ordinary solution. Try your hardest to practice creative solutions whenever possible. Deal with buyers and sellers who are creative. You can learn from them.

Brainstorming. Discuss your problem. The real estate agent, the seller, the seller's attorney, and anyone else who could have an impact on the decision to sell or buy should be involved. Search for solutions other than using your own cash. Ask probing questions. Forget that investing your own cash is even a solution.

Deep thinking. Ponder. Don't give up—you'll learn the excitement of flashes of creative genius.

Cultivate a creative mind. Treasure it. Some people will tell you that the only avenue that leads to successful real estate investments is paved with cash. Don't believe it. You will eventually run out of cash—probably very soon. You'll never run out of creativity. Plunderers can rob you of your cash, no one can steal your creativity. Cash loses value. Creativity never will.

It is your most vital asset.

Commit to it now.

CHAPTER 3

They're Not Making
Any New Land

"My biggest, quickest, and easiest profits were on two homes in rural areas unfamiliar to me. I told the sellers my fear of the slow market in rural areas, and said my best offer is such and such. I was pleasantly shocked that the sellers just wanted to cash out. The amount of cash was not the criteria. I was able to resell the homes quickly for a profit of $60,000 on one and $35,000 on the other."

—NEELD J. MESSLER SR.

Back in the Middle Ages, struggling inventors tried to make a perpetual-motion-machine—a device that would keep moving forever. The quest failed because it tried to break the laws of physics. But in the twenty-first century, smart investors have discovered something even better: a "money machine" based on the universal laws of supply and demand. This very practical way of producing money is called investment real estate.

Every year, it seems as if demand for real estate goes up. Young families are having children, more newcomers are coming here, and even older people are looking for new homes and new lifestyles. But while demand is constantly increasing, the supply of real estate is limited.

What *is* real estate? Real estate is the home you live in. It's the building you work in. It's the factory or warehouse you see next to the freeway. It's the store where you shop. It's the community center where your children play. It's the field where your uncle plants his wheat crop. It's where you park your car. It's the mountain cabin or beachfront condominium where you spend your vacation.

The common denominator of real estate is land—and land is everywhere. Well-selected real estate almost always increases in value. Why? Because, as Mark Twain put it, "They ain't makin' any more land."

But certain kinds of real estate are a better investment than others. Some types of land are more valuable, and have a greater potential to grow in value, than others. Here's a story to illustrate my point.

Three wealthy old poker buffs were playing a very important game. The stakes were high. After several hours of playing, there came a hand in which all three had been dealt excellent cards. The betting increased, and finally each of them ran out of cash and began to gamble with the deeds to their various real estate holdings. A rancher from Montana began the last round by pledging his entire fifty-thousand-acre ranch, including all of his cattle and equipment. An oil baron from Oklahoma met the challenge by pledging his two thousand acres of oil-producing wells with all of his oil derricks and equipment. A wealthy New Yorker ended the bidding by putting his one building into the poker pot.

"One building!" gasped the other two players. "Here we have pledged thousands of acres, and you expect us to accept your building?"

"Sure," replied the New Yorker. "My building is right on Fifth Avenue in midtown Manhattan."

Obviously, the value of land can vary from "dirt cheap" to "astronomical." But high demand and a short supply usually means a higher sales price, and a higher probability that the property will continue to rise in value.

While financial opportunities exist for every type of real estate, the best choices are different for beginning, intermediate, and advanced investors. Therefore, in considering a real estate investment, you need to understand the pluses and minuses of the following four major categories of land.

1. *Undeveloped land.* Located far away from metropolitan centers, this type of property has no immediate potential for development. In fact, about the only thing this kind of ground is good for is holding the earth together.
2. *Recreational land,* such as forests or mountains. This type of land has legal restrictions that prevent it from being developed or being used for anything other than recreation or conservation purposes. Unless you are a seasoned investor, stay away from recreational property.
3. *Agricultural land.* Unless you're planning to become a farmer, this type of land is usually less than an ideal investment. Many farms have restrictions that require the land to be used for agricultural purposes rather than for commercial development.
4. *Urban/suburban land.* Virtually all real estate investors focus on some type of urban or suburban property. This land is valuable because it is located in a town or city with a significant number of people. Those people need homes, stores, offices, warehouses, and apartments. This is the kind of property you should consider for your Nothing Down investment strategy. With this kind of land the factors of supply and demand will almost always be working in your favor.

Think of Income

For the beginning investor, the safest investment is a property that produces some type of income, especially if you're making an investment with little or nothing down. Income-producing properties come in all shapes and sizes, including rental homes, apartment buildings, vacation condominiums, office buildings, shopping centers, hotels, motels, rest homes, warehouses, and industrial parks.

By definition, income-producing property is any kind of real estate that is rented out to a tenant: an apartment building, rental home, commercial retail space, office building, or industrial-warehouse building. The tenant pays you a monthly or quarterly rental amount that should be enough to cover your mortgage payment, pay your operating expenses, and produce a small cash flow as a return on your investment.

Of these types of properties, rental homes and apartment buildings typically offer the least risk and require the least amount of expertise. There are three important advantages to income-producing residential properties that make them highly desirable to an investor like you.

First, there is usually a fairly sizable pool of homes and apartments in most urban and suburban settings. That gives you more properties to consider as possible purchases, and may provide you with an advantage later on when negotiating with the seller.

Second, the volume of sales of residential properties is much higher than for commercial properties. That makes it easier for you, as an investor, to determine the market value of the house or apartment building. Knowing the market value is essential in recognizing a true "bargain" when it comes on the market and in preparing your offer to purchase the property.

Third, it is easier to obtain a mortgage loan or get other financial help in purchasing a residential property. Lenders generally see the risks as lower than in buying an office building, shopping center, or warehouse and are more likely to approve your mortgage application. If you're seeking money from family and friends—or using one of the creative approaches we'll get to in future chapters—it's easier to build a convincing case.

Within the residential investment arena, you may be able to make a great deal of money by finding older homes or poorly maintained apartment buildings, adding fresh carpeting or a coat of paint, and giving the property a general facelift. If all goes well, you can turn around and resell the property for a much higher price to a new buyer. This type of investing is called the "fixer-upper." While it's a great way to make money in a relatively short time frame, it does take a dedicated individual who knows something about fixing up buildings. Personally, this is not my cup of tea. In fact, I can barely tell which is the right end of a hammer.

But there is a type of investment that is universally beneficial, whether or not you have the special training and personality to fix up run-down real estate, and that is choosing well-constructed residential properties in a growing area. The long-run appreciation from such an investment may be slow, but it will be steady and relatively predictable. And it does not require a lot of supervision or work to bring such a building up to usable standards. Don't be frightened away from investing in real estate because you don't understand a thing about repairs. Just buy solid property at a bargain price and hang on to it.

Your first purchases of income-producing property will give you the knowledge, experience, and confidence you need to venture into other areas, such as business and commercial properties. These commercial properties are dependent upon a healthy economy and sound business management for success. This last requires sophisticated knowledge and experience. On the other hand, homes and apartment buildings will always be in demand, regardless of what the economy may do. Housing is a basic need. People must live somewhere; they have no choice. It might as well be in your property.

I would also advise you to stay away from raw land, at least at first. This does not mean that land in predevelopment stages is a bad investment; it simply means that predeveloped land has some basic disadvantages that increase the risk for the beginning investor. One big disadvantage is that land does not generate a cash flow. Mortgage payments and property taxes must be made out of your pocket. That's why it's called an "alligator" investment—it eats up an investor's capital through monthly payments, and it does not produce any cash flow. The beginning investor soon runs out of money to feed his alligator a daily diet of principal, interest, and taxes. When you don't feed an alligator, it becomes very hungry and it eats you alive; many a piece of land has been foreclosed because the owner couldn't keep the payments current.

In addition to starting with income-producing residential properties, here are several other general principles to guide you in tapping into the financial rewards of real estate. First, become more familiar with your own local real estate market by studying properties now up for sale. Learn all about your particular city, its growth patterns, its depressed areas, and the most likely paths of future growth. The more you know, the more prepared you will be to invest. And the more prepared you are to invest, the more confident you will become in your ability to spot a good opportunity.

How do you obtain this information? Explore your community on the Internet, taking advantage of neighborhood and real estate–related websites. Your local newspaper, for instance, probably offers an online edition complete with real estate features, property listings, and ads from brokers and agents. Or you could go to a broker's site and learn more about the prices and features of homes and apartment buildings now on the market.

Talk to real estate agents. Pick an area of town and drive through the neighborhoods noting all of the "for sale" signs . . . and stop and ask questions. Check with your city or county planning departments, which will be more than happy to tell an interested citizen about real estate areas. Use your common sense and always ask questions. Is this area growing or declining? How fast will the city grow and in which directions? Would I like to live here myself?

A good opportunity always goes to the investor who knows how to locate a good investment (something that only comes through practice) and has the courage to act quickly. As often as you can, you should try to buy properties with as much leverage as possible—in other words, with little or none of your own money. This book was written to tell you how. And since well-selected income-producing properties are steadily increasing in value, the sooner you buy, the sooner you will reach your financial goals.

It all sounds so easy. But if anyone can become wealthy through real estate investing, why isn't everybody doing it? I think it would be safe to say that most of us do recognize that real estate investment is one of the surest and safest ways to financial freedom. So there is only one real explanation for why so few of us fail to reach financial independence: Only a few are willing to pay the price. Only a few are willing to take the risks (no matter how slight those may be). Only a few are willing to set their sights high and start climbing. And only a small number of those who read this book will actually buy any investment real estate, even though they may agree with the concept. And the difference between the failures and the successes is the subject of the next chapter.

CHAPTER 4

It's Time to Pursue Your Passions

"One of my lifelong goals has been to become wealthy enough that I might help those that are in need and struggling. Thank you for giving me a tool to accomplish that dream and help those that are without."
—WILLIAM C. DAVIS

Most people choose real estate because it's the fastest, safest way to financial freedom. And who doesn't want financial freedom? If you make enough money, the world is yours! Right?

That's one of the reasons a lot of people go to work each day. In the back of their minds they say, "If I work and save long enough, I can retire and do what I really love." Some yearn for a faster way. They play the lottery. Or get caught up in some get-rich-quick scheme. Or turn to legitimate investments such as stocks or real estate. The underlying assumption is always the same: First make some money, then you'll be able to do what you love—pursue your passion. It's the American way. In fact, it's so ingrained in the American psyche that we could almost call it the Great American Formula:

Money = Happiness, Fulfillment, and Freedom to Pursue Your Passion

So what's the first step in making money? All success books preach the same thing: You must set a goal. Make it specific. Write it down. Visualize it. Read it every day. Magnetize your subconscious mind with single-minded, moneymaking determination. Simple.

Well, if it's so simple, why aren't more people financially independent? Is it because so few set financial goals? Or is it a faulty goal-setting technique? Perhaps they need to visualize the money better—smell those dollar bills and see them stacked in neat bundles as high as a house. Maybe they have to read their goals more regularly. Or to cut their goals up into bite-size pieces. What's the answer?

Well, one of the problems is that most people set goals based upon external motivation or whim. They see an advertisement for a new car and their "greed glands" fire up. "I want that car and I won't be happy until I get it!" That's a goal. A goal is wanting to become a doctor or lawyer because it will please your parents. A goal is often fueled by fear, such as: "Real estate prices are jumping upward. I better get in and make some money before it's too late."

I think it's far more important to talk about "intentions" than goals. That's because your intentions are guided by your "inner voice." An intention is fueled by a sense of purpose. For instance, "I've always wanted to be a real estate investor. I would love the personal freedom it could provide."

Here are some other differences between goals and intentions:

GOALS	INTENTIONS
External motivation	Internal motivation
Whim, fancies, appetites	Deep needs, desires
Happiness in end result	Journey is the reward
Future oriented	Now-oriented
Unnatural	Second nature
Dissatisfaction	Fulfillment
Imitation	Uniqueness
Mediocrity	Excellence

Many years ago, before I understood why goals don't always work, I was teaching a seminar in Dallas, Texas, on the power of setting goals. A woman came up to me afterward with a puzzled look on her face. "Mr. Allen, I'm a full-time real estate investor. I get up in the morning excited. I love to make deals. I have so much fun making money that I hate to go to bed at night. And yet I've never written down a financial goal in my life. What am I doing wrong?"

I was stumped for a moment. She didn't fit my picture of a successful person (since all successful people have financial goals, right?). I stammered something about how much more successful she would be if she did set goals. She nodded wisely. And I shrugged off the whole incident.

About this time, a good friend and fellow real estate investor told me that he was going to liquidate his small portfolio of properties and concentrate on his painting. I said, "But Sam, if you stick with real estate for five more years, you can retire and be free to paint for the rest of your life." His answer was mildly unsettling. "Bob, I've discovered I don't like real estate. But I love to paint." I walked away shaking my head at this soon-to-be-a-poor-and-starving artist. But a year later he was doing rather well financially—and loving every minute of it.

And then, one day these seemingly unrelated incidents coalesced into one gigantic "aha" moment. It happened while I was watching a golf tournament on TV featuring Jack Nicklaus, Lee Trevino, Fuzzy Zoeller, and Arnold Palmer. As these four great golfers were asked why they golfed, I suddenly knew why they were so successful: "I love the game of golf." "I love the competition." "I love to try to beat the best players in the world." "I love the people you meet in the game of golf." "Challenge is important to me." "I could play golf every day, all day long." "I'm one of the luckiest guys in the world. There are very few of us who get to do what we love and make a lot of money doing it."

That was it! These guys weren't playing for money! They were playing because they loved to play. Sure, maybe in the beginning money was a part of it—maybe even a big part—but money was never the primary motivator. First and foremost, their intention was to play golf, and they were passionate about playing the game. I doubt any one of them had a written financial goal: "I want to become a millionaire playing golf before my thirty-fifth birthday." What's more, I bet golfers who play just for money rarely make it to the leader board. It's not that their financial goals don't work; they've just got the formula backwards! Remember the Great American Formula?

Money = Happiness, Fulfillment, and Freedom to Pursue Your Passion

In truth, that formula should be just exactly the opposite.

24

Pursuing Your Passion = Fulfillment and Leads to Financial Freedom

When you're doing what you love to do, the money comes naturally. Maybe not at first, but eventually—if you stick with it. Do you think great comedians like Charlie Chaplin, Bob Hope, or Steve Martin started out with the goal "I want to become a millionaire by making people laugh, then I'll retire to do what I really want"? I doubt it. They just did what they did best. And the money came. Slowly at first, but then in truckloads. Comedian Jim Carrey has often told his story of being down-and-out and writing himself a twenty-million-dollar check. Then he sought his goal by doing what he loved doing—and he eventually was able to cash that check for real. When you're living your dream, no matter how financially successful you are, why would you want to retire?

What about the presidents of the Fortune 500? They make several million dollars a year. Why do they do so well financially? It's because they love the game of business, and they have polished the skills necessary for success in the corporate world. The financial results are just how they keep score.

I read a study in which the employees and executives of a major company were asked what they would do if they won $10 million in a lottery. Eighty percent of the rank-and-file employees said they would immediately quit their jobs. Asked the same question, only 20 percent of the executives said they would quit. Why would 80 percent stay even though they were now financially independent? Because they find a lot of happiness and fulfillment in their day-to-day activities. They love what they're doing. They're not leaders because they make so much money. They make so much money because they love to lead.

Imagine what you would do if you won $10 million in your state lottery. Would this make you happy? Sure. (Whoever said money doesn't bring happiness doesn't know where to shop!) What would you spend it on? A larger house in a better neighborhood? How about a nicer car? Pay off those debts? Buy some new clothes? Give a little away to your favorite charitable cause? Blow a few thousand for the heck of it? Sock some away for a rainy day? And, of course, you'd quit your job and do what you love to do, right?

Seriously, how would you spend your time if you didn't have to worry about money? Want to know a secret? Most people never bother to ask themselves that question. They just assume that if they win that $10 million jackpot, they'll be happy forever.

But wait! Is that what really happens? After all, the lottery doesn't pay you $10 million in one big chunk. The money is usually spread out over twenty years at $500,000 a year. Still, that's a lot of money. But what about taxes? Let's say you have to knock off about a third of that amount for state and federal taxes. That still leaves you with $350,000 a year after taxes or about $29,000 a month. Now, you can retire in comfort.

Or can you? Now that you feel more wealthy, you will probably acquire some wealthy spending habits: a $10,000 Rolex watch, an $80,000 Mercedes, a second home in Florida or Hawaii—you name it. Your standard of living is likely to go through the roof, absorbing all the extra money, and before you know it, you feel broke again. And what are you going to do in twenty years when the money runs out? Obviously, you're going to have to make more money in order to stay happy.

But wait! *That's the trap!* More money in order to stay happy. (Not that any of us wouldn't want that kind of misery. "Oh well," you say to yourself, "I always knew money couldn't buy lasting happiness, but I wanted to find out for myself.") But it's not the money that you want, really.

At the Robert Allen Institute (www.robertalleninstitute.com), one of the most important lessons I teach is money doesn't come first. What most people are really seeking is the ability to spend each day doing something they love. Rather than looking for happiness in some future goal of financial freedom (like almost all Americans), you want to find something that fulfills you every step of the way. Obviously, there's more to your personal success than just writing down your goals and dabbling in real estate.

A Sense of Purpose

People who achieve success and maintain it, whether in real estate investing, corporate boardrooms, or show business, have something that gives power to their goals—something I call "purpose." In my opinion, without purpose, goals aren't worth the paper they're written on. In fact, without purpose, goals ruin a perfectly good piece of blank paper.

So what is purpose?

Purpose is knowing what you want and doing it because it expresses who you really are. From world-famous celebrities who can't wait to be in front of the camera to the person who truly enjoys cutting your hair or the teenager who has dedicated her life to dance, you can find people every day who are "on purpose." They are living the life they were born to live. It's hard to imagine them doing anything else. They don't need goals to motivate themselves. They would do it anyway. And if they do set goals, it's just to keep score.

I've spent a lot of my time studying highly effective people, including graduates of my Creating Wealth with Real Estate program, and I find four threads that run through all of their conversations:

1. *Passion:* They love what they do. If they weren't making so much money, they would be tempted to do it for free.
2. *Values:* Their daily activities are extremely important to them.
3. *Talent:* They are good at what they do—call it talent, ability, skill, a special gift. Although they may have to work at it, they have got what it takes to be one of the best.
4. *Destiny:* They have a sense that they are doing what they were born to do, making their own unique contribution. It's almost a spiritual thing. They're fulfilling their destiny.

Is purpose only found in the lives of movie stars, corporate executives, artists, and dancers? Absolutely not. I believe every person has a unique purpose. And that includes you. You have unique talents, abilities, and values that only *you* can bring into greatness. You have a destiny that only *you* can fulfill.

So how do you tap into this sense of purpose? Actually, there are three distinct steps.

Step One: Ask Yourself the Purpose Questions

What do I love to do? What am I good at? What is important to me? What was I born to do? Complete the following Purpose Finder Exercise to help you find out.

Write down the top seven answers to each of the four questions. I've given you some additional clues to get you started. Don't be too serious. Enjoy yourself. When you're finished, rank each item in each list in order of importance assuming you have only five years to live. I encourage you to spend at least one uninterrupted half hour completing this exercise.

Purpose Finder Exercise
What Do I Love to Do?
Additional Clues

What has given me the most satisfaction in the past?
What excites me about life?
What activities give me the most satisfaction and inner peace?
What are my hobbies?
What have I been happiest doing?
What is my secret ambition?

RANK   ACTIVITY

1. _____
2. _____
3. _____
4. _____
5. _____
6. _____
7. _____

What Is Important to Me?
Additional Clues

What would I commit myself to if money were not an object?
If I only had five years to live, what would I absolutely have to accomplish for my life to have been meaningful?
What do I stand for?
What won't I stand for?
What has caused me to make great sacrifices in the past?
What would I be willing to risk my life for?

RANK   ACTIVITY

1. _____
2. _____
3. _____
4. _____
5. _____

6. _____
7. _____

WHAT AM I GOOD AT?
Additional Clues

What have other people told me I'm good at?
What have I excelled at in the past? (e.g., sports, entertaining, relationships, communicating, problem solving, persuading, leading)?
What are some of my strengths?
What have I been successful at?

RANK   ACTIVITY

1. _____
2. _____
3. _____
4. _____
5. _____
6. _____
7. _____

WHAT WAS I BORN TO DO?
Additional Clues

What is my unique mission in life?
What can I do that will make a difference?
What specifically does God want me to do?
What can I contribute?
What is my niche?
What unique opportunities have been placed in my path?

RANK   ACTIVITY

1. _____
2. _____
3. _____
4. _____
5. _____
6. _____
7. _____

Step Two: Prepare a Purpose Statement

Using the information from the Purpose Finder Exercise, try to find the thread that runs through your life and connects you to your life's energy. What activities make you come alive? What values guide your daily decisions? Most people complete this exercise and are amazed at what they discover. Try to see patterns in your answers. See how many of the top priorities in one quadrant are similar to those found in other quadrants. These are good clues. Use this information to construct a Purpose Statement, a short description of the priorities that guide your life and give it meaning (see below).

Don't let this intimidate you. You're not trying to discover the meaning of life, just what motivates you at this point in your life.

By the way, my own Purpose Statement used to be a page long. I finally honed it to one sentence: "My purpose is to inspire and empower people to achieve real wealth."

This one sentence says it all for me. I love to teach. I love to write. And I love to create new ways to help people live life to the fullest. Real estate just happens to be one of the vehicles I use. These things are really important to me. It is where my talents lie. The principles of real wealth are ideas that I feel I have been born to teach. And one of those principles is Purpose.

Purpose Statement

_____

_____

_____

_____

_____

_____

_____

_____

_____

_____

_____

_____

_____

_____

_____

_____

_____

_____

_____

_____

_____

So what does all this have to do with a book on real estate? Actually there are several reasons why it's necessary to link purpose to your real estate activities. You may be one of those fortunate souls who has the real estate "knack," who is a "natural" for this kind of business in the same way Van Gogh was a natural artist or Mozart was a natural composer. If so, your investment career may not bring you fame, but it will certainly bring you more fulfillment and financial success. To determine this, ask yourself the following questions:

- Do I like real estate? Or am I choosing real estate just because I want to be rich?
- Do I enjoy taking risks?
- Do I like to negotiate?
- If real estate made me wealthy, what would I do if and when I retired?
- If I were wealthy, would I still do real estate?
- Do I like the challenge of doing deals?
- Am I an entrepreneur?
- Does the thought of being an investor give me a surge of excitement?
- Is business important to me?
- Will real estate help me express who I really am?
- Is real estate my equivalent of an artist's canvas?
- Am I good at creative problem solving?
- Do I have the drive to grow my real estate business bigger and bigger?
- Is real estate in my blood?
- Would I be "on purpose" as a real estate investor?

If real estate is a big part of your purpose, then the odds of your success go up dramatically. You see, purpose is like your favorite dessert. Have you ever noticed that no matter how full you are, there is always room for your favorite dessert. You always find time for the things you really want to do, no matter how busy you are. When you are "on purpose," nothing stops you. When you aren't, any distraction, problem, obstacle, disappointment, or negative thought or feeling can divert you.

So what if you weren't "born" to be a passionate real estate investor? What if you just want to make some fast, safe money to pursue some other dream or passion? Moreover, what if you don't want to be financially free at all but just want some extra financial security? That's okay, too, as long as you link your intentions to a sufficiently motivating reason.

Step Three: Link Your Intentions to a Compelling Reason

There is an old saying that I will paraphrase: "If the 'why' is important enough, then no 'how' is too difficult."

In other words, a lot of us would be reluctant to sky dive from three thousand feet in the air for a mere $10 reward. But if we had to jump in order to save our child's life, we would strap on that parachute, close our eyes, and step right out of that plane.

The basic principles of real estate investing are simple to understand but not easy to implement. It takes commitment, dedication, time, and effort. If your only reason for starting is because you want to get rich, then you don't have a compelling enough "why." You need a reason that motivates you to go through the "gravel digging" until you uncover a real estate nugget. What is your major reason for wanting to be financially free? The more specific your are, the more compelling the drive and the more probable the success.

At a recent Creating Wealth seminar, I asked a middle-aged woman why she was there. She explained that she had a handicapped son who required substantial government assistance. This assistance was scheduled to run out in a few years. At that time, she "had to be a millionaire" just to be able to take care of him. In other words, her reason for investing was so compelling that she will be motivated to do whatever it takes to become successful. Whether she is dealing with a banker, seller, or real estate agent, her commitment is going to radiate from every cell of her body. This will transfer into more investment opportunities and successful transactions.

I encourage you to think clearly about your purpose in life. For most people, it will take time, dedication, and a steady flow of income in order to fulfill your purpose. So, let's take a moment to take stock in ourselves, as we move closer to creating a sound financial strategy to help you achieve your purpose.

CHAPTER 5

Let's Take a
Personal Inventory

*"Bob Allen's seminar opened my world to a new vision. I started two
weeks ago, took a look at my skills and where I was going. It has helped
me acquire more useful knowledge than my whole college career."*

—DR. JAMES OEVERMANN

Okay. You've spent some time focusing on your unique purpose in
life. Now it's time to look at the factors that may determine how
quickly and smoothly you will move ahead toward fulfilling that purpose.

Before dipping your toe into the real estate investment "swimming pool," I believe it's essential to pause for a moment. Just as
you would apply sunscreen before stepping out of that poolside
cabana, you need to inventory your personal traits, your individual
skills and your financial resources. After all, you are about to
embark on one of the most important journeys in your life, and you
have to know your starting point. Otherwise, the investment strategy you devise—your road map, so to speak—may send you off in
the wrong direction.

Let's look at those three "inventory" topics in order, starting
with your personal traits and skills. In many years of helping others

find success in my Creating Wealth seminars, I've noticed that success in the field of real estate usually goes hand in hand with certain types of personal characteristics.

First, a real estate investor has courage. Time after time, you will make decisions that carry a certain degree of risk. (If you've applied this book's teachings correctly, then the risk should be small!) But you may be the kind of person who thinks the only safe place for your investment money is a savings account, certificate of deposit, or T-bill.

If you are going to lie awake at night worrying if your money isn't 100 percent insured at the local bank on Main Street, then you have two choices. First, you should content yourself with that small return on your savings and move on with your financial life. Or second, find another field that you're passionate about, and invest your time and energy there.

But you don't have to let your fears keep you out of the real estate world. After all, an investment that offers "100 percent security" probably won't grow quickly enough to cover the rising costs of inflation. That's what millions of retirees have discovered in recent years—low interest rates just don't provide enough for a comfortable living.

Of course, you don't want to risk everything you own on one throw of the dice. That's far too risky in Las Vegas *or* in a real estate investment. But without taking some calculated, limited risks, you are extremely unlikely to achieve the financial freedom that will allow you to pursue your passion for the rest of your life.

Another vital trait for real estate investors is a sense of imagination. One person might pull up to an empty warehouse with a "for sale" sign, and drive away after seeing the scruffy landscaping and run-down appearance. Another investor, one with a better imagination and a good understanding of the marketplace, might picture the scene in a different way. He or she can envision the busy trucks pulling up to the loading dock, day and night, then rushing away loaded with products that are in high demand in the local market. Guess which person is most likely to make the investment and upgrade the property so it can achieve its true potential.

A third essential quality for success is the ability to be a critic. It's not enough to be a risk taker and to have a creative imagination. You must also use your critical skills to sift through the facts and the emotional issues involved in any real estate transaction and determine if it makes financial sense for you. It's easy for the seller or the seller's agent to paint a rosy picture. Perhaps a small shopping center is up for sale at a price that seems like a "steal." But you have to be able to analyze the situation, and find out whether the seller is painting a realistic picture or a weird masterpiece of modern art!

In most of my seminars, there are people who like to sit in the back. They tend to listen quietly and never say a word to other attendees. Of course, the opposite is also true. Some people like to sit in the front rows, talk to anyone within listening distance, and exchange business cards—long before the class starts. If you are a "people person" like my front-row attendees, you may have a long and happy career ahead of you in real estate. Despite the Internet and all the other wonderful technology tools of today, real estate is ultimately a people business. If you are a "people person," or can develop those traits, your chances of financial success are much higher. Thankfully, even those "quiet types" in the back row can (and often do) learn how to break out of their shells, gaining the necessary "people" skills to have a productive and profitable real estate career.

When thinking of "people" skills, put communication right at the top of the list. To reach your goals, you will need to communicate frequently with other people. And that's not just being able to talk up a storm. You will have to use your fingers, too—typing a letter, a proposal, or an email message. The other aspect of communication skills is the ability to listen. A really good real estate investor knows how to listen to what the speaker is saying, and to "read between the lines" to get a clearer picture of the situation.

Negotiating ability is another great trait for a real estate investor. We will cover that topic in greater detail a little later in this book, but if you're a person who loves to bargain at flea markets, haggle for the best price on a new car, or pick up a discount at every opportunity, you will probably do just fine in the real estate world.

Generosity is another important trait that all too often goes unrecognized. If you are the kind of person who likes to help others, if you go out of your way to take care of a sick neighbor, help a business associate with a problem, or give your child a little extra TLC, you have the "right stuff" for success. I truly believe that you have to "give" in order to get—and that applies in the financial arena just as it does in your family and your community.

Finally, I would like to mention the importance of having a sense of humor. Once in a while you are going to have a bad day, you will make a mistake, and you will run across a person you just can't stand. Now is the time to shake your head, smile at the situation, and laugh it off. A sense of humor will be your salvation on those black days when everything seems to be going wrong. It helps you keep things in perspective—and there will be another day, a brighter day, ahead of you!

So let's recap. Here are some of the key traits associated with success in real estate investing:

- Courage
- Imagination
- Critical thinking
- People skills
- Communication
- Negotiating ability
- Generosity
- A sense of humor

On a scale of 1 to 10, how would you rate yourself on each of these eight traits? I would hope that you would be at least a 5 on all of them, but be honest here, nobody else has to see the results!

If there are one or two traits that might need improvement—perhaps your negotiation skills—you can take a class or read a book and polish up those skills. Just as a shy person in my seminar can learn to speak up to the entire group, you can cultivate all those personal traits that lead to success.

Find Out Where You Are Financially

It certainly helps for a real estate investor to have a good sense of numbers. Now, I don't mean that you have to be a math wizard—someone who can calculate a complex algebra formula in your head. But you should be able to add and subtract, and to develop a sense of when the numbers add up and when they don't. Now, math is one thing that can certainly be taught—and I am going to give you a little practice right now.

As part of your preparation for financial success, I would like you to sit down and prepare a realistic financial statement. You will find a blank copy of an excellent financial file on the next pages. You should fill it out.

I know you're tempted to skip over this step. *You can't.* It is essential to this process. As you prepare your financial statement, remember to list all of your assets whether or not you think they are valuable.

Confidential Check List and
Survey of Investment Objectives

PERSONAL AND FAMILY DATA

Name_____ Date_____

Mailing Address_____ Phone_____

Employer/Position_____ Phone_____

Spouse's Employer_____ Phone_____

	Age	Date of Birth	Health	Occupation	Social Security No.
Self					
Spouse					
Children					

Other Dependents_____

	Firm	Phone
Attorney		
Banker		
C.P.A.		
Insurance Broker		
Property Manager		
Other Financial Adviser		

When was your present will executed?_____ Spouse's?_____

Do you have a trust arrangement? ☐ Yes ☐ No   Type_____ Trustee_____

INCOME AND TAXATION

Current Annual Taxable Income	Self	Spouse	Total
From salary, fees, bonuses, etc.	$_____	$_____	$_____
From interest	$_____	$_____	$_____
From dividends	$_____	$_____	$_____
From real estate	$_____	$_____	$_____
From capital gains (½)	$_____	$_____	$_____
Other (trusts, etc.)	$_____	$_____	$_____
Total taxable income	$_____	$_____	$_____

Expected future income?_____ When?_____

What income increases or decreases do you expect?_____

Do you receive additional non-taxable income?_____

Do you have a regular savings or investment program now? ☐ Yes ☐ No

Present monthly savings $_____ Could comfortably save $_____ monthly.

TAX RETURN SUMMARY (LAST 4 YEARS)

	19___	19___	19___	19___
Adjusted gross income	$_____	$_____	$_____	$_____
Taxable income	$_____	$_____	$_____	$_____
Federal taxes paid	$_____	$_____	$_____	$_____
State ( ) taxes paid	$_____	$_____	$_____	$_____
Exemptions claimed	_____	_____	_____	_____

How many exemptions this year?_____ Estimated personal deductions $ _____

Do you have any personal carry-over losses from last year?_____

Factors affecting future income _____
_____
_____
_____
_____
_____

Comments _____
_____
_____
_____
_____

ASSETS AND LIABILITIES (EXCEPT INSURANCE)

_____ Lender and Loan Number _____

REAL ESTATE

Type of Property and Location	How Acquired	Title Held In Name Of	Date Acquired	Adjusted Basis	Market Value	Amount of Mortgages	Present Equity	Monthly Cash Flow Before Taxes
				$	$	$	$	$
						TOTAL	$	$

SECURITIES (Listed and Unlisted)

Company and Type of Security	Registered In Name Of	Date Acquired	Cost Basis	Market Value	Margin or Loans	Present Equity	Annual Cash Flow Before Taxes
			$	$	$	$	$
					TOTAL	$	$

BUSINESS INTERESTS

Name of Company	Form of Organization	Date of Organization	Number of Employees	Percent Ownership	Client's Current Net Value	Client's Annual Net Income
					$	$
				TOTAL	$	$

39

ROBERT G. ALLEN

EMPLOYEE BENEFITS

Type of Plan Company	Tax Qualified?	Retirement Age	Retirement Benefits	Voluntary Contributions	Current Value	Death Benefit Now
Pension			$	$	$	$
Profit Sharing						
Savings						
Tax Sheltered Annuity						

LIFE AND HEALTH INSURANCE

LIFE INSURANCE

Company	Type	Date Acquired	Insured	Owner	Beneficiary	Face Amount	Cash Value	Loans	Annual Premium
						$	$	$	$
					TOTAL	$	$	$	$

MEDICAL AND DISABILITY INSURANCE

Type	Cancelled? Yes No	Insurer	Insured	Periodic Benefit	Maximum Benefit	Exclusion	Annual Premium
Disability Income							$
Disability Income							
Hospitalization							
Major Medical							
Business Overhead							

FINANCIAL STATEMENT

ASSETS

cash and checking $_____
savings accounts _____
real estate owned _____
securities _____
notes receivable _____
bonds – face value _____
furniture & personal _____
automobiles _____
life ins. cash value _____
net worth business _____
net lease value _____
boats, trailers _____
alimony _____
deposits on real estate _____
pension & annuity value _____
other_____ _____
_____ _____
_____ _____

TOTAL ASSETS $_____

LIABILITIES

mortgages $_____
notes payable _____
loans on life ins. _____
debts, unsecured _____
installment purchases _____
property tax reserves _____
income tax reserves _____
long-term leases _____

TOTAL LIABILITIES $_____

NET WORTH $_____

INVESTMENT OBJECTIVES

What priority do you assign to the following investment objectives?
- ____ Additional current monthly income of $_____ .
- ____ Capital growth/inflation hedge. ☐ Short Term ☐ Long Term
- ____ Tax shelter for ☐ Income ☐ Capital gain ☐ _____ .
- ____ Professional management for ☐ Property ☐ Securities ☐ Trust
- ____ Safety of investment.
- ____ Maintain minimum cash reserve of $_____ .
- ____ Diversification of investment program.
- ____ Provision for family in event of premature death or disability.
- ____ Other

At what age do you anticipate full retirement? _____

What do you consider to be a minimum retirement income (Today's dollars) $_____

What do you consider to be a comfortable retirement income (Today's dollars) $_____

Comments (Education funds, etc.): _____

COMMENTS

_____

BUDGETING - create your own wealth for pyramiding

Gross Income - including interest, dividends, rents $_____

    Less deductions - Federal _____ F.I.C.A. _____

                 State   _____ Others _____ (_____)

                                         $_____

Spendable Income

		BUDGET	SPENT
1. Savings for investment = at least 10% of gross income			
2. Committed expenses:	a. Charitable		
	b. Housing		
	c. House maintenance		
	d. Utilities		
	e. Life insurance		
	f. Automotive		
	g. Medical		
	h. Others:		
3. Manageable expenses:	a. Food		
	b. Clothing		
	c. Personal expenses		
	d. Appliances		
	e. Furnishings		
	f. Building and grounds		
	g. Entertainment		
	h. Others:		

Total Expenses $_____

Spendable less expenses $_____

If there is income remaining apply to your savings. If there is a deficiency of income find ways to alter your expenses or increase income. Do not decrease savings!

Now that you have a clear picture of your traits and skills, as well as your overall financial situation, it's time to start on your own personal game plan. This will help keep you firmly on the road to success in life!

CHAPTER 6

Formulate Your Game Plan for Success

"Embrace change as our golden opportunity."
—ERIN L. DAVIS

Let's imagine that you're an artist who is passionate about painting beautiful landscapes. In fact, you might say that's your *purpose* in life. You have traveled to the scene of a snowcapped mountain and your *intention* is to capture that beauty on your canvas. You have set up your easel and *taken inventory* of the various paints you will need. Now you need a *game plan* for that painting—just where do you start?

Just like that artist, you are now ready to create a game plan for your own personal and financial success in life. This game plan will outline the specific steps you must take to make your purpose and your intention come to life. Try this on for size:

Purpose: I have always felt a need to own my own business.

Intention: I will be a full-time real estate investor within two years.

Game plan: I will remain in my job and spend five hours a week for the next six months learning, studying, and going to seminars to acquire the basics of real estate investing. Then I'll buy one property in the following six months. I will remain a part-time successful investor until I can afford to do it full time. I intend to make the leap to full-time status when I have accumulated a "safety net" of at least six months of cash and become experienced enough to earn at least twice my current salary from my investment activities. This should happen in the next twenty-four months. Within five years I intend to own properties with accumulated equities exceeding $1 million. Then I will broaden my focus to include the following additional intentions:

- Teaching kids about the importance of the free-market system
- Increasing support for my church organization
- Finding reasonable approaches to saving the environment
- Writing a book
- Pursuing my talent for singing

Got the idea? Let's try another one.

Purpose: I have always wanted to work with underprivileged children.

Intention: I intent to start a safe house for younger teenagers on drugs.

Game plan: I will establish myself with a solid financial base through my current occupation. At the same time, I will learn how to master the basics of real estate investment by study and experience. I will buy my first investment property within one year. With the profits generated from this property, I will start my youth program. I will approach "at risk" youth and encourage them to work with me as I invest, fix up, and manage my growing investment portfolio. Within two years, I intend to buy one property to use as a group home. The profits generated from investing will be used to expand the program. Within five years, I will be "saving" a hundred youths per year from the horrors of drugs and alcohol, and training them how to go back into the community to repeat this process with other youths. Within ten years, I intend to create an education program to be taught in schools citywide that shows young people a legitimate way to "make it" in America besides selling drugs. From this educational program, at least a thousand youths per year will be involved in summer work programs.

Here's another one:

Purpose: I feel a deep responsibility to provide financial security for my family.

Intention: Within one year I will embark on a specific real estate investment program.

Game plan: I will build my investment program on the sound financial foundation of adequate insurance, emergency preparedness, savings, credit protection, and company retirement benefits. Then I will protect my career by becoming an increasingly productive team player. In my spare time, I will acquire information and experience about small real estate investments. Within one year I will buy my first property and will add at least one property per year to this portfolio for the next ten years. This portfolio will appreciate in value as well as provide added cash flow. I will involve my family in the details of the program so they can learn by doing. Give a man a fish and you feed him for a day. Teach a man to fish and you feed him for a lifetime.

Get the idea?

Now, when it comes to real estate, whether you're buying and holding for appreciation, renovating run-down properties, or concentrating on finding a super bargain, it is possible to earn 25 to 100 percent on your investment within a short time, especially when you follow the Nothing Down approach.

The key to a good real estate investment game plan is to be specific with dates, time frames, and activities (the more specific the better). With this in mind, let's play around with some numbers just for fun.

Since 1968, prices of single-family homes have gone up in value every year, according to median sale price figures provided by the National Association of Realtors. Over the decades, the annual increase has been as small as 0.2 percent, or as much as 14.4 percent, with an average growth of 6.3 percent a year. That means a house that cost $62,200 in 1980 grew in value to more than $155,000 in less than twenty-five years.

Now, it's important to remember that these figures are national averages. In some cities the rates of return have been much less than average. If you live in a town or city where real estate values are rising slowly, you may want to look around for a "hotter" market for your investment dollars. On the other hand, there are many communities or neighborhoods where values have risen by 10 percent or more annually for a multiyear period. In the next chapter, we will discuss how to research the marketplace; for now, we are just looking at possible returns on a real estate investment.

44

Depending on where you live, you can organize your buying strategy to create opportunities for your entire real estate portfolio to grow by 10 percent each year. *At that rate of appreciation, a well-selected property would double in value in just over seven years!* Obviously, not all real estate appreciates in value, and some types of properties go up much faster than others.

To be safe, you shouldn't expect more than a 5 percent growth rate—and you should be financially prepared if prices decline in your market. But just to show you what a 10 percent appreciation can do to your real estate portfolio, take a look at the Gross Equity Appreciation Schedule below.

GROSS EQUITY APPRECIATION SCHEDULE

Gross Value of Real Estate	$250,000	$500,000	$750,000	$1,000,000	$1,250,000	$1,500,000	$1,750,000	$2,000,000	$10,000,000
$2,000,000	1.3	2.4	3.4	4.3	5.1	5.9	6.6	7.3	18.8
$1,750,000	1.4	2.7	3.8	4.8	5.7	6.5	7.3	8.0	20.0
$1,500,000	1.7	3.1	4.3	5.4	6.4	7.3	8.2	8.9	21.4
$1,250,000	2.0	3.6	5.0	6.2	7.3	8.3	9.2	10.1	23.1
$1,000,000	2.4	4.3	5.87	7.3	8.6	9.7	10.7	11.6	25.2
$750,000	3.1	5.4	7.3	8.9	10.3	11.6	12.7	13.7	28.0
$500,000	4.3	7.3	9.7	11.6	13.2	14.6	15.8	16.9	32.0
$250,000	7.3	11.6	14.6	16.9	18.8	20.5	21.9	23.1	39.0

Net Equity Columns

Assumptions :
- Property values increase by 10 % per year
- All of your purchases are nothing down
- Equity build-up is not counted in equity
- Figures are rounded to highest tenth

For example, suppose you buy a $200,000 building today with nothing down. Within seven to ten years, if conditions have been favorable, that building will be worth approximately $400,000. Depending on how you structured your purchase, your profit will be several hundred percent!

This chart was created to teach you an important concept: The compounding effect of relatively low real estate price increases over time. You can see by playing with the numbers on the chart that there are countless ways to create a fortune. You just need to decide how wealthy you want to become.

However, most investors don't just walk into the market and buy $1 million worth of real estate, then wait for ten to fifteen years to become wealthy. The normal process is to buy properties in incre-

GROSS EQUITY ACCUMULATION SCHEDULE

$300,000	3.5	5	6	7	8	8.5	9	9.5
$250,000	4	5.5	6.5	7.5	8.5	9	10	10.5
$200,000	4.5	6	7.5	8.5	9.5	10	11	11.5
$150,000	5	7	8.5	9.5	10.5	11.5	12.2	13
$100,000	6	8.5	10	11.5	12.5	13.5	14.5	15
$75,000	7	10	11.5	13	14	15	16	17
$50,000	8.5	11.5	13.5	15	16.5	17.5	18.5	19.5
$40,000	9.5	12.5	14.5	16.5	18	19	20	21
	$250,000	$500,000	$750,000	$1,000,000	$1,250,000	$1,500,000	$1,750,000	$2,000,000

Annual Accumulation (left axis)

Net Equity Columns

Assumptions :
• Property values increase by 10 % per year
• All of your purchases are nothing down
• Equity build-up is not counted in equity
• Figures are rounded to nearest one half

ments—to eat the elephant bite by bite rather than at one sitting. This fact necessitates the use of another chart, which I call the Gross Equity Accumulation Schedule (see above).

This more closely approaches the actual real-life situation of the average investor—that is, the purchase of individual properties slowly with building equities. This second chart provides you with a quick and easy way to find out how much you can be worth in a prescribed time period.

How do these charts work? Say you want to have a net equity of $1 million in 5½ years. Find $1 million in the Net Equity column of the Gross Equity Appreciation Schedule; now follow the column up until you find something close to 5½ years—5.4. Now go across to the Gross Value of Real Estate column. You'll have to buy $1.5 million worth of property to reach your goal. What if you now have $250,000 worth of property? Find $1 million in the Net Equity column and the $250,000 point in the Gross Value of Real Estate column. The point at which the two intersect is the number of years it will take your property to appreciate to a $1 million net equity—16.9 years. Make sure you note the assumptions listed at the bottom of the chart.

Let me explain a little more about how the chart works. Let's assume that you want to generate a steady cash flow of $100,000 per year for the rest of your life. We'll also assume that this $100,000 income represents a return on your investment ten years from now. If you could successfully invest your money to yield 10 percent, then your $100,000 income would represent your yield on a $1 million net worth ($1,000,000 x .10 = $100,000). What you will need to have ten years from now, therefore, is a net worth of $1 million which can be invested to yield you 10 percent.

The next question is: How can I attain a net worth of $1 million in ten years? This takes you to the Gross Equity Accumulation Schedule. Look for a net worth of $1 million in the Net Equity column in the table. Then follow the column upward until you find the number of years until your intended retirement date—in this case ten years (use the 9.5-year figure). Then follow the column horizontally to the left to find the yearly purchase quota—in this case $150,000. This tells you that in order for you to accumulate a net worth of $1,000,000 within ten years, it will be necessary for you to purchase at least $150,000 worth of real estate each year for the next ten years. This should be held and not sold. If property values increase at an average rate of at least 10 percent per year for the next ten years, the $1 million goal is feasible and realistic.

If you want to get fancy, you can use both charts to make a prediction on your future net worth. But the important concept to grasp here is that the building of a fortune is accomplished steadily, gradually, one step at a time. For some the purchase of even one property each year for ten years seems as formidable as climbing Mount Everest.

You must realize that every little step counts—one single-family home adds to your quota, as does a small apartment building. Some years you will not be able to find anything. The very next month you could locate an excellent property to satisfy two or three years' quotas. I found that during one six-month period, when I could not locate anything that fit within my investment guidelines. Then, in one week, I located a "don't-wanter" who had five smaller homes to sell in one transaction. And I was able to negotiate a *nothing-down* purchase! It's either feast or famine.

As your confidence and experience increase, you'll learn that you can pyramid your investment. Make sure you buy solid real estate in good neighborhoods in growing areas. You should begin by purchasing small homes and apartment buildings until you get the hang of it (and so you don't get stung by risking your investment capital in unknown areas). You must choose each property carefully—with legal protection, assurance from professionals, and some conservative long-range objectives for creative appreciation and cash flow. As you learn to master the techniques, you will eventually purchase larger apartment buildings, small office buildings, and land for subdivisions. Give yourself time. Most of all, give yourself optimism.

Whatever your dream is, take time to fill out the commitment form at the end of this chapter. Don't pass up this opportunity to commit yourself in writing—and have your spouse witness it with his or her signature so he or she can be part of the process. This step could well be the most important thing you do in your goal to obtain financial independence.

With a completed Commitment form to focus your attention like a laser beam, you're ready for the next step.

Flood Your Imagination with Vision

In addition to a specific regimen of physical training, every Olympic athlete also incorporates a scientifically designed program of visualization. It is impossible to achieve world-class status without it. Why?

Nearly a century ago, the French scientist Emile Coué uttered a statement that provides an insight into why visualization is essential to long-term success: *"When the will comes in conflict with the imagination, the imagination always carried the day."*

In other words, no matter how determined you say you are, if your imagination is not in harmony, then you are doomed to failure. To say this in a more positive way: If your deepest needs, values, and internal beliefs agree with your direction, then you are more likely to succeed.

Have you ever sabotaged yourself? Ever come close to victory only to slide back into the jaws of defeat? When you are fighting yourself, you can't win. Suppose you desire financial success but a part of you thinks that rich people are "all bad." It's going to be a tough fight all the way to the bank. What if some part of you feels that you don't deserve to be wealthy. That's obviously going to slow you down.

There is a way to rechannel your imagination so that you are completely aiming in the right direction. I call it Neurobics, a specialized way of visualizing. Obviously, there is not space here to share the complete program with you, but here, in general, is the way it works.

I recommend that you spend five minutes a day quietly visualizing your future. Imagine you are in a movie theater watching a film of your successful future. See yourself up there on the screen as the principal actor. Notice how you behave now that you have achieved what you set out to achieve. Notice how happy you look. Notice how you walk and talk and interact with the other people in the film. Notice the material benefits of success. Tinker with the imagined scene by adding color, moving images as well as sound. Adjust the imagined scene until it feels right to you, until it reflects the most real representation of your successful future. Then, move out of your seat in the theater, step into the body of the "future you" on the screen, and notice what it feels like to have achieved your dream. Look through your future eyes and notice, from this perspective, how others react to you. Notice the surrounding trappings of success. Concentrate on how it feels to have "made it."

Step back out of the screen and take your seat once again in the theater. Then scan the various steps in your game plan that brought you to your ultimate success. Notice exactly how you "made it" in such a way that all parts of you were in agreement. Notice what it's like to close on each property in your game plan from the last back to the first. Especially notice how you developed as an individual. Notice how you transcended each of the major obstacles in your path. Imagine how you overcame each fear.

Now return to the present, bringing with you the insights of your journey into the future. Each day you can focus on a different aspect of that future. For instance, you might create in your mind a "mastermind" council or board of directors to advise you. This imaginary board might consist of your heroes past and present. At each barrier, you could convene your internal mastermind team to counsel you.

That should be enough to get you started. Once your purpose, intention, and game plan are in place and you have begun a regular Neurobics regimen, there is only one final step.

Take at least one small step a day toward achieving your purpose.

Don't let a day go by without doing something, no matter how small. I call this my "bottom line" for the day. A bottom line is saying to yourself, "When this day is done, no matter what else I accomplish, I must at least do this: _____ (fill in)." So to review:

- Determine your purpose
- Establish a specific intention
- Take inventory
- Develop your game plan
- Practice your Neurobics
- Put your game plan into action by accomplishing at least one daily bottom line

My purpose, and the purpose of this book, is to teach you the principles of real wealth through investing in real estate. Once you have mastered these principles, make me a promise that you will buy at least one piece of real estate a year—skipping a year or even two if there is no reasonable investment no matter how hard you look, but making up for it by buying two or more properties in a year when opportunities are plentiful, so that you average at least one purchase per year. That's a challenge! You will be amazed at how fast your real estate garden will grow.

And don't be worried by the fact that you don't have a lot of money to invest. You bought this book because you didn't have a lot of cash in the bank. Few people do. But you can still reach your investment goals. Keep reading, and you will learn how to do it with little or none of your own money.

Commitment

I, _____ hereby acknowledge the following:

My destiny is to weave the following principles, values, and talents into the fabric of my daily life:

_____

_____

_____

_____

_____

_____

_____

_____

_____

_____

_____

SPECIFIC INTENTION

Drawing upon the strength of my purpose, I intend to focus my efforts on the following specific intention:

_____

_____

_____

_____

_____

_____

_____

_____

_____

_____

_____

GAME PLAN

I will pursue my specific intention through the following game plan. I acknowledge that the game plan may change as circumstances change. I will be open to flexibility and intuition as my intention becomes clearer and clearer.

_____

_____

_____

_____
_____
_____
_____
_____
_____
_____
_____

ADDITIONAL INTENTIONS

Upon achieving my primary intention, I may choose to focus more effort on achieving the following additional intentions:

1. _____
2. _____
3. _____
4. _____
5. _____

Signed this _____ day of 20 _____.

_____

_____

Witnessed by:

_____

　　If you'd like a commitment certificate suitable for framing, just call me at 801-852-8711 or visit www.robertallenrealestate.com, and I'll be glad to send you one.

CHAPTER 7

The Bargains Are Out There!

"Don't wait until you feel confident, self-assured, and competent before you make your first deal. That day will never come. Feel the fear today, and do it anyway."

—ROBERT LYNN

Now that you've determined your overall goals, it's time to start looking for your first once-in-a-lifetime deal. I use that phrase because bargain properties exist in every town and in every price range. But finding the right property for your limited investment dollars is like panning for gold: You have to sift through a lot of gravel before you find that valuable nugget.

In your local market, there are probably many properties that *appear,* like fool's gold, to be a rich find. Only close inspection will tell you for sure if you've located a true bargain. For this reason I try to maintain a very neutral, aloof attitude whenever I go looking for properties. If I get too emotionally involved in any investment decision, I may find myself swayed by too much nonfinancial detail.

One of the first assignments for students in my Creating Wealth with Real Estate course is to find a property they think has potential, analyze it as best they can, and make an offer to the owner. We

53

start them right off digging for information on the Internet and in the classified section of the local newspaper. It isn't long before an excited student comes up with something that seems like a golden opportunity.

Student: "Bob, I think I've really found a winner!"
Me: "Have you done your analysis yet?"
Student: "Not really, but his ad sounds real desperate. I'll bet he'll take any price to get this property off his hands."
Me: "Now, don't get too excited until you've finished your homework."
Student: "Well, I can already smell the money."
(Everything smells like money to a beginning investor who hasn't yet learned to sift the real stuff from the fool's gold.)

Before you know for sure that a particular income-producing property is genuine gold, you need to analyze the possible sale from three different points of view: (1) location analysis, (2) market analysis, and (3) seller analysis. In this chapter, we'll look closely at the first two types of analysis. We'll look at the seller more closely in the next chapter.

Location Analysis

Location is the first and most critical element in studying a particular property. Ask any real estate agent, broker, or investor about the three cardinal rules in buying real estate, and you'll hear "location, location, and location." Pick a property in the right location, and you can almost watch its value rise day by day. Many homes in desirable locations have gone up 10, 15, 20 percent, or even more in just one year. Of course, the market may slow down for a year or two, but unless you have to sell at that point, you can simply wait for values to start rising again.

On the other hand, if the property is in a bad location, a "bargain" sales price or attractive financing won't make up for the high price you'll eventually have to pay in terms of bad tenants, measly rents, and poor resale profits. You can't move toward your goal of financial independence if you're throwing away your precious money, time, and effort on a home or apartment building in a poor location. I have owned property in a bad location before, and before long I was willing to give it away. In fact, I would have paid someone to take it off my hands. My bad location attracted the worst tenants and commanded the lowest rents. My expenses were higher because of these tenants, and that doesn't include the cost of antacids for my unsettled stomach.

So, how do you analyze a property's location? A great way to get started is on the Internet. Today, there is a wealth of real estate and community information right at your fingertips. For instance, the National Association of Realtors provides a wealth of "for sale" listings, as well as information for buyers and sellers on its site, www.realtor.com. Or you could go to one of the popular search engines and simply type in the name of your city or town and the words "real estate." You might get dozens or hundreds of sites that contain just the information you want. You could narrow your search even more by typing in the name of a particular neighborhood that interests you, or a certain type of property.

Of course, some of the information you'll find on the Internet is likely to be outdated. And other information may be misleading, posted by someone eager to promote a particular development or community. So you have to be careful in compiling information you find online. Make note of any sites or other sources that seem to be particularly helpful or knowledgeable. That will make it easier for you to find your second and third "deals of a lifetime."

But, you can't rely on the Internet for everything. Ultimately, there's no substitute for hopping into your car and driving around the neighborhood—unless you prefer to travel by train, bus, bicycle, or "foot power." Whichever way you travel, bring along a notebook or a laptop computer and a camera to help you remember and record exactly what you see. Remember, at this point, you're just trying to get general information about a community or neighborhood, trying to identify the best locations within your target market for a potential purchase.

So take a good look around. Is the neighborhood deteriorating or improving? A drive down the street should answer this question easily enough. You don't have to be an expert to recognize unkempt homes, uncut lawns, and debris in the street. If that's the case, just keep driving. In a bad area, your property will only decline in value along with the rest of the neighborhood. Remember, you're buying a neighborhood, not just a property.

Keep going until you find a neighborhood where the residents seem to care about maintaining the value of their properties. Now you're getting somewhere! One of the cardinal rules in real estate is to buy the worst property in the best neighborhood, *not* the best property in the worst neighborhood. That's because if you buy the worst property in the best neighborhood, you can upgrade the property to match the standards of the neighborhood, and your property value will increase. It's a formula that has worked for homeowners throughout America—and it will work for you, too.

Nearby amenities provide another clue to a good location. Apartments and homes need to be close to shopping centers, churches, schools, and other services. If your tenants can walk to a convenience store or elementary school, that's definitely a plus. And pull out a map to see where this neighborhood is situated in relation to major expressways and highways—if your tenants will spend an hour driving to work, you might want to explore a "closer-in" location.

When it comes to location, the value of properties generally conforms to what I call the concentric circle theory. For example, let's assume you're analyzing an apartment building that is rented to single students who are attending the local university. The closer the apartment is to campus, the higher the rents and the higher the sale price. By the same token, the vacancy rates will be lower, and you will probably have less tenant turnover. The same theory applies to homes. To repeat: How close are they to places of employment, shopping centers, and churches?

The diagram on page 57 illustrates the concentric circle theory. Buildings in Section A would command the highest rents; buildings in Section D would be the lowest. Generally, I try to avoid properties in Section D unless it's for a quick turnover. I try as much as possible to buy properties in A, close to the center of demand. Thus, my rents are higher and my property values increase more quickly.

If you're still in doubt about the best location in your market, there are several types of professionals who can give you insights into your prospective purchase. First, ask the city's planning department what is planned for the area you're considering. The planning staff will be glad to answer your questions; just let them know you want the answers to be blunt. Or call a local property management firm, and ask one of its account managers to discuss the pros and cons of the area.

Another source of expert advice is a knowledgeable local real

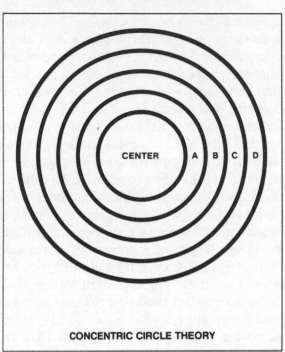

CONCENTRIC CIRCLE THEORY

estate agent. Talk to several agents on the phone or check their websites; then arrange a face-to-face meeting or two. Once you tell the agent that you're considering buying an income-producing property in the area, you'll get all kinds of advice. After all, an agent who puts you in touch with the buyer or the buyer's agent can expect to receive a commission on the sale.

So, if you want a firsthand, objective opinion about a possible property, start knocking on doors in the neighborhood. Ask some of the owners what they think about their investment. Or ask the tenants themselves. They know better than anyone what the neighborhood is really like.

Market Analysis

As a savvy investor, your second major step is to conduct a market analysis. I usually don't start to get excited about any particular property until I determine that it can be purchased for below market price. *This implies that I first know what the market is!*

ROBERT G. ALLEN

When you are seeking to buy income-producing homes, condo-miniums, duplexes, or apartment buildings, you must know the "going price" in your ideal location. The best source for up-to-date market information is a local real estate agent. Ask the agent about recent sales and present listings—in a hot real estate market, prices can rise substantially in just a couple of months.

Pay close attention to the real estate section in your local news-paper. Many papers carry a list of recent transactions on a weekly or monthly basis. Your county courthouse may also post recent sales on its website—take a look online or give them a call.

If you want to know the market values of homes or buildings in a specific neighborhood, stop and ask a property owner. We all keep our ear to the ground and we have a fairly good idea what our own property is worth by comparing it to recent nearby sales. Just ask around. In a few short minutes you'll know approximate values.

As you gather your data, it's important to keep track of every recent sale. Keep a record of the sale price and terms of the prop-erty; classify the information under number and type of units, spe-cial amenities, price per unit, and available terms. The form on page 98 should help you in compiling any comparable sales information you should happen to find.

There's one important formula that will help you determine com-parative market values: the price per square foot. Let's say a duplex with 2,000 square feet of space recently sold for $250,000 in your tar-get neighborhood. The price per square foot would be $125. If another seller offered a duplex with 1,750 square feet for $200,000, the comparable price would be about $114 per square foot. That means if the conditions of the two properties were identical, the sec-ond duplex, priced at $114, would be a bargain—its true market value (based on the $125 figure) would be $218,750.

So be sure to keep track of the price per square foot. It's proba-bly the best way to compare different investment properties of dif-ferent sizes and types—and using this figure in conversation tells others that you're serious about becoming a real estate investor.

If you still aren't sure what kind of a deal you're getting, hire an appraiser who will give you a professional opinion. Use any infor-mation you have already gathered to help you judge the validity of the appraiser's estimate.

There is, however, one more important step to take in your market analysis—and don't buy a single piece of income-producing property until you perform this essential calculation.

It's not enough for a particular property to be a true bargain, it must also provide you with enough income to cover all or nearly all of your expenses, including the mortgage, taxes, insurance, repairs, and other operating costs. Otherwise, you'll be feeding the alligator until it finishes off your investment.

Determining if a property will actually produce income for you is a two-step process. First, you need to have a clear picture of exactly what you can expect to pay each year on your purchase. That means talking to a lender—or using an online mortgage calculator—to determine how much you will pay in principal and interest on the mortgage (assuming you choose this route to buy the property). Talk to an insurance agent to determine the annual premium payment and if any increases are likely in the next year or two.

Next, check the annual property taxes assessed on the building. This is a public record and should be available online or at the courthouse. However, be aware that in some areas the sale of a property will cause a reassessment that may well result in a tax bill that is much more than you expected.

Once you calculate your total expenses for the year, just divide by twelve to determine how much your property will cost each month. In other words, if your total expenses are $120,000, your monthly expenses would be $10,000. Then divide the monthly expenses by the number of units available to rent in the building. So, if your building has ten apartments, the cost per apartment would be $1,000 each.

This means you would need to rent each apartment for at least $1,000 a month—and keep them fully occupied every month—just to cover your annual expenses. Now, $1,000 a month may seem like a fortune to your potential tenants, or it might be the greatest bargain in the marketplace.

So, to complete your calculations, you need to know rental rates in your target area. Simply call other rental properties and ask—it's a logical question and almost everyone will give you an answer. Their comments will tell you how your property compares with others in the neighborhood. Hopefully, you'll be able to charge your tenants more in rent than you'll pay in expenses, so you'll start earning profits right away.

If not, you'll need to consider if all the other advantages of owning rental property—such as higher tax deductions, increased property value—outweigh a negative cash flow at the start.

And in many cases, a lower purchase price can make all the difference between a successful and unsuccessful real estate investment. That's why we will be looking at buying bargain-priced properties next.

CHAPTER 8

The Don't-Wanter Seller: You Pick the Price and the Terms

"I couldn't believe it! All I had to do was sign the papers and I would have a check in my hand for $5,000. A three-unit apartment building that needed some roof repairs was now mine. They paid me to take it!"

—DANIEL SCOTT FREEBAIRN

If you're looking to buy a property on your own price and terms, search the Internet, the classified ads, and the for-sale-by-owner listings for the "don't-wanter." This is a seller who will do almost anything to get rid of his property. He might take a personal note from you secured only by your signature. He might take your SUV or pickup truck in exchange. He probably will give you a price that's well below the market average because he needs to sell now. He wants out!

This is the kind of seller you need to find. He won't care if your MasterCard account is maxed out, because he won't even check your credit. He's irrational. He is flexible. Don't-wanters are on their knees every night praying for deliverance, and you could be the answer to their prayers.

How many don't-wanters are there? Even in extremely tight sellers' markets there are still plenty of don't-wanters. Perhaps 5 percent of all sellers are willing to be flexible enough to be called

61

don't-wanters. And when things slow down in your local market—say a local company closes its doors or announces a big layoff—you'll find the percentage of don't-wanters will jump dramatically. Most neophyte investors become discouraged because they haven't learned that 95 percent of the sellers are not flexible. They need to be dealing with the 5 percent who are don't-wanters.

A word of caution: Sometimes a don't-wanter is a don't-wanter for a very legitimate reason. Sometimes the problems that go with a property aren't easily solved. If you are not careful in analyzing what has made the seller a don't-wanter, you could buy the property and end up being a don't-wanter for the very same reasons.

But often a don't-wanter's problems aren't as serious as she perceives them. They're only serious to the owner's situation, and you may be able to overcome them quite easily.

What makes someone a don't-wanter?

Management problems lead the list of reasons why people want to sell their income-producing property quickly. Some people cannot deal with tenants on a daily basis; they bought the property hoping to make a profit and didn't anticipate all the headaches that come with management.

The first multiple unit I purchased was a seven-unit building located in a fairly decent part of town on a busy street. The building was a converted home and had seven furnished apartments. Since the original structure was at least fifty years old, the plumbing was just beginning to cause weekly problems.

It took only a couple of months for me to realize that the excellent terms I received when I bought the building were the only good thing about owning the place. One morning at about 1:30 I was awakened by a telephone call from an upset tenant. She whispered, "Mr. Allen, I think you'd better get over here right away. The tenants in number seven are having an orgy." I rushed over immediately to find a drunken party in full progress. Since this was the third time this had happened, I called the police and went home.

All that summer I received similar complaints once or twice a week. "Mr. Allen, Ben in number three is running a heroin operation. He's smoking marijuana right now. I think you should do something before he harms one of us."

"Mr. Allen, the unwed mother in number seven is having a brawl with her friends on the lawn."

"Mr. Allen, the girl in number six moved out in the middle of the night and from what I can tell her apartment will sure need a lot of repairs."

"Mr. Allen, someone broke into our apartment last night and stole our television set." (As it turned out, Ben in number three, my resident manager, who *was* running a heroin operation, was arrested two days later with the television set in his possession. He was stealing from the tenants to help buy heroin.)

"Mr. Allen, I'm moving out of here unless you ask the people in number seven to leave immediately."

The last straw was when I cosigned with my trustworthy Ben of number three on a small loan to help him buy a pickup truck. Of course, at the time, I had no idea that he had been stealing things from the other tenants. When the police caught him with the stolen TV set they gave him two alternatives: leave town before the sun set, or go to jail. And so he left town that night. In my truck! Every month when I made out a check to the bank to cover the loan to Ben, I remembered the seven-unit building, and I swore I would never get involved in another situation like that. I was a don't-wanter.

Early that fall I put the building on the market for exactly the same price I had paid for it eighteen months earlier. I was suffering from a severe advanced case of don't-wanteritis. I wanted to get rid of my property at all costs. Luckily, I soon found someone to buy the building and cash out my equity.

But my decision was irrational—and it ended up costing me money. Rather than selling, I should have solved the real problem, which was the management of the property. At that time, though, I simply did not know how to manage. Even so, it would have been much better for me to keep the property and hire a professional management company. This same property I so hastily bought for $69,000 and resold for $69,000 a short while later sold again, one year after I sold it, for $85,000. A few years later, it had shot up to over $150,000, and I cringe to think about how much it's worth today.

Like most don't-wanters, I was very shortsighted. I concentrated only on my immediate problem. If I had solved my problem without selling, I would have more than doubled my investment in just a couple of years!

Types of Management Problems

If you're considering a real estate investment, you should know that management problems come in all shapes and sizes, including:

- Vacancy problems (Your tenants move into a competitor's apartment.)
- Tenant problems (Your tenants refuse to pay the rent.)
- Current expenses (Your tenants' air conditioner just broke.)
- Anticipated future expenses (Your building's old water heaters need replacing next year.)
- Distance problems (An absentee landlord living in a neighboring state has to travel to the property to solve the problems that crop up.)
- Time problems (The owner is too busy with other business matters to pay attention to managing the apartment building.)

There is one very simple solution to every one of these management problems. Wherever you live, you have access to professional management companies. You can do a quick search on the Internet or look in the telephone directory under "Professional Property Management." For a fee—usually around 10 percent of the gross income—the professionals will take responsibility for the maintenance, collect the rents, handle minor and major problems, evict bad tenants, advertise vacancies, and handle bookkeeping. In short, they will do everything for you. If you are building your own real estate portfolio, living in another city, or short on available time, the management-company route may be just what you need. Just make sure to watch over the management company.

Financial headaches can turn any owner into a don't-wanter. Maybe he's been hit with a tax bill he wasn't expecting, maybe he has discovered another, better investment and needs cash to make the move, or maybe he's in trouble—needs to reduce indebtedness, pay a note that is coming due, or save himself from foreclosure. With experience you'll be able to recognize these symptoms of don't-wanteritis. This kind of owner will usually negotiate willingly just to move his property quickly.

Not long after I'd sold my first multiunit property, I came across a twelve-unit building owned by an attorney. He had recently bought his partners out by placing a heavy wraparound mortgage on the building. The time he needed to manage the property, coupled with a negative monthly cash flow, made him a serious don't-wanter. I purchased the property with a down payment of less than $4,500, taking a mortgage for the balance. I promptly did some minor repairs and cosmetic work to the building, raised the rents by a couple of hundred dollars a month, and soon generated a positive cash flow from the building. Best of all, the building's value soon went right through the roof because it was generating so much more income each month. The reason I was able to get such a good deal on the purchase was that I understood the attorney's problem, which was largely financial. He simply couldn't continue to feed his monthly alligator and still make ends meet with his family obligations. He was the perfect example of a don't-wanter.

A third reason an owner becomes a don't-wanter is that his property is suffering from physical problems—the building doesn't meet fire codes, the plumbing is deteriorating, or the parking lot is too small. Like property management problems, physical problems also come in a variety of shapes. For instance:

- The competition is offering a newer or better building. Perhaps the nearby rental properties have been installing new swimming pools or fitness centers to attract new tenants, and the building's tenants are moving out.
- The building is aging—and not gracefully. Structural elements like a roof or plumbing system may need replacing at great expense to the owner.
- A deteriorating location. The neighborhood is going to the dogs. Even if the building's owner throws you a bone, the property may still be a turkey.
- Functional obsolescence. Appraisers use this term to describe the particular faults and out-of-date features of a building that cannot be easily corrected, such as small units, lack of electrical outlets, or wiring that won't support cable TV or high-speed Internet access.

If you suspect physical problems, the guiding phrase is "buyer beware." Physical problems are the most serious that confront any property owner. If you decide to help the don't-wanter by buying his dilapidated building, you may end up making his incurable problem your incurable problem.

Owners Have Problems, Too

Individual property owners have all sorts of personal problems, either real or imaginary, that turn them into don't-wanters. Fortunately, these owners want to sell badly, even if their property is making money, even if it's in great condition. If you spot this kind of motivated seller, make a low-ball offer quickly!

Here are some things to look for:

- *Retirement.* The seller decides he has worked long enough; it's about time he sold his rental units and lived a more relaxed lifestyle.
- *Health.* Some owners who have actively managed their own real estate portfolios may be stricken with serious health problems. One such owner, who couldn't leave her home, refused to relinquish management of her lifetime investment. Unfortunately, her units rapidly became a slum area in town because of lack of attention, and her children were forced to take over management to avoid catastrophe. They became don't-wanters when they saw the units' state of disrepair.
- *Marriage or divorce.* A property owner often changes his or her lifestyle following a marriage or divorce. The owner may be forced to sell for financial reasons, such as splitting an estate with an ex-spouse. Or a new marriage may mean a move to a different part of town or across the country, and the rental building goes on the market.
- *Transfers.* When a property owner who is still employed gets transferred to a new location, he usually must dispose of all his holdings. The time and distance factors make it difficult for him to hold on to the property, giving you an opportunity to buy a good property at a distressed price.
- *Social activities and status changes.* Some owners would rather have the cash in hand than the ongoing investment. They sell to buy a better lifestyle for themselves.
- *Inheritance.* When an owner passes away, the heirs frequently decide to sell the income-producing property. A sale may be necessary to pay the taxes, or the attorneys! Or the sale of a large piece of property may be the only way to fairly divide the assets in the estate. Whatever the reason, it usually doesn't take long for heirs to become don't-wanters. If you're a buyer,

chances are good that the heirs may not know the real value of the property, or if they do know, they simply don't care. Since the property was just a gift anyway, they are often inclined to sell for a good price.

- *Partnership problems.* I have discovered more good buys as the result of partnership problems than almost anything else. In such a situation, the property itself isn't bad, the partnership is bad. The partners disagree about how funds should be spent or dispersed as dividends; one partner wants to sell, while the other partner can't because of tax problems. A don't-wanter partner will do almost anything to get out of a bad relationship.

Several years ago I was involved in the sale of a beautiful twelve-unit apartment building in an excellent location. The two partners had decided to sell; each wanted to keep the building, but neither could tolerate the other. And neither would allow the other partner to buy him out for fear of being cheated. They put the property on the market, and I was there immediately with an offer they accepted. They knew that the property was worth more than the price we agreed on, but they both realized they could go on no longer. They sold for a price that was $30,000 under market, but they solved their problem.

Every fisherman has his "big fish that got away" story, and I have my "great deal that fell through" story. A partnership of seven brothers and sisters was left with a collection of more than forty apartment units in one small midwestern town. They were living in different cities all over the West and had no way to manage the properties effectively. They jointly decided that they would not sell the property to any family member for fear of what the future might bring. In addition, none of them wanted to be responsible for any litigation should anything happen to one of their tenants. They had sold the buildings once before, but that buyer had gone belly up in another enterprise and could not keep the units; the brothers and sisters reluctantly proceeded to try to sell the units again. They were serious don't-wanters. The symptoms were all there: They were willing to sell for 30 percent below the appraised price, willing to subordinate their interest to a second trust deed secured by other property, willing to deliver free-and-clear title to their property, willing to close immediately, and willing to sell with 10 percent down and carry the rest on excellent terms with 7 percent interest.

They were willing to do almost anything to get rid of the property. They knew that the property was worth more than the eventual sales price, but that was of little consequence—they were don't-wanters; they just didn't want the property.

Because of my heavy time commitments and because of a very conservative banker, I wasn't able to secure a loan for the down payment and the money required for repairs to bring the units up to rentable condition. I know that this banker's decision cost me tens of thousands of dollars in lost profits—in the first year alone. (He is no longer my banker.)

Keep Your Eyes Open

Keep your eyes open for good property that is being sold because of partnership problems—a family that can't agree on terms, a group who have become heirs to an estate, or property splits caused by a divorce. Casually ask the seller or the seller's agent why the property is now on the market.

While it's probably not a good idea to team up with a current partner in an already poor situation, you can often make an offer and take the disputed property off their hands—at a good price!

Remember, whenever you get involved with a don't-wanter, you must be sure that the problems you are buying are solvable; otherwise, you'll end up being a don't-wanter for the very same piece of property and for the very same reason.

Here's my best advice. When you recognize why the owner is a don't-wanter, ask yourself, "Is this problem real or imaginary?" If the problem is real, try to determine if a new owner can solve it. You have to realize that certain problems are not solvable. Sometimes the neighborhood is bad; sometimes the building has deteriorated too far to repair simply and easily. Use your best judgment, and if the situation looks right for you, jump in!

CHAPTER 9

Become a Prospector for "Golden" Real Estate

"After returning from Robert Allen's seminar I made seven offers on different houses, and bought number seven. I made two phone calls and got private financing. I bought it with no money down, and received $1,500 back at closing. I smiled all the way to the bank!"

—DON ROACH

Now that you know how to *recognize* a bargain, how do you go about *finding* one?

One primary source, of course, is to enlist a real estate broker or agent to help you find the right property. I consider real estate agents so important that I discuss them in detail in chapter 12. But what are other sources?

The classified section of your local newspaper lists all the don't-wanters in town. Isn't the newspaper just a collection of "cries for help"? People are paying good money to let you know they want to sell. Most of the people advertising won't have what you're looking for, but I can guarantee that at least one out of twenty has a good piece of property and wants to sell it badly enough that he will lower his price drastically for your all-cash offer! Try it.

Respond to every ad in the paper one night, and make verbal all-cash offers of at least 20 percent below the advertised price on every property. Even if you have no cash, you will have satisfied yourself that such bargains do exist. You can then do some serious searching and secure enough money to take advantage of the best buys. *I guarantee you'll run out of cash before you run out of good properties to buy!*

The newspaper is one of the cheapest and most productive tools for finding properties for sale. Use it wisely and often. You might even consider running an ad yourself. Try something like this:

I BUY PROPERTIES.

WILL PAY FAIR PRICE WITH SMALL DOWN

QUICK CLOSINGS. CALL BOB, 555-555-5555

You probably won't get a lot of responses, but when someone *does* call, you'll know the caller is genuinely interested and you'll be able to close if you want to. Run the ad in the "Real Estate Wanted" section of your newspaper. You won't be the only ad there, so write creative copy that will attract callers. It takes only one transaction to repay all your advertising costs.

The Internet offers another great way to prospect for sellers. Almost any town of any size will have a website or two—often owned by the local paper—that provides an online opportunity for motivated sellers to list their properties. In many cases, you can read a description of the property, see a photo or two, contact the seller via e-mail and even make an offer—without leaving the comfort of your home or office. Because you can travel so quickly from one "virtual" property to another, the Internet is ideal for serious prospecting, especially when your time is limited.

Of course, if you're like most people you do have to drive to work, the supermarket, a nearby playground, and your church or synagogue. Whenever you're in your car, pay attention to those "for sale by owner" signs. When you see one, make a habit of stopping and asking the owner about the details of the sale. Many times you can even pick up a flyer or brochure from a tube or drop box on the front lawn.

Don't be afraid to stop; the fact that the property has a "for sale" sign is an indication that the owner welcomes passersby to stop and inquire. Walk in, inspect the property, and ask every question that comes to mind. It's the best free education available. When the property sells and the sign comes down, stop again and ask the new owner about the terms and conditions of the purchase. And, of course, if you should happen to find a bargain, buy it yourself!

Create a Listing Farm

Another good source is to establish a *listing farm*. Real estate agents choose one area of town they feel they can service well, and they contact every property owner in that area. They tell the owners that they are specializing in properties in that particular area, and they offer to help property owners either buy or sell property. The real estate agent will then visit each owner occasionally to learn about recent sales in the area and to discover any pending plans to sell.

The listing farm is a very successful technique for real estate agents, and it can be useful to you as well. Just call it your "buying farm." Find a neighborhood you're interested in, and circulate a flyer similar to this:

> Property owners! I buy real estate. If you are planning to sell in the near future, call me before you list with a real estate agent. I just might be able to save you a commission and the anxiety of waiting for the right buyer to come along. Call me at [phone number] or email me at [email address].

When you're prospecting, you can find a wealth of information in your local county courthouse (or county government website). If you walk into the courthouse, you can look at legal notices filed on the bulletin board. They will list individuals and companies that have had judgments rendered against them, that have had properties foreclosed, or that are behind on their payments. The same location could list individuals who are seriously delinquent in payment of property taxes. All of these people are don't-wanters; most would welcome your help.

Another good source of don't-wanters is the divorce file kept at the courthouse as a matter of public record. Look for recent divorces. You can examine the complete files, which give information about property jointly owned (and probably available for sale).

Here's another proven suggestion for building your portfolio.

Compile a list of recent divorce filings and addresses of the parties involved. Then try sending each individual a letter that reads something like this:

Dear _____:

I understand that you have had some recent changes in your life and that you may need to sell some of your property. I buy real estate and will be more than happy to make an offer on your property. If you are interested, please contact me at your earliest convenience.

Sincerely,
[Your Name, Phone, and Email Address]

At the courthouse, you will also be able to obtain the addresses of individuals who own property in your buying farm. You may want to send each of them a letter expressing your interest in buying his property. If you want to see what a property looks like on the official plats of the county, tell the county recorder. Be sure to ask questions; it's the only way to learn.

Still another good way to find bargains is to search your local business or commercial newspaper. This is usually a small daily or weekly publication that lists all of the divorces, judgments, bankruptcies, foreclosures, deaths, and probate cases for the benefit of attorneys and title companies. A subscription usually costs less than $100 annually and can be a very valuable listing of don't-wanters. Ask your attorney if he knows about such a publication, or go to the public library, which should have copies available for you.

Seek Out Attorneys and Accountants

Here's another tip: Talk to as many attorneys and accountants as you can. That's because the first person a seller talks to about selling his property is usually his accountant or lawyer. And of course, if you become the buyer, you could hire the referring attorney to handle the paperwork in the sale or the accountant to review the books. As Humphrey Bogart once said in the classic movie *Casablanca,* "This could be the start of a beautiful friendship."

And don't stop with attorneys and accountants. Be sure to let all your friends, neighbors, and business acquaintances know that you're interested in buying property—one of them just might give you a good lead. Some prospectors distribute printed cards that say:

I Buy Real Estate.
Call [Your name] at [Phone number]

Others send out occasional email reminders—being careful to respect the recipients' wishes about whether or not they want to hear from you in this way.

If you are really creative, try T-shirts and bumper stickers. Or contact your local apartment owner's association for a list of all apartment owners in your city. Contact them all, one by one, and explore the possibilities. Some people even try billboards.

Those of you who have teenage children might try involving them in the search for your real estate. It's great training for adulthood, and they could get really excited if you paid them a reasonable fee for every super buy they locate. I have used students between semesters or in the summer months to act as finders for me in locating real estate. These college students learn quickly and can make excellent money while they help you reach your financial goals. If you are extremely busy in your present job, this might be just what you need.

There are hundreds of ways to find out where property is for sale. Keep looking. Keep prospecting. Spend a few minutes a day on a regular schedule, and you're bound to discover a vein of pure gold.

Just remember that only a small percentage of the property on the market will be right for you. Don't get discouraged; don't get overanxious. Finding exactly the right property is a numbers game. I'll bet your money will run out long before you run out of buying opportunities, if you just keep at it!

Here's a classic example of a "don't-wanter" flyer that came across my desk.

El Dumpo Apartments

Property description: Ten-unit apartment building located at ADDRESS in the western city of ANYTOWN. The building was completed last year and is fully furnished, but is still totally vacant.

Asking price: $400,000

Current loans: A $300,000 fixed-rate 30-year loan payable at $1,995 per month at an interest rate of 7 percent. The mortgage can be assumed with no qualifying.

Special information: The current owner purchased the building from the developer upon completion. But while the sale was still pending, the owner received a job offer in another state that he couldn't refuse. Although he closed on the property rather than lose his own down payment, the owner cannot manage the building because of the distance problem. Therefore, he listed his property at 33 percent under its true market value to ensure a quick sale. His ad in the local newspaper says, "This is a good opportunity for an individual with initiative and ability to solve problems."

Market conditions: City officials are expecting a housing shortage in the near future due to construction of several new resorts and shopping centers in this tourist-oriented community. Current rents in the neighborhood are $600–800 a month per comparable unit.

Terms: The owner will exchange his $100,000 equity in this property for land, paper, boat, vacation condominium, or personal property. There are no geographic limitations. In other words, make me an offer. I won't refuse.

Sweeteners: In order to make a deal, the seller will lease back the property at $1,500 per month until the occupancy reaches at least 60 percent or for one year, whichever comes first. And he will also provide for a resident manager on the property on or before the date of possession.

Do you get the picture? This is an actual example of a few years ago. This owner is a don't-wanter—and he can't wait to hand you the keys to his property!

CHAPTER 10

Financial Analysis: Here's How to Read the Numbers

"I bought a home from a bank for $50,000 under market, using techniques I learned from Bob Allen. It generated a $280-a-month positive cash flow, and I was able to sell the house for a $32,000 profit."

—TIM BOGERT

Once you've located a promising property, your next step is to conduct a financial analysis. You want to be sure the deal is as good as it sounds. If not, this simple exercise can save you thousands and thousands of dollars, not to mention what you'll save in aspirin by avoiding a bad-buy headache!

Let's examine an income-producing piece of real estate to see how it operates. Even if you don't consider yourself a numbers person, it's really not that difficult. In fact, about all you'll probably need are a good calculator and your common sense. The figures I use in my examples may not be representative of your particular area, but these principles should apply anywhere.

For our example, you are considering making an offer on a five-unit apartment building that is well located in a growing city. The rental situation is excellent because the building is in good condition. Each of the apartments has two bedrooms and is rented for $600 a month. The renter pays the electric and gas bills.

How do you determine if this investment is a good one? To help with our analysis, consult the Annual Property Operating Data form on page 79. This will help you determine the cash flow situation for the building based on the annual property operating data. The top one third of the form provides space for all the important data you will need to learn about the property.

The purchase price is $200,000, and the seller owns the property free and clear of any mortgages. (All figures are rounded to the nearest dollar.) The seller is extremely motivated and wants a quick sale. He realizes that the value of his property is close to $240,000, but he needs out and settles for a price of $200,000, which is about 20 percent below market.

At this price, the seller's equity is $200,000. The seller has even agreed to sell the building to you with a down payment of only $20,000, and issue you a mortgage for the balance of the purchase price. This will result in a new loan of $180,000 from the seller—and you won't even need to go to the bank for approval! Over a thirty-year period, with an interest rate of 7 percent, your payments on the mortgage loan will be $1,200 a month. The illustration below illustrates your financial situation.

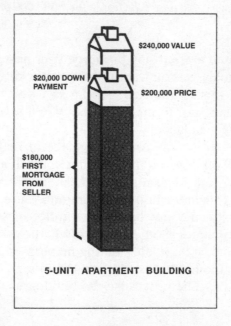

$240,000 VALUE

$20,000 DOWN PAYMENT

$200,000 PRICE

$180,000 FIRST MORTGAGE FROM SELLER

5-UNIT APARTMENT BUILDING

This type of sale is referred to as a Uniform Real Estate Contract, a seller first mortgage, or "seller carries the financing," depending on which area of the country you are in. The seller receives monthly payments of $1,200 from you (the buyer) on the new loan.

The 7 percent the seller receives is certainly better than the interest he could earn from a savings account. In addition, depending on his tax situation, he may even prefer to give you a mortgage and receive the payments over an extended period of time, rather than getting all his equity in cash. You can turn these situations to your benefit if you don't want to invest a lot of your own cash in the property—and that's the main point of the nothing-down approach.

Let's continue this example, filling in the top of the form. The seller has agreed to accept a small down payment ($20,000) and to have the rest of his equity paid to him over a thirty-year period. If your seller has an existing mortgage, fill in that balance, payment, period, interest, and term as well.

We have also found out that the property has an assessed value for tax purposes as follows:

Land	$ 50,000	33.3 percent of value
Improvements	$100,000	66.7 percent of value
Total	$150,000	100 percent of value

You can obtain this information, which is important for computing property tax consequences, by looking at the county tax notice the seller should have in his files. If the seller doesn't have the information, call the county tax assessor and ask for the assessed value of the property. The assessor can also give you a projection for the coming year's taxes.

You will notice that the assessed value is usually lower than the actual market value of the property. Each state has a different method of calculating property taxes, but generally the county assessor determines an assessed value for each property. The assessor may or may not revise this assessed value every few years, meaning that the appraised market value is likely to climb much more quickly. However, it is the county's assessed value that is used to calculate the county taxes.

After you have completed the information for the first third of the form, it's time to gather information for the income and expenses analysis (lines 1 through 34). This information is vital and *must* be verified whenever possible. The seller usually doesn't have readily available financial data on the operation of his building. He may estimate, projecting figures far from reality. He might not be lying (although this could be the case), but the tendency is to project high rents and low expenses, and neither figure is accurate. After all, he wants to portray a positive situation to the buyer.

Therefore, be wary of the seller's figures; double-check *everything* yourself. If possible, try to obtain the seller's income tax records—the seller may balk at showing you these records, but it doesn't hurt to ask. The tax records will probably be closer to the truth; the seller will tend to report the lowest income and the highest expenses.

Let's examine each of the items in the Annual Property Operating Data form on page 79 to see how each is calculated:

1. Gross Scheduled Rental Income

This is the amount of income the property would generate if the building were rented all year with no vacancies. In our example, the five-unit building is rented for $600 per apartment.

$$\$\,600 \times 5 = \$\,3,000 \text{ monthly income}$$
$$\$3,000 \times 12 = \$36,000 \text{ yearly income}$$

If every apartment in the building were rented all year, you could expect to collect $36,000 in rents.

2. Other Income

This income might include cash from vending machines (soft drinks, candy, or washers and dryers in the laundry room). It might also cover furniture rentals, pet fees, rental of parking spaces, or forfeited deposits. In our example, the building has a small candy-vending machine that generates about $50 a month net profit. Yearly income from this source is $600.

3. Total Gross Income

List here the total of all money collected from the operation of the building—add lines 1 and 2.

Annual Property Operating Data

SAMPLE

Purpose _____ Date ____ September 1 _____

Name ___ Hidden Valley Apartments ___

Location ___ 100 Main St. ___ Price $ ___ 200,000 _____

Type of Property _5 units_ _____ Loans $ _____ 0 _____

Assessed/Appraised Values Equity $ ___ 200,000 _____

Land	$ 50,000	33 %
Improvements	$ 100,000	67 %
Personal Property	$	%
Total	$ 150,000	100 %

Adjusted Basis as of _____ $ _____

	Balance	Payment	Period	Interest	Term
Existing $					
1st $				%	
2nd $				%	
3rd $				%	
Potential					
1st $	180,000	1,200	mo.	7 %	30 yrs.
2nd $				%	

		%		2		3		Comments
1	GROSS SCHEDULED RENTAL INCOME					36	000	5 x 600 x 12
2	Plus: Other Income						600	
3	TOTAL GROSS INCOME					36	600	
4	Less: Vacancy and Credit Losses	5%				1	830	
5	GROSS OPERATING INCOME					34	770	
6	Less: Operating Expenses							
7	Accounting and Legal			750				
8	Advertising, Licenses and Permits	2%		695				
9	Property Insurance			2	000			
10	Property Management	7%		2	434			
11	Payroll - Resident Management							
12	Other							
13	Taxes - Workmen's Compensation							
14	Personal Property Taxes							
15	Real Estate Taxes	12%		4	000			
16	Repairs and Maintenance	5%		1	738			
17	Services - Elevator							
18	Janitorial							
19	Lawn							
20	Pool							
21	Rubbish							
22	Other							
23	Supplies approx.	1%		350				
24	Utilities - Electricity			1	200			
25	Gas and Oil			1	500			
26	Sewer and Water			3	000			
27	Telephone			500				
28	Other			260				
29	Miscellaneous	4.1%		1	440			
30								
31	TOTAL OPERATING EXPENSES	57%				19	867	
32	NET OPERATING INCOME					14	903	
33	Less: Total Annual Debt Service					14	400	1,200 x 12
34	CASH FLOW BEFORE TAXES						503	

The statements and figures presented herein, while not guaranteed, are secured from sources we believe authorative.

Prepared by _____

Nothing Down Seminar Manual

4. Less Vacancy and Credit Losses

Unless you are in an extremely tight rental market, your building will always have some vacancy. Even if the seller tells you that he hasn't had a vacancy in three years, you should reduce your estimated income to cover the vacancies you can expect. To do so, multiply the gross scheduled income by 3 to 5 percent to account for the lost days in rent between tenants or lost income when one of the tenants moves out in the middle of the night without paying the rent. It is almost impossible to have 100 percent rent collection, so plan accordingly.

There may be some markets where overbuilding of apartments has occurred. In this case, you should call up your local rental agency or several professional property management companies (listed in the Yellow Pages of the phone book under "Real Estate Rental Services" and "Property Management Firms"). These people are experts in the field and will be able to give you valuable and free information concerning current rental rates and current vacancy rates in various areas of your city. You can also do your own rental and vacancy study by asking other area resident managers some pertinent questions about their rental projects. But seek professional advice early so you cut your risk and increase your safety.

5. Gross Operating Income

After vacancy and credit losses are subtracted from the gross income, you will have the total amount of income this property should generate in a year's time.

6. Operating Expenses

Subtract all the expenses you will incur during the year from the gross operating income. These operating expenses include:

Accounting and legal
Advertising, licenses, and permits
Property insurance
Property management
Payroll and resident management
Taxes
Repairs and maintenance

Services
Supplies
Utilities

7. Accounting and Legal

Make an estimate here based on your own situation. In this example, we have included $750 for an accountant to balance your books at the end of the year and for some minor legal work. It could be higher but I doubt it would be much lower.

8. Advertising, Licenses, and Permits

This expense will vary from state to state and will depend on the various laws and rental markets. We have made provision here for about 2 percent of the gross scheduled income to be used for these purposes.

9. Property Insurance

Here's an area where prices tend to rise very quickly. In our example, we are assuming your annual premium would be $2,000. The seller may let you assume the existing insurance on the property. It would be wiser, however, to have your own insurance agent make a bid; the seller may have underinsured the property, and the building may not be fully protected. It pays to have several insurance bids; you will be amazed at the difference in rates. Bids are free, so you have nothing to lose. There are sites on the Internet that will help you compare rates from various insurance carriers without even picking up a phone!

10. Property Management

If you plan to manage the property yourself, you will not have to include any fee here for outside professional management services. Although fees for such services vary from state to state, they range from 5 to 10 percent of the gross operating income. If you own many units, your rates can be negotiated even lower.

A professional management firm takes care of everything that has to do with operating the property, including the collection of rents, payment of expenses, and making sure the mortgage is paid each month. If requested, the firm will send you a check each month with an accounting of all expenses and income. You never

81

have to worry about plugged toilets or leaking roofs; your management company will take care of everything and will call you only for major decisions, if that's what you want. In addition, a management firm usually has maintenance personnel on its staff. They may be cheaper to hire than you can afford on your own. A management firm may even help you by purchasing supplies at wholesale prices.

Now, that's the good news. The bad news is that not all management companies are as competent as I describe. I encourage you to do some in-depth checking before you decide on your company and to monitor their service monthly until you feel they are honest, trustworthy, capable, and professional. Whatever you do, don't walk away from your property after you have turned it over to a manager and forget about it. Inspect your property monthly and read your reports from the management company faithfully. After you have acquired a number of properties, you may decide to hire your own management team. This way you can maintain a firmer control over expenses and income, while taking advantage of every possible cost saving.

As a novice investor, it's a good idea to manage your own property for at least the first several months. That way you can learn firsthand all about the problems of managing an apartment building.

As you grow, you may decide to turn over all of the headaches (and believe me, there are headaches!) to a professional company. The professionals know their business and will perform well as long as you monitor them carefully. And if you're spending all your time managing one property, you won't have enough spare time to go out looking for more properties to buy. Therefore, in our example, I have included professional management at 7 percent.

11, 12, and 13. Payroll and Resident Management

The larger the apartment building, the more people you will need on your staff. For a building of up to about twenty-five apartment units, you can probably expect your resident manager to handle all minor repairs and problems. The resident manager should be trained to collect rents and handle minor problems without calling in outside help; it's important to find a handyman for this position. His salary should be enough to motivate him to do his job well. A typical arrangement is to provide the manager with free rent plus a small salary. This will depend on your area. This amount is not paid by a management company, if you choose to hire one. As the owner, you pay this expense, although the management company may provide training and support for your resident managers.

14 and 15. Taxes

Depending on your county, you will have to pay some type of property or real estate tax on your investment. You can determine the seller's tax bill by calling the county assessor and asking for the tax assessment for the current year. Don't rely on the seller's estimate of the past year's taxes. Also, be aware that in some states the real estate tax bill can go up significantly after a property changes ownership. Check with your tax assessor to see if this situation might apply to you—there's no need for "sticker shock" when next year's tax bill arrives. If you are getting a mortgage from a lending company, usually the taxes, as well as the insurance payments, are paid monthly into an escrow account. You should know if that's the case; otherwise, you will be deducting these expenses twice. Count on about 12 percent of the gross operating income.

16. Repairs and Maintenance

These expenses usually amount to between 5 and 10 percent of the gross operating income. On newer buildings, the figure will be closer to 5 percent; it could be 10 percent or more on older buildings. Try to obtain the seller's receipts for major repairs during the past several years so you can see the trend. For our example, repairs were calculated at 5 percent.

17 to 22. Services

Each of these expenses should be verified as closely as possible. Calls to various experts can help immensely. You might also check with the firms that are currently providing the service to the seller. A resident manager can take care of some of these services, such as mowing the lawn.

23. Supplies

There is always a need for small items such as tools, faucet rings, fertilizer, and so on. You should budget about 1 percent of your gross operating income for such expenditures. After a year's operation you can make a more accurate projection. You may give your resident manager a small petty cash fund so he can take care of these small items without having to bother you; if your property is professionally managed, all of these items will be handled through the management firm.

24 to 28. Utilities

The cost of each utility item should be verified by going to the local agency and asking for the past several years' utilities records for the building. In my area the gas company will give you (with the seller's permission) a computer printout of the past twelve months' gas bills. This can reveal any trends and can help you make projections for the coming year. In our example, I have made an estimate for various utility expenses. The tenants pay for their own electricity, gas, and garbage collection.

29 and 30. Miscellaneous

This is just an estimate of expenses that have not been included in other categories. It will amount to at least 1 percent of gross operating income. We are going to be conservative and plan on 4 percent.

31. Total Operating Expenses

Here is where you total up all the expenses we have listed so far. Usually, this total will be from 30 to 60 percent of your total operating income—a ratio that varies in different parts of the country. In other words, from 30 to 60 percent of your total collected income will eventually be paid out as operating expenses. If the seller gives you a projection for expenses that is lower than 30 percent, something is not right somewhere. It is possible to have expenses lower than 30 percent if the building is new, if the tenants pay all of their own utilities, and if you do your own management. But if property taxes are high in your state, your expense ratio will be 40 percent or higher. I have used 57 percent expense ratio on our example. Check with your local management firm to determine what your local expense ratio will be.

32. Net Operating Income

Subtract all your expenses (line 31) from your gross operating income. What's left is called your net operating income. If you have been conservative in your projections and have verified as many figures as possible, this net operating income will be the amount of money you should collect for a year's operation of the building—before making the mortgage payment. This figure is a critical one in judging the value of the investment, as you will see later.

33. Total Annual Debt Service or Mortgage Payments

Take your monthly mortgage payment and multiply by twelve to get your total debt service figure—in other words, the amount you'll pay each year on your mortgage (principal and interest).

34. Cash Flow Before Taxes

After you have totaled all these expenses and mortgage payments, you should wind up with a small positive cash flow. Obviously, the higher the cash flow, the more likely you are to make money right off the bat. However, any positive result from your projections, no matter how small, is a good thing!

Just as in a land investment, it is possible to have a negative cash flow—an alligator—in an income property. If the mortgage payments are too high because of small down payments, or if the expenses are inordinately high because the building is an older one (or income is very low because of low rents), there could be a negative cash flow. The only ways to eliminate a negative cash flow are to restructure the mortgage payments, pay less for the property, increase the rents, or lower the expenses. More on this later.

If you determine after your analysis that the property has a heavy negative cash flow, and it will not be possible to raise rents in the immediate future, you will have to be prepared to subsidize your investment on a monthly basis until the cash flow can be improved. If you are not prepared to subsidize the investment, then don't buy the property. It is better not to buy something than to lose it to foreclosure for failure to make the payments.

By filling out the Annual Property Operating Data form in this example, you have learned some of the valuable information needed to make a good investment. First of all, you have collected *all* of the necessary information needed to enable you to make a wise decision based on costs. The figures have all been verified and are conservative. The bottom line of the analysis form tells how much debt you can amortize without going in the hole. This one sheet is all any investor needs to do a preliminary investment analysis. Blank copies of this form are available by writing my company, Robert Allen Real Estate, 5072 North 300 West, Provo, UT 84604. Ask for information about APOD forms.

Remember, your projections on any income-producing property should be conservative and based on reliable information. Make sure you do your homework at this stage of your investment planning. It's the best way to avoid costly mistakes later.

CHAPTER 11

Just How Much Money Are You Going to Make?

"Bob Allen's strategies gave me the information and confidence I needed to net $30,000 in equity and $1,400 a month in cash flow on my first deal. I'll never have to rely on a J-O-B again."

—STEVE ECHOLS

Now that you've put your calculator to good use in determining how much of a cash flow you might expect from buying an income-producing property, let's do a few more calculations. After all, it's fun figuring out how much money you're going to make!

One of the most important concepts is how much of a financial return you might expect to receive on your investment—a concept called return on investment, or ROI. Let's use the same example. You have invested $20,000 as a down payment toward the purchase price of the five-unit building. If you had taken the same $20,000 and invested it in a savings account at a local bank, you would be lucky to earn a few extra dollars for one year. How well does real estate compare to a savings account's guaranteed return? For well-priced, well-situated properties, the return on your investment is likely to be surprisingly higher!

There are four kinds of financial returns you might receive from a normal income-producing property investment:

- *Cash flow.* This is the money left over after all expenses and mortgage payments have been made. This is what you determined in the previous chapter.
- *Equity buildup.* This is the money that builds up as your mortgage payments gradually reduce the loan. If you hold the property long enough, you may wind up paying off the loan entirely.
- *Tax savings.* These come from the favorable tax advantages of owning real estate. For instance, the interest you pay on your mortgage loan may be deductible—check with your tax advisor.
- *Appreciation.* This is the financial benefit of owning a property that increases in value over time.

If we analyze the five-unit building with respect to these four kinds of investment return, we discover some very interesting things. In fact, when you look at all four types of return on your investment, you will probably never again put a dime into a bank savings account!

1. Cash Flow

$$\frac{\text{Annual net cash flow}}{\text{Down payment}} = \frac{\$500}{\$20,000} = 2.5 \text{ percent}$$

This kind of cash on cash return seems extremely low. But let's keep going; this is only the start.

2. Equity Buildup

A portion of every one of your mortgage payments of $1,200 a month is applied toward the reduction of the $180,000 loan. Using your calculator, it is possible to determine that at the end of the first year of ownership and after paying the interest, the loan balance will be $178,171. If you then sold the building, you would collect an extra $1,828 from the reduction in principal that took place during your ownership of the property.

$$\frac{\text{Loan principal reduction}}{\text{Down payment}} = \frac{\$1,828}{\$20,000} = 9.1 \text{ percent}$$

3. Tax Savings

$$\frac{\text{Tax savings}}{\text{Down payment}} = \frac{\$500}{\$20,000} = 2.5 \text{ percent}$$

We will assume a $500 tax savings and let your accountant show you how to work out the specific details. Again, your tax return savings could be much higher than this; we're just taking a conservative approach.

4. Appreciation

Appreciation is the gravy in real estate investing. It is not possible to project the increase in property values accurately since the increase depends on inflation, investor demand, and supply of available units. But property values should at least keep pace with inflation. If appreciation rates change, so will your rate of return. But let's conservatively figure an appreciation rate of 5 percent.

That doesn't seem like much, but because you bought your property with just $20,000 down, that appreciation alone would give you an investment return of almost 60 percent. And think how much higher that return would be if you bought the apartment building with nothing down!

$$\frac{\text{Rate of increase in value} \times \text{value}}{\text{Down payment}} = \frac{5\% \times \$240,000 \text{ value}}{\$20,000} = 60 \text{ percent}$$

Remember, by carefully searching for the don't-wanter seller, you were able to buy this property at $40,000 below the market price. You thus made an immediate profit. If you were to put the property back on the market, you could recoup this profit and gain a 200 percent return on your $20,000 investment before sales costs, without waiting for any appreciation (assuming you sold it yourself without paying a commission to a real estate agent). But if you decided to hold on to the property, then your rate of return from appreciation would be calculated by multiplying the appreciation rate (5 percent) by the value ($240,000) and dividing this by your investment ($20,000).

When all of the above rates of return are combined, your total rate of return from this real estate investment after one full year is:

Cash flow	2.5 percent
Equity buildup	9.1 percent

Tax savings	2.5 percent
Discount bonus	200.0 percent
Appreciation	60.0 percent
TOTAL RETURN	274.1 percent

That's right! *Almost 275 percent!* Compared to your measly return at the bank, 275 percent looks rather exciting. This is, of course, your return on investment in the first year of ownership. The ROI will decline each year thereafter.

By investing $20,000 in an apartment building, you have turned your initial down payment into almost $75,000. While real estate returns are not locked in like a bank savings account or certificate of deposit, you can achieve much higher returns in real estate in return for your efforts and willingness to take on a few uncertainties.

Now, before you go charging out into the world to buy your first property, here's a word or two of caution. First, you can't expect every property you analyze to give you a 275 percent return on your investment. You can't even expect to buy every property with a small down payment. Do not misunderstand me. My system involves buying property from highly motivated sellers who, because of their flexible circumstances, are willing to sell their property with excellent terms or at excellent prices or both.

You must be willing to get turned down dozens of times before you find the right seller with the right property. This is a numbers game. Most sellers will reject you. Real estate agents will tell you that what you are looking for is almost impossible to find. Almost everyone will tell you that you are crazy for wasting your time. But I assure you, from my own experience and from that of tens of thousands of graduates of my seminars, that the bargains are there, right now. Those great deals are found every day . . . by buyers who are willing to persist until they find them. If you want to play safe, put your money in a bank.

But safe as it may seem, there is no profit in keeping your money in a savings account (unless you are waiting for the right real estate investment), because inflation and taxes render your investment useless. You must take the risk that real estate investment requires. You must cope with management problems (or give them to a management company for a fee). You will learn that your financial independence comes at a price, but the price is well worth it. Nothing worth anything is free.

The Power of Leverage

Two final elements that need to be considered in an analysis of a real estate investment are the power of leverage and the determination of value.

Leverage makes real estate an extremely advantageous investment under most circumstances. Think of using a small lever to move a large boulder. You could never move the boulder by yourself. But if you use a lever, the job becomes easy. Leverage in real estate is the ability to control a large number of investment dollars with a small amount of your own money. Without leverage, the $240,000 investment in our example would not have been nearly as exciting. In the example, you could control $240,000 worth of real estate with only $20,000 (and for which you paid approximately 80 cents on the dollar). You borrowed the remaining $180,000 from the seller (or you could have used a lending company's money). If you had purchased the building with your own money—$200,000 cash—then the return on your investment would have been very different.

Cash flow without mortgage payments:

$$\frac{\$14,903}{\$200,000} = 7.5 \text{ percent}$$

Equity buildup: Since there is no mortgage, there is no equity buildup.

Tax savings:

$$\frac{\text{Tax savings}}{\text{Down payment}} = \frac{\$500}{\$200,000} = 0.25$$

Appreciation:

$$\frac{\$12,000}{\$240,000} = 5 \text{ percent}$$

Discount Bonus:

$$\frac{\$40,000}{\$200,000} = 20 \text{ percent}$$

TOTAL RETURN: 7.5 + 0.25 + 5 + 20 = 32.75 percent

With leverage your return is almost 275 percent; without leverage, it's only about 32.75 percent. That is the power of leverage. The more you can buy with the least amount of money, the greater your rate of return. That's why the nothing-down approach is so effective for so many investors. Of course, the more leverage, the greater the risk—an element that must be overcome. But real estate is one of the few areas in which an average investor with average knowledge can borrow other people's money, then use leverage to increase your own return. That's what the nothing-down concept is all about.

Determination of Value

The final area of analysis is determination of value. After all, who is to say the building you buy today for $300,000 on fairly good terms isn't really an $250,000 building? How do you make sure you're not losing $50,000? Real estate sellers have been notorious for pricing their property much higher than market value—if they can get away with it. One of my clients insisted on purchasing sixty acres of desert property for $60,000, a price that is still too high twenty years later. How can you avoid making the same mistake?

There are several ways to find this bit of information—information that is crucial to your entire investment decision. The easiest way to determine a building's accurate value is to hire a professional real estate appraiser. You will find them listed on the Internet, just do a search for appraisers and "your town." You can also look in the Yellow Pages, or contact the American Society of Appraisers (www.appraisers.org) at 555 Herndon Parkway, Suite 125, Herndon, VA 20170. Appraisal costs will vary from several hundred to several thousand dollars depending on the size and complexity of the property.

A less expensive—and probably free—way to determine value is to ask a local real estate agent to do a comparative market analysis. In this case, the agent consults the area's multiple listing service (MLS) or county recorder's office to find three to five recent sales that can be compared to this particular property.

Or, you can do your own estimate of value by employing the same processes as a professional appraiser. If you have the time, try working out the numbers yourself first, then see how your results compare to the professional's. Here are the three approaches you can use to determine the property's value:

Cost approach. Determine what it would cost at present rates to replace the building by talking with local building contractors. In other words, if an earthquake, a hurricane, or a fire destroyed the building tomorrow, how much would it cost you to rebuild the same structure on the same spot.

Income approach. Determine value by analyzing the income the building generates. This involves some additional calculations based on the formulas you have practiced so far. We will discuss this in a few moments under "capitalization rate."

Market approach. Find similar properties in your market and find out their sale prices. This will give an indication of what investors in the marketplace will pay for a similar building.

Of these three approaches, the market approach is the most effective method of determining current value, especially in "hot" real estate markets where prices keep going up month after month. Or if prices suddenly turn downward, keeping an eye on your local market could prevent you from overpaying as well.

The prize for investing in real estate goes to the investor who *knows,* not who guesses, the current market price of similar units. The more time you spend studying the local market, the more you will know about market prices and the more prepared you will be to judge them. This must be a continual process, one that you conduct every time you consider making a purchase.

Capitalization Rates

Until recently, sophisticated investors usually arrived at a determination of value by looking at the stream of cash flow they could expect in the future from an investment. They used this formula:

$$\text{Value} = \frac{\text{Income (net operating income)}}{\text{Capitalization rate (or V)}} = \frac{I}{CR}$$

If a property had a net operating income of $10,000 and a capitalization rate of 10 percent, then its value would be calculated by dividing the net income by 0.10 (which is the same as multiplying it by 10). Therefore, if the annual net operating income was $20,000, the value of the property would be $200,000, assuming a 10 percent capitalization rate.

Now, there's another way to approach this formula. If you want to determine the capitalization rate, all you have to do is divide the net operating income by the purchase price, according to this formula:

$$\text{Capitalization (cap rate)} = \frac{\text{Net operating income (NOI)}}{\text{Price}}$$

Playing with the numbers in this way, you know that the net operating income is $20,000, and the purchase price is $200,000, giving you a cap rate of 10 percent.

Now, what is the value of performing this little calculation? The cap rate is one of the ways you can compare the potential benefits of purchasing different income-producing properties—the higher the cap rate, the better!

For example, you might be comparing that first property to a second property with a net operating income of $12,600. If the seller is asking $194,000 for the second property, then the cap rate (shortened in real estate lingo) is:

$12,600 / $194,000 = .065 or 6.5 percent. Clearly, in this case, the first property, with its much higher cash flow, would appear to be a better buy.

Be sure to analyze each property carefully on its financial merits before presenting an offer to the seller. Follow the steps outlined in the previous chapter, and summarized below:

1. Determine the gross operating income of the property you are considering buying (gross yearly rents less vacancy estimate).
2. As a rough guess, estimate what percentage of your gross rents will be spent on expenses. As you learned earlier, this may be as low as 30 percent or as high as 60 percent. As you gain experience on your particular area, you will learn how to estimate accurately. For the time being, use 50 percent until you learn if your area has a higher or lower average expense ratio. Of course, as soon as possible, your estimate of annual expenses should be replaced with the actual expense projection obtained through a more detailed analysis of the property operating expenses.

3. Subtract the expenses (2) from the gross operating income (1) to come up with net operating income. Once you have this all-important figure, you are ready to use the capitalization formula to determine the property value.
4. Using the formula, determine the property capitalization rate. This is done as follows:

Net operating income/Seller asking price = Capitalization rate

In most areas of the country, a property with a cap rate of 10 percent or higher won't last long at such a price. On the other end of the scale, if a property has a cap rate of 5 percent or less, it's possible something might be wrong:

• The rents are too low.
• The expenses are too high.
• The price of the property is out of line.

You may still be safe in buying the property with a low cap rate if you are certain that you can immediately raise rents or lower expenses significantly and therefore raise your cash flow. Generally, however, a property with a low cap rate is being sold by an individual who is trying to make a killing in the real estate market. Make sure you don't become his victim.

The higher the cap rate, the greater the possibility of a positive cash flow even with small down payments. The lower the cap rate, the greater the possibility that you will have an alligator on your hands. Since the price of real estate is going up continually (and thereby causing lower cap rates), it is easy to see why it is more and more difficult these days to find a property with a positive cash flow.

In many markets, buyers are willing to purchase properties with a negative cash flow. By doing this, they are speculating on the potential for appreciation. As investors began to expect prices to increase automatically, they sacrificed cash-flow returns in anticipation of high appreciation profits. Since rents haven't kept pace with property values, cash flows from real estate can be low and even be negative, depending on financing. What you must remember is not to get caught up in the feverish purchase of highly overpriced properties just for the sake of investing.

I am of the opinion that a once-in-a-lifetime buy comes on the market about every seven days. I would rather be investing my time finding the best buys than spending my money feeding an alligator property that is overpriced.

One last word about using the cap-rate formula. It is generally very difficult to find a home, duplex, or four-unit apartment building that has an adequate capitalization rate. This is not because the smaller property is not a good buy; it is because the smaller property has an additional reason for being built. The rationale for the smaller unit is to provide the owner with a way to live in his property and have renters pay enough to make the owner's mortgage payment.

As a rule, it is better to rely on the market sales approach when purchasing small units. What have similar properties sold for recently? On properties of over four units, the capitalization-rate formula will begin to be more accurate.

This is a rather simplistic view of an extremely complicated subject. If you are a beginner and don't quite understand the valuation process, hire a professional appraiser, or use a real estate agent who knows his investment market well. The best real estate agent to deal with will have a CCIM designation (Certified Commercial Investment Member). This is a strenuous program of certification, which is granted by the Realtors' National Marketing Institute. Through practice, your confidence will grow, and you will be able to make accurate market-value estimates yourself.

Check the Property's Condition

Now, let's summarize. It goes without saying that the location should be good, the price in line with the market, the seller anxious to sell and flexible, and the financial details favorable. However, if property condition is poor, then you should not buy. The condition of the property is extremely important to making sound investment decisions.

As you inspect a property, you should focus on potential structural problems—the most difficult and costly items to repair. Is the roof sound? Is the foundation solid? Are the plumbing and heating systems adequate and in good condition? Is the electrical system working? Does the property meet current building codes? (A call to the city might help here.) Are there adequate parking spaces? What about termites?

You can hire an inspection company to come in and check each of these areas for you and give you an estimate of cost to repair any deficiencies. I highly recommend such an inspection. It's cheap insurance. You should be less concerned with cosmetic problems. These things include landscaping, painting, draperies, small appliances, carpets, and minor repairs. The cost of these items is small in comparison to the increase in value resulting from a minor fix-up (or touch-up).

With this in mind, how do you proceed? How do you gain confidence? Look at several properties each month and take note of their net operating income, their prices, and their other amenities. I use a Comparative Market Analysis Form whenever I do market research (page 98). Whenever I hear of another building being sold, I try to find out what the sale price was and what the special terms of sale were. This gives me ammunition against sellers whose prices may be out of line with the current market value.

There is another benefit: If I know that two-bedroom four-unit buildings are selling for $300,000 (or $75,000 per unit) in a certain part of town, I can be on the lookout for anything priced lower. If I happen to find a seller who hasn't kept abreast of the market and has priced his building at $275,000 for a quick sale, I know I am looking at an immediate profit of $25,000—and that I had better act quickly before someone else comes along with the same intent.

I can't stress enough the importance of learning the market. Go out and compare prices. This one simple exercise will prepare you for wise investments better than any other thing you can do.

Choose several pieces of property from the classified or the listings on the Internet. Call or email the owners, then visit the properties. When you are driving around, stop whenever you see a "for sale" sign posted on a lawn. Ask the owner questions, and record the answers on your comparative analysis form. Get a feeling for which areas of town have the best and the worst properties. Always be on the lookout for a don't-wanter.

In the process, you'll get the best education in the nation.

Remember, you don't need a lot of cash in the bank before you start your search for the right investment . . . practice first. Practice makes perfect.

COMPARATIVE MARKET ANALYSIS FORM

Subject Property Address _____ Date _____

Information on other properties which are located in the same general area and have the same approximate value as the subject property:

FOR SALE NOW	Bed-rooms	Baths	Den	Sq.Ft.	Mtgs.	Price	Days on Mkt.	Terms

SOLD PAST 12 MONTHS

EXPIRED PAST 12 MONTHS

Realtors can be of great help in finding sold and expired information.

CHAPTER 12

It's Too Complicated for Me: Putting the Professionals on Your Side

"It took me three agents and three brokers to get the deal I wanted, and six months to close everything. But I got what I wanted."

—JOSEPH PAZCOGUIN

Now you're excited about real estate. You have learned that income-producing property is the wisest way to invest your money. You feel you are ready to venture into the marketplace and make an investment or two. But then you encounter a problem you hadn't anticipated: You can't understand what everyone is talking about.

What's a trust deed? A warrantee deed? A title policy? A legal description? A contract of sale? A land contract? A wraparound mortgage?

Your head is swimming. You may even be tempted to put your money in a mutual fund or the stock market, where at least you understand the jargon.

Stop! Don't do anything foolish. There is a simple solution.

First, you can use the Internet to find answers to almost every basic question you might have about real estate investing. There are sites that will provide you with definitions of the words and concepts you need to know as a real estate investor. While you could also go to the local library and ask for help, today's technology lets you educate yourself right at your home or office. For instance, you could type a phrase like "title insurance" into one of the popular search engines. With another click or two, you can get a definition, an explanation, or a detailed example.

If you prefer human contact, you can also call on hundreds of professionals in your area who spend their entire lives answering questions just like yours. And in many cases, these services are free of charge. With a few phone calls or emailed messages, you can create your own private team of investment consultants and "leverage" their expertise, just as you can use financial leverage to buy your properties.

Let's see how these experts can help you.

Real Estate Brokers and Agents

An experienced real estate broker or agent is one of the most important consultants on your team. A good real estate professional may have walked his or her clients through the entire buying or selling process dozens of times, and can probably answer virtually all of your questions.

Before we go further, let me explain that a broker is a person who brings a buyer and seller together and assists in negotiating contracts between them. For this service, the broker receives a commission or a fee that may range from hundreds to tens of thousands of dollars, depending on the size and complexity of the transaction.

While many brokers own their own companies, others work for the large regional or national real estate chains. A licensed broker has received extensive training about real estate transactions, and may well be familiar with apartment buildings and other types of commercial investment properties.

Closely allied with real estate brokers are real estate agents, who handle the overwhelming majority of residential transactions in America. Agents represent the interests of the buyer, the seller, both parties, or the entire "transaction," depending on individual state laws and regulations, as well as customary practices in local markets. You may want to talk to several brokers and agents about how these "agency" laws work in your state—it will help you

PUTTING THE PROFESSIONALS ON YOUR SIDE

REAL ESTATE BROKERS AND AGENTS
BANK LOAN OFFICERS
LAWYERS
APPRAISERS
PROPERTY RENTAL COMPANIES
THE INVESTOR
BUILDING INSPECTORS
INSURANCE AGENTS
MANAGEMENT COMPANIES
ACCOUNTANTS
TITLE COMPANIES

understand what an agent can (and cannot) do for you in your local market.

For a beginning investor, the best service a real estate agent provides is market analysis. A good agent understands current trends in the market. She knows what properties are selling for, how fast they sell, and for what terms, and where the hottest areas are. She has access to the local multiple listing service (MLS), where she can check information on recent sales and what's now for sale in the market.

A real estate agent is a watchdog on the lookout for bargain properties that come on the market, and provides you with an estimate of market value for properties you are thinking about buying.

In addition to the market knowledge, the real estate agent has a great deal of information about preparing contracts and arranging the financial details of the purchase. Your agent knows which banks are easiest to deal with and which loan officers most readily lend money for real estate mortgages. This information could save you hours of research and legwork.

As a source of help, a real estate agent is a great benefit. But don't let that blind you to some of the disadvantages of working with real estate agents. A real estate agent's services are not free. He charges commissions, so you need to be prepared to pay him if you intend to use his services. Generally, the seller pays the real estate commission, but the cash to pay the fee comes out of the buyer's down payment.

There are other drawbacks to using a real estate agent. The real estate agent is legally and morally obligated to act on behalf of the person with whom he has a signed contractual agreement. This person is usually the seller, who typically signs a binding listing agreement usually lasting from three to six months. In exchange for his services, the real estate agent is paid a commission in cash ranging from 3 to 10 percent of the sale value at the time of closing. A seller's agent is paid by the seller. He is working for the seller. He is under a signed agreement to represent *only* the seller.

This means that a real estate agent who represents the seller will not be looking out for your best interests first. Generally, it is illegal for him even to tell you if a seller is considering lowering the price or offering more favorable terms. He must relate to you only what has been put in writing, only what is already in the signed listing agreement. Anything else is taboo. (But just because he is not supposed to tell you a lot of these details does not mean that he won't. Each real estate agent is individually responsible for upholding professional standards. Some simply do not.)

Worst of all, a real estate agent who represents the seller is going to be reluctant to present the seller with the kinds of creative transactions you want to offer.

So, what can you do? One of the possible solutions is to offer a real estate agent a buyer's broker employment agreement. You, as buyer, agree in advance to pay the real estate agent a specific fee if he is able to locate the kind of property you are seeking, and you close on the transactions.

I have included an example of a complete Buyer's Broker Employment Agreement for your examination on page 103; it is much like an attorney's retainer agreement.

In recent years, a growing number of agents have specialized in representing buyers. A buyer's agent has the buyer's best interests in mind throughout the entire real estate transaction. A buyer's agent may use a representation agreement (similar to the form I have provided) that specifies the services the agent will provide and the way he will be compensated.

Some agents may be willing to assist you for a time as a buyer's agent without asking you to sign a written agreement. But you

NCR (No Carbon Required)   **BUYER'S BROKER EMPLOYMENT AGREEMENT** *

The undersigned _____, hereinafter designated as CLIENT,
hereby employs _____, hereinafter designated as BROKER,
for the purpose of exclusively assisting Client to locate property of a nature outlined below or other property acceptable to Client, and to negotiate terms and
conditions acceptable to Client for purchase, exchange, lease, or option of or on such property. This agreement shall commence this date and terminate at
midnight of _____, 19____.

GENERAL NATURE, LOCATION, AND REQUIREMENTS OF PROPERTY.
Apartment units and commercial building located in California preferably
San Diego but not excluding Orange County or other areas depending upon the
particular investment.

Size: Up to 36 units.

PRICE RANGE, AND OTHER TERMS AND CONDITIONS.
Price range/rental: Anything up to $75,000 down payment with maximum
leverage for tax purposes.
If client or agent of client locates a piece of real estate in California
without aid of Broker the 3% fee will be waived.
It is Broker's responsibility to analyze and do research and act as an investment counselor with the objective of determining the long-term value of the
property as compared to other valuable properties. A $500.00 retainer will
be paid by client as credit for a $50.00 per hour fee that Broker will charge
for all time spent locating, organizing and closing the purchase of property.
The rider attached hereto is an integral part of this agreement.

RETAINER FEE. Client agrees to pay, and Broker acknowledges receipt of a retainer fee of $_____N/A_____ as compensation for initial
professional counseling, consultations and research. Said fee is non-refundable, but shall be credited against the Brokerage Fee.
In the event state law so requires, Broker shall deposit and account for said Retainer Fee in Broker's Trust Account.

COMPENSATION TO BROKER. Client agrees to pay Broker, as compensation:
a) For locating property acceptable to Client and for negotiating the purchase or exchange, a fee of $___N/A___, or ___3___% of the acquisition
price, or $___N/A___ per hour.
b) For obtaining an option on a property acceptable to Client, a fee of $___N/A___, and to pay Broker the balance of a fee equal to ___N/A___% of the
purchase price in the event the option is exercised or assigned prior to expiration of the option.
c) For locating a property acceptable to Client and negotiating a lease thereon, a fee of _____not applicable_____.

IF:
1. Client or any other person acting for Client or in Client's behalf, purchases, exchanges, obtains an option for, or leases any real property of the nature
described herein, during the term hereof, through the services of Broker or otherwise.
2. Client or any other person acting for Client or in Client's behalf, purchases, exchanges, obtains an option for, or leases any real property of the nature
described herein, within one year after termination of this agreement, which property Broker, Broker's agent, or cooperating brokers presented or
submitted to Client during the term hereof and the description of which Broker shall have submitted in writing to Client, either in person or by mail, **within
ten (10) days after termination of this agreement.**

**NOTICE: The amount or rate of real estate commissions is not fixed by law. They are set by each broker individually
and may be negotiable between the buyer and the broker.**

AGENCY RELATIONSHIP. Broker agrees to act as agent for Client only in any resulting transaction, provided that Broker may cooperate with other
brokers and their agents in an effort to locate property or properties in accordance with this agreement, and may divide fees in any manner acceptable to them.
If Broker receives compensation from anyone other than Client, Broker shall make full disclosure, and such compensation shall be credited against Client's
obligation hereunder.
In addition, Broker will provide appropriate Agency Disclosure as required by law.

BROKER'S OBLIGATIONS. In consideration of Client's agreement set forth above, Broker agrees to use diligence to achieve the purpose of this
agreement.

CLIENT'S OBLIGATIONS. Client agrees to provide Broker, upon request, relevant personal and financial information to assure Client's ability to
acquire property outlined above. Client further agrees to view or consider property of the general nature set forth in this Agreement, and to negotiate in good
faith to acquire such property if acceptable to Client. In the event completion of any resulting transaction is prevented by Client's default, Client shall pay Broker
the compensation provided for herein upon such default.

ATTORNEY FEE. If any action is brought to enforce the terms of this agreement, or arising out of the execution of this agreement, or to collect fees, the
prevailing party shall be entitled to receive from the other party a reasonable attorney fee to be determined by the court in which such action is brought.

ENTIRE AGREEMENT. Time is of the essence. The terms hereof constitute the entire agreement and supersede all prior agreements, negotiations and
discussions between the parties. This Agreement may be modified only by a writing signed by each of the parties.

Receipt of a copy of this agreement is hereby acknowledged.   DATED: _____ TIME: _____
Buyer's Broker: _____   _____ Client
By: Robert Allen   _____ Client
Address: 5931 Priestly Dr. Carlsbad CA   Address: _____
                                92008   Phone: _____
Phone: 1-800-345-3648

FORM 100 (2-89)   COPYRIGHT © 1989, BY PROFESSIONAL PUBLISHING CORP., 122 PAUL DR., SAN RAFAEL, CA 94903 (415) 472-1964   **PROFESSIONAL
                                                                                                                              PUBLISHING**

* **For a free Buyer's Broker Employment Agreement form call 1-800-345-3648.**

should always put your agreement in writing before you make an offer to purchase a particular property—and be sure you understand how your agent will be compensated.

By using the buyer's broker agreement you accomplish two very important things. First, you put the real estate agent on your side legally and morally. Now the real estate agent can be aggressive with any seller he meets, even if the seller has already signed a listing agreement with another broker! If that is the case, your broker will receive his buying commission directly from you, and the seller's listing broker will receive his normal percentage of listing commission from the seller.

Second, a buyer's broker agreement gives you and your real estate agent greater flexibility in helping to find good properties for you. Since you're not obligated to buy anything, you only have to sit back and wait until the real estate agent brings you a piece of property you think is valuable enough to invest in. This puts you in the driver's seat all the way. It also puts the agent in a stronger negotiating position with sellers who have not listed their property. He doesn't have to beg for a listing but can negotiate on your behalf, knowing that if you buy the property he will get paid.

One weakness with most buyers' agents is that they may lack an in-depth understanding of the many kinds of creative financial transactions you will need to make. Most real estate agents are accustomed to "normal" transactions: Seller has property. Buyer has lots of cash, or a friendly banker. Buyer gives seller lots of cash in exchange for the property. Real estate agent gets cash commission from seller. All live happily ever after.

Most inexperienced buyers become discouraged when they first approach a real estate agent about finding property for them with no down payment; the real estate agent usually listens to their story and then tells them that it can't be done.

I'm telling you that it *can* be done.

Picture how difficult it must be to have an unbelieving real estate agent present a creative offer to purchase to a seller who is not desperate. The real estate agent is flustered, perhaps even embarrassed, to have to present such an unconventional offer to the seller. The seller is equally upset, because the real estate agent virtually promised a cash customer. The seller counters with an angry full-cash, full-price deal. The real estate agent just looks at you hopelessly and says, "See, I told you so!"

Despite these drawbacks, there are ways to work effectively with a real estate agent and overcome any lack of understanding. Use these guidelines:

1. Give the real estate agent specifics.

Whenever I work with a real estate agent, I give her the following restrictions: I tell her I am very interested in any property she brings me when the seller will

- Sell for a 10 percent or less down payment
- Carry back at least a 25 percent second mortgage subordinated to new financing
- Sell his property for 15 to 20 percent below the market value for a quick cash-out.

Now my real estate agent has something concrete to use. Whenever she finds a suitable property, she calls me up; I inspect the property exterior within twenty-four hours. To maximize my time, my real estate agent will usually give me several properties to inspect at one time. I drive by and do the exterior inspection by myself without the real estate agent present. She doesn't have to give a tour of the town or spend her valuable time giving me a sales pitch.

I reject most of these properties because of their poor location or physical appearance. But if I'm interested I have her arrange for an interior inspection of the building. I also let all the real estate agents who act as my "scouts" know that when they find a property that interests me, I will act immediately to prepare a written offer through the real estate agent. I let them know I appreciate their efforts and that I will be fair with them.

2. If you have the time, always do your own negotiating.

If the real estate agent is not familiar with the way you do business, he will try to convince you that he must act as a go-between, and he will try to present your earnest-money agreement to the seller himself. This is not always the best approach. When you talk to the seller face-to-face you can determine for yourself what kinds of things he wants and needs; you don't have to try to interpret his wants and needs through the eyes of a third party. Take the time to explain this to your agent.

3. Work with several good real estate agents simultaneously.

To give yourself maximum exposure in the marketplace, you should have good relationships with several real estate agents. The only way to do this is to talk to several agents every week. Explain your guidelines and let them know you will not give them a runaround. If you talk to twenty-five or thirty real estate agents, you will probably only have two or three who will eventually begin bringing you properties, because of your strict guidelines and because many real estate agents are looking for the same kinds of properties for themselves.

Don't get discouraged.

The last major problem in dealing with a real estate agent is the fact that he makes his living from selling properties. Since your criteria for buying property are rather unusual and strict, working with you will cut down his chances of making a sale. What's more, he needs to be paid in cash for his services. Therefore, if you want to get into a property with little or nothing down, your approach usually varies from what he considers his best interests.

I find that the only kinds of properties I can work with a real estate agent on are those that require some kind of cash down payment and are too good to pass up. Since I am always buying properties with the same real estate agents, they know they can make money serving my account. Once I have established that, I can ask my real estate agent to let me give him a short-term note for his commission, which I can pay off as soon as I can find the partners.

And now a few words to those real estate agents who may find themselves reading this chapter: You are in the best position of all to find the kind of properties I have been discussing. You have first access to the new listings in your office, to well-known investors who may want to become partners with you, and so on. To top it off, you can use your commissions as part of the down payment on any listed property. This puts you a jump ahead of the rest of the world.

But having a license has its drawbacks. When I had my license I found that my liability was greater. Whenever I bought a property from a client and thereby received a commission, the seller had more grounds to sue me by maintaining that I acted with superior knowledge, took advantage of the seller, and was even paid for it. I also found that fellow real estate agents would not deal with me as eagerly because I wanted a piece of the action for myself. And finally, I found that sellers who had not listed their properties would always want to know if I was a real estate agent; when they found out I was, they were always more reluctant to deal with me.

Because of all these disadvantages, I decided I would be better off surrendering my license and working as an investor on a full-time basis. You might consider doing the same, especially if your current broker frowns on your investment practices. If you are a full-time sales professional and you love what you do, I see no reason to stop selling. Keep your license and use it in your investment activities.

Other Professionals

The real estate agent is only one member of your private team of consultants. Let's take a quick look at what the rest of them can do to help you.

1. Accountants

Don't undertake any major real estate venture without establishing a relationship with a good real estate–oriented tax accountant. He will keep you from paying all of your income to the government as taxes. It doesn't *cost* to have help from an accountant, it *pays!*

If you run into a property owner who doesn't want to sell his property because of the tax ramifications, you should find out as much as you can about the details and discuss them with your accountant. He may give you an idea as to how the seller could sell his property without major tax consequences.

I consult with my accountant constantly, and I have never regretted it. Don't be shy.

2. Attorneys

Attorneys are oriented to finding out what could possibly go wrong with any given real estate transaction or agreement and to preparing ways to avoid them. Because of their cautious stance, they are known among real estate investors as "deal killers." But you need to know what could go wrong and how to avoid it. You need to know how the deal should be written up to offer you the greatest possible protection.

Not all real estate transactions require the help of an attorney, but it is worth the extra money in most cases. The amount of an attorney's fee is minuscule compared to the potential problems that can crop up before, during, or after the closing.

If you have any doubt about what is taking place, get an attorney to review your problem with you. Young attorneys just establishing themselves might offer you a free hour of counseling in the hope that you will become a permanent client. If you have never visited an attorney because of the cost involved, you should look for one with reasonable rates who offers a free first visit, so that you can get acquainted and comfortable. If that attorney is both knowledgeable and trustworthy, then stick with that legal professional throughout the rest of your real estate lifetime.

3. Title Companies

Title companies check the legal records associated with a particular piece of property to be sure that the seller does own the property legally, and has the right to transfer the ownership to you. The title company prepares a title insurance policy that indicates all of the liens, mortgages, and encumbrances on the legal record against the property. Then, if there is a problem with that property, the title insurance policy will compensate you.

Title companies provide an invaluable service to buyers. Can you imagine the problems that would result if you didn't know who was the legal owner of a piece of real estate? There have been many cases where a con artist sold one piece of property several times to different individuals, each time collecting a down payment. Then the thief left town, leaving no forwarding address. There were several angry investors when they found out that they had been swindled, and that none of them owned the property because the seller didn't either!

Even though title insurance is expensive, it is obviously critical. You must get title insurance for every property you buy. In most states the responsibility for paying the costs of title insurance is borne by the seller. If this is true in your state, you shouldn't hesitate to require that the seller purchase title insurance.

Ask your title insurance company if it offers research services, sometimes called a "listing package." That means that if you promise to purchase title insurance through that company, it will research the title to any property you are considering buying. You can get information, such as current taxes, legal descriptions, a photocopy of the property and its boundary lines as they appear on the county records, and the names and addresses of current owners. Some researchers even find out what the property originally sold for and on what terms. Such information will be helpful in preparing an analysis of a potential investment.

Title companies also usually act as escrow agents and closing officers. If you have a complicated transaction, a title officer will give you information you need to complete the transaction. If you have questions about trust deeds or warrantee deeds, your first source of free information is a title company officer. He will be glad to help you with any real estate problem.

4. Appraisers

A professional real estate appraiser can give you an accurate (and legally recognized) figure detailing the value of a commercial or residential property. The appraiser can let you know whether the property is overpriced or underpriced, and you can use the appraiser's estimate as the basis to obtain funding.

5. Management Companies

No one enjoys being woken in the middle of the night by a frantic renter with a backed-up toilet. Management companies handle all maintenance details. They're professionals. They have staff members (or contacts) who can do repair work at the lowest possible prices. They have connections, too, so they can often purchase supplies at wholesale prices—all of which means a lower cost for you.

In addition to handling maintenance, management companies also collect rents, pay utility bills (with collected rent money), and make mortgage payments (with collected rent money). In short, they will handle all aspects of building operation. They'll even provide you with a monthly financial statement, including bills and a cash-flow check. In theory, all you have to do is wash your hands of the whole matter and concentrate your energy and creativity on your next investment. But you would be unwise to choose a management company without shopping. And by all means, watch over their shoulder. Don't delegate complete control and responsibility for your money to anyone.

6. Property Rental Firms

Every town has small companies that charge potential renters a fee for the privilege of examining their listings of vacant rental properties. If you are trying to rent some of your properties, contact one of these rental agencies. They are listed in the phone directory, their services are often free to property owners, and they usually refer good tenants (those who are willing to pay money to find a good place to live).

7. Bankers

The role of bankers is so important and so involved that several chapters are dedicated to a discussion of their services and methods of working with them.

It is normal for a fledgling investor to feel overwhelmed with the details of the real estate business. After all, you're just starting to spread your wings. Go to the professionals in the business and ask their advice. There are plenty of people who are ready to help you. Use them!

CHAPTER 13

Negotiations: The First Person to Mention a Number Loses

"In the absence of communication, suspicion is king."
—CHARLES WHITE

All right, you've found a property with promise. Now what do you do? Hang on. Here comes the fun—and critical—part of investing in real estate: negotiating with the seller.

Negotiating is an art that becomes easier the more motivated the seller is to sell his property. In other words, it's necessary to find a don't-wanter if you want to have a successful negotiating experience.

1. If a seller is firm on his price, you must be able to negotiate flexible terms! If a seller is firm on his terms (usually meaning all cash), then you must be able to choose the price (usually lower). Whenever possible, try to choose both the price and terms.

If you can't obtain either your price or your terms, move on. The only time you should deal with an inflexible seller is when his original price and terms are already good enough to get excited about. You can't afford to waste precious time dealing with a seller who might not budge. Move on to the next deal.

2. Destroy all expectation of high profit in the seller's mind!

You must subtly and gently poke holes in the seller's expectations of high profit. Don't let the seller blind you with his fancy reasons why his property is worth a fortune. Go over the property with a fine-toothed comb and observe every single negative thing you can. You do this for two reasons. First, you may not really want the property after all. It may be just too much of a hassle; you may decide against it. Second, you want to show the seller that you are thorough enough to observe that his property has flaws and problems that need correcting. Later on, as a point for negotiation, you might require the seller to correct all the faults you found in your examination before you buy his property if you decide to invest.

Almost every property owner (except the don't-wanter) has learned to ignore the flaws in his property and to overemphasize the good aspects. Bring the seller gently back to reality. You might be able to bring his price back into the real world, too.

And if you sincerely follow my advice and notice all the flaws in the property, you may do yourself a big favor: You may destroy your *own* expectations of high profit. Don't buy a property if you can see all your profit going into deferred maintenance.

There are other ways of destroying the seller's expectations of high profits: Act uninterested in the seller's property. Let the seller know directly or indirectly that his property is only one of several you will be visiting that day. Also let him know that there are competitive properties on the market every bit as attractive as his property. You might say to the real estate agent who is with you, "What time is our appointment to visit that ten-unit building on Charles Avenue?" Or "The bedrooms in his unit are not as big as the bedrooms in the Terrace Apartments." Or "This house is priced $4,000 more than the identical one on Seventh Street." Do your homework and let the seller know in no uncertain terms that the marketplace does not command a price as high as he is asking. Show him comparable figures on comparable units. If your figures are accurate and your analysis is convincing, you may cut thousands of dollars off the seller's asking price.

Teach the seller whose property has been on the market for some time a lesson that neither he nor you should ever forget: *The only reason a property doesn't sell is that the price is too high.* Any property in the world will sell immediately if it is put on the market at the right price. If a property has been on the market for more than three months, the property is not worth what the seller is asking, no matter what the terms are. Before I negotiate any transaction I always ask:

"How long has this property been listed or been offered for sale?"

"Before you listed this property, did you try to sell it by yourself? At what price?"

"How many offers have you had for your property? Why didn't you accept them?"

Don't be shy about asking questions like these. It's your right to have them answered before you buy the property. Don't stay silent out of a fear of offending the seller—as long as the questions are questions you wouldn't hesitate to ask in any normal, causal conversation. These are bold questions and should be asked carefully and with great sensitivity to the feelings of the seller. Don't push. Just ask in a straightforward manner. Notice the seller's reaction. Your objective here is not to offend the seller, but to obtain sensitive information. It may require time for the seller to "soften up" before he will respond to such questions. Give him space. Make a joke. Try again later. Remember, *your money* is at stake here. You need answers.

There are plenty of other questions that might affect your purchase decision. It's a good idea to make a list of the questions before you meet with the seller. Some that might help are:

"When did you buy the property and from whom?"

"What did you pay for the property?" (Even though this is a very personal question, more often than not the seller will answer you without hesitation.)

"How much did you spend on repairs and capital improvements during your ownership? What structural changes did you make?"

"Why did you list your property for sale with XYZ Realty?"

"What is the worst thing you can think of about your ownership of these apartments?"

"Are there any major improvements that will have to be made shortly?"

The seller will more than likely answer these questions without hesitation because you asked in a straightforward manner. If he balks at any, ask him, "Is there any reason why I shouldn't know that information? Would the answer to that question keep me from buying your property?" Be sure to smile while you are asking this, to break the ice. If he says no, repeat the question and wait for his answer.

Success during this questioning phase requires that you visit the seller personally. A real estate agent, or any other third party, will reduce the effectiveness of this technique and will probably affect the honesty of the seller's answer. The more flexible the seller, the more effective the face-to-face negotiation becomes. If a real estate company lists the property for sale, you may have difficulty getting a face-to-face meeting with the seller. The agent feels an obligation to act as go-between in the negotiations and generally does not want the two parties to meet. This sets up an adversarial frame of mind—with you, the buyer, and the seller. And if this frame of mind prevails, it is difficult to create a problem-solving spirit that makes the seller your ally or friend. If the real estate agent refuses to let you visit his client, you can do one of three things: (1) You can try to get as much information about the seller's flexibility from the real estate agent and make your best offer. (2) You can try to find out the whereabouts of the seller and arrange your own meeting (realizing, of course, that the real estate agent may not appreciate this; also, that there is no legal or ethical way to cut the agent out of the commission the seller has agreed to pay). (3) You can decide to look for don't-wanters who are selling their properties without the aid of a real estate company,

3. Interpret and relieve the seller's fears.

In essence, try to understand why the seller is selling his property. The answers you get will provide you with invaluable information, and may even surprise the seller. Chances are good the seller probably hasn't really been asked these kinds of questions before. As you probe deeper into the seller's motivations and show an interest in his needs, he will become more confident in your ability to solve his problems.

You need to ask and understand the answers to questions like:

"What would happen if you didn't sell for six months?" The answer will help you determine just how much the seller wants to sell. If he says he can wait as long as necessary, he's probably just speculating and hoping someone will come along and pay his price. If he says he must sell before the first of the month, your seller might consider creative terms. The closer you are to the deadline the seller sets, the more anxious the seller will become.

"Do you have other property for sale?" This might lead you to a property that isn't listed but might better suit your needs.

"What are you going to do with the cash proceeds of this sale?" The seller may say that he intends to pay off some nagging debts. Offer to pay the debts for him; you might be able to prolong the payment of these debts, thus allowing you to come up with less cash at the closing. If the seller says that he plans to buy a plane ticket to Rome, offer to buy it for him as part of the down payment. Then buy the ticket with your Visa or MasterCard—another way to defer the payment of cash at the closing. Do you get the point? Try to find ways of solving the seller's dilemma without investing any of your precious cash. Probe deeply. It can probably be done.

"What is the lowest cash price that you will accept if I give you all of your equity within forty-eight hours?" This is a critical question as it usually reveals the rock-bottom price. Sometimes you should look for a way to raise the cash quickly instead of pressing for terms. Your profit potential may be much greater this way. Don't avoid the question. You might make a lot of money as a result.

"What is the real reason why you want to sell?" Now you'll really find out if you have a don't-wanter. He'll tell you he has management headaches, financial headaches, physical-plant problems, personal problems, or partnership problems. You solve his problem, but don't oversolve! Remember the last time you had an itch? You could scratch all around the itch, but until you scratched the itch itself you still had that nagging itch. The don't-wanter has the same problem: an itch of sorts. And all you have to do is listen, determine where the itch is, and scratch *only* the itch, no more. Whatever he says, solve his exact problem. If the management of the property is too much for him, stress your management skills. If he has a deadline to meet, stress your ability to close now, today. If he is afraid to sell with a low down payment, offer him security on other property you own. If he is concerned about closing costs, sell him on the fact that he will pay no closing costs whatsoever (of course, you lower the price as compensation for paying the seller's closing costs). If he is afraid of tax consequences, take him to your accountant; let your accountant show the seller the many avenues open for him to reduce his tax liability. Whatever his problem or fear, come up with a solution. This technique will be your strongest selling point.

Once you understand the seller's position, you will be in a better position to proceed with the negotiations. Remember these rules for the buyer:

1. Decide beforehand the benefits you want for yourself. Pick a price and terms beyond which you will not bend. Get up and walk out graciously when you can see that you are not getting what you had hoped to gain.

The seller may realize that you are not bluffing and back down on his terms so he won't lose a good prospect.

2. The first person to mention a number loses.

If you wait long enough, the seller will tell you exactly where he will go. You don't need to mention any number; if you do you may weaken your position. An anxious seller becomes even more anxious in the presence of a silent negotiator. Your conversation might go something like this: "I've got to have $200,000 or I won't sell." Silence. "Because that's the figure that I said I needed." Silence. "Well, I guess I could settle for $190,000 if you pay all the closing costs." Silence. "I won't go a penny below $185,000." Let the seller do the talking. Silence is devastating when used in the right places.

3. Keep it simple.

Don't say, "We'll have to draw up a wraparound mortgage with a substitution of collateral agreement and we'll place them in escrow." Using the vernacular of real estate with a novice seller will just confuse him; remember, a confused mind always says "no." Keep it simple. Say, "We'll have everything done legally so that you won't have anything to worry about."

4. Make sure the seller is well aware of the problems you will be saving him from.

5. *Try the would-you-take technique.*

Once you have listened to the seller's reasons, try the would-you-take technique (pronounced "woodjatake," a term used frequently by real estate buyers). Would-you-take questions expose the flexibility of a don't-wanter. For example:

"Would-you-take a duplex equity for your quadplex equity?"

"Would-you-take some raw ground instead of cash?"

"Would-you-take a new car in exchange for the equity in your home?"

"Would-you-take a note due in a year for part of your equity?"

Try to give the seller a number of alternatives from which to choose. This will prepare him for your final offer, which will probably incorporate some of the successful would-you-takes. The seller needs to be reminded that cash is only one form of payment for equity. Point out that there may be other more suitable solutions short of a large cash down payment. Use the would-you-take technique to give you a little advantage in the final round of negotiations.

6. As soon as you have as much information as you need, leave the seller, go somewhere where you can analyze all the data you have collected, and prepare a formal offer to purchase.

Now you're ready to start the final round of negotiations.

CHAPTER 14

The Final Round of Negotiations: How to Get What You Want Without Using Cash

"Robert Allen's techniques work beyond real estate, too! Not only did I get a $5,500 discount on the purchase price of my car, I put nothing down and negotiated a lower interest rate with no credit check."

—ANN R. HUMPHREY

You've had some time alone to consider your investment, and you've decided to go ahead. Even though you've negotiated verbally, nothing's legal yet. You still need to make final negotiations.

In most states, negotiations become legally binding when both the seller and the buyer have affixed their signatures to a written agreement called an Earnest Money Receipt (also referred to as an Offer to Purchase, a Contract for Sale or Purchase, a Purchase Money Receipt, or a Deposit Receipt). Any real estate agent in your city can show you one of the state-approved forms, or you can obtain one at any stationery or office-supply store.

Even if a particular form is not legally required in your state, the law still requires that you show your earnestness to buy the property by giving the seller a cash deposit; the seller or the seller's agent will hold the deposit, and the seller will keep this deposit as liquidated damages if the buyer defaults.

Three rules will serve as guidelines as you fill out an Offer to Purchase. First, try to negotiate price. Get it as low as you can before you do anything else. Second, start to think of your cash as a precious commodity—a disappearing species, so to speak. One millionaire referred to his tightfisted policy as the Effective Nonuse of Cash. Many of us, on the other hand, spend our cash as if our policy were the Noneffective Use of Cash. Guard your investment capital with your life. Negotiate for low-down or nothing-down deals. Set this goal now. You'll be more successful. Third, you need to be aware of a hierarchy of negotiation. What does that mean? Examine the chart below:

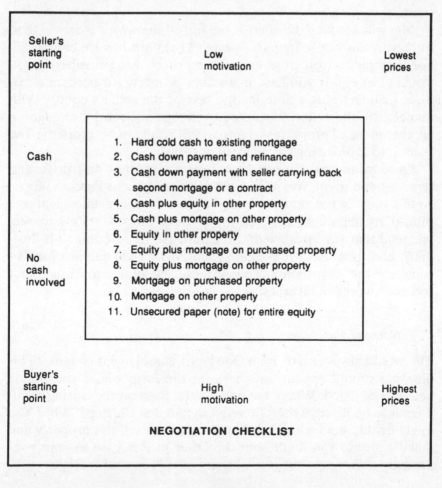

Seller's starting point	Low motivation	Lowest prices

Cash

1. Hard cold cash to existing mortgage
2. Cash down payment and refinance
3. Cash down payment with seller carrying back second mortgage or a contract
4. Cash plus equity in other property
5. Cash plus mortgage on other property
6. Equity in other property
7. Equity plus mortgage on purchased property
8. Equity plus mortgage on other property
9. Mortgage on purchased property
10. Mortgage on other property
11. Unsecured paper (note) for entire equity

No cash involved

Buyer's starting point	High motivation	Highest prices

NEGOTIATION CHECKLIST

A Negotiation Checklist

This checklist has eleven basic alternatives for you and the seller as you negotiate the price and terms for the final purchase.

At the top of the list is the seller's first choice: The buyer pays all cash. The buyer, of course, wants to start at the bottom of the list at number eleven. The seller accepts an unsecured note for his equity with no cash changing hands. You will learn soon enough that neither the buyer nor the seller ever gets exactly what he wants.

In between the top and the bottom are nine other choices. As you conduct your negotiation, always begin at the bottom, and don't get too close to the top! Stick to your guns. If your seller is a don't-wanter, he'll come down to meet you closer to the bottom of the chart.

You will see why the chart is organized the way it is as you read further in this book. Items 6 through 11 do not involve cash at all. For example, if you were to make an offer using number 7, you would offer equity you have in another property (or perhaps a car, SUV, or boat) plus a note for the rest of the seller's equity. With number 10, the seller may agree to accept a second mortgage on another piece of property you own as full equity in his property. The point is to avoid using cash if at all possible

Once your negotiations have been completed and price and terms agreed upon, you need to fill out the Offer to Purchase form. At this stage in the game, you may involve the real estate agent as a third-party negotiator between yourself and the seller. I always recommend that you speak with the seller first, to determine his flexibility, and then use a real estate agent, if there is one involved, to complete the negotiation. Follow these guidelines to ensure that you are covered in all cases:

1. Name of Purchaser

This would always read "John Doe [your name] or his assigns." This phrasing should appear anywhere on the form where your name needs to be listed. Where the name to be used on the closing document is to be listed, write "To Be Designated at Closing." Why? You might decide before closing that you want to sell the property and make a profit. You don't want the Offer to Purchase to limit your flexibility. Your new buyer can legally qualify as your "assigns."

2. Amount of Earnest Money or Deposit

Start low ($1,000 or less). The law says that $1 is legal and binding, so offer as little over that as possible. This limits your liability; if for some reason you are forced to default, you want to suffer as small a loss as possible. Early in my career I put up $1,000 with a partner as earnest money and committed to coming up with financing for a duplex in one week. It was sheer stupidity on my part. I ended up paying back the $500 I borrowed from the bank to make up for not coming through with the money. That taught me to be stingy with my earnest money. If a seller asks why you offer so little in earnest money, you might reply, "I often make several offers on different properties at the same time, and I don't want to tie up my capital needlessly."

If the seller demands more earnest money, tell the real estate agent that the seller can request this in a written counteroffer. Stress that you have good reasons for the small amount. Let the seller give you a good reason that justifies coming up with more money. If you do come up with more, designate it as "additional deposit, not to be called earnest money." Then if you default you'll forfeit only your original earnest money depending on the laws in your state, of course.

If you are working through a real estate agency, it will collect the earnest money from you and hold it in a trust account until fulfillment of the terms and conditions of the Offer to Purchase is completed. If you are dealing directly with a seller, you can either give the funds to the seller or to a third party. I feel more comfortable giving the money to my title company, which acts as an escrow agent between the seller and me; I know that my money is safe with an independent third party. I have been known to give a $500 check to a seller with instructions not to cash the check until the closing. This way I could use the funds until closing, but I also had to trust that the seller wouldn't cash my check and disappear. It's a risky proposition at best.

3. Closing Date

Sometimes it is best to prolong the closing as long as possible. This gives you the flexibility to raise the needed capital for the down payment, to search for a partner, or to sell the property to another individual for a higher price. If, however, you can sense that the seller will not last long in an extended closing situation, negotiate a short closing. Use your judgment. I generally allow myself at least four weeks to close; longer if I have to get conventional financing.

Engineer the closing to fall on the day the rents are due if you are buying a rental property. You are normally not required to make your first mortgage payment for thirty days after closing, but you are allowed to collect all of the rents on the first day of ownership. In some cases you will have thousands of dollars' worth of rents and tenant deposits, and no obligation to make a first mortgage payment for thirty days. Depending on the laws in your state, you could even use the money as part of your down payment!

4. "Subject-to" Clauses

These are better known as "escape clauses." They are clauses that you insert into the Offer to Purchase (wherever indicated on your form) that limit your liability even further. Here you state that the offer is *subject to* certain limitations and conditions that must be fulfilled before the offer is valid, such as:

- Subject to the inspection of my partner, whoever he may be, within three days of the seller's acceptance of this offer. (If you decided within three days that you don't want the property after all, just have your partner write a letter saying that he does not give approval to the purchase. Your partner can be anyone—your wife, your doctor, your next-door neighbor, a friend.)
- Subject to all appliances, heaters, refrigerators, stoves, air conditioners, and all other equipment pertaining to the operation of the property being in good working order as of the day of the closing. (Then, if anything goes wrong before the closing day, the seller has to pay for repairs or replacement, not you!)
- Subject to the seller's obtaining a termite inspection of the property. (This applies equally to a building-code inspection, a roofing inspection, or any other kind of inspection you want conducted.)
- Subject to having all the things done to the property that need to be done to bring it up to standard. Be specific—list repairs to cracked foundation, grounds cleanup, and so on. Make the seller bring the property up to your standards.

- Subject to obtaining suitable and adequate financing (specify the amount and interest rate) on or before the day of closing. (If you can't obtain financing, you can get your earnest money back.)
- Subject to the seller's providing clear and marketable title to his property. (You might request a survey to verify the title search.)

Your possibilities are limitless.

Of course, the real estate agent, acting as the seller's agent, will try to get you to eliminate most of these "subject tos" because they stand in the way of an easy closing. But be sure that you include enough of the clauses to limit your liability. Make sure that if anything goes wrong, you've got something to fall back on.

One last "subject to" negotiation technique: the front porch offer. Among many creative investors, a "front porch" inserted in an Offer to Purchase refers to a final concession you want the seller to make (such as painting the front porch). While the main points of your offer require you to obtain an excellent price and/or excellent terms, the front porch is not critical to the negotiation. Some common front porch clauses are:

- Seller must pay all closing costs.
- Seller must relinquish all of his tax and insurance impounds.
- Seller must paint the property inside and out.
- Seller must pay any FHA or VA points.

If the seller accepts your front-porch offer without any changes, then you just got a free paint job for the front porch. If he refuses your offer, it's no skin off your teeth.

Visit your local office-supply store and ask to see its supply of legal forms. Buy a large supply of Offers to Purchase real estate forms and put them in your car. Carry them in your briefcase or purse; in short, have one with you at all times. You never can tell when you'll need one. Look at as many properties that are for sale as time permits.

Make offers on everything. Even if you don't have the time to go through the long process of formal negotiation, at least get in the habit of making acceptable offers. Set a goal to write a certain number of offers each week. Be specific. This is a numbers game: The more offers you write, the greater will be your chances of buying property. Make as many offers as you can, and don't be afraid to offer low. You might find a taker. One real estate agent I know wrote offers to over seventeen hundred properties in a California listing book, offering all cash down to the existing mortgage with a price 20 percent below the listed price. Forty of his offers were ultimately accepted!

Is There a Counteroffer?

What about a counteroffer? Suppose the seller doesn't like your offer, which is not uncommon. What do you do next? The seller will inform you, usually in writing, that your offer is unacceptable, and he will usually propose a counteroffer. This process of offer/counteroffer is a critical one, as both you and the seller are jockeying for position, seeing just how far the other party will bend. If you have had previous discussions with the seller personally, you will have a fairly good idea of how flexible he will be. Just remember not to bend yourself beyond your limit to pay. If you can't see the light at the end of the tunnel, you may decide to back out of the negotiations quickly and move on to your next project. You can't afford to waste time and mental energy with an inflexible seller. If the property is an excellent buy, then I would suggest moving rapidly. I have known properties to be sold out from underneath a negotiating buyer because he persisted in demanding a minor concession. Remember, you snooze, you lose. If you find a seller who completely refuses to negotiate because he is offended by your first "creative" offer, you should respond in this manner:

"I have taken considerable time and spent precious money analyzing your property. I have even been courteous enough to put my offer in writing. Please be courteous enough to give me a written counteroffer if my original offer is not acceptable to you. Don't tell me what you won't do; tell me what you will do."

Practice making your offers. The chance of your being able to negotiate and close properly when you do find a good buy will be greatly increased.

Now it's time to get ready to buy your property!

CHAPTER 15

Home Buyers—
For Your Personal Use

"Using a lease-purchase strategy, I was able to sign a contract on a new home, locking in a purchase price with part of the monthly rent going toward the down payment at the end of the contract. All this occurred while in the middle of foreclosure on our old home."

—STEPHEN MARTINEK

If you're renting an apartment or still living at home, there's one step I urge you to take: Buy a home for yourself, using the no-down-payment approach.

Owning your own home is undoubtedly the best investment most people ever make for themselves and their families. Owning a home creates a solid foundation for your financial future, and going through the home-buying process will provide invaluable experience as you invest in income-producing real estate.

Best of all, there are countless ways you can buy your home with little or no down payment. And even if you do have cash, the creative techniques described here may help you to locate and negotiate a better deal.

When it comes to buying a home, there are two major financial obstacles that must be overcome. In the face of rising home prices, many Americans are unable to qualify for a long-term loan, called a mortgage, because their incomes are too low or because their credit rating is poor. Second, many people have no money in their savings accounts and are unable to make even a minimal down payment. These problems are real. The goal and dream of the older generation was to pay off the mortgage. The goal and dream of this generation is just to get a mortgage.

That ever-elusive creature called a mortgage, however, can be yours even if your income is low and your credit rating isn't quite up to snuff. There are plenty of federal, state, and local programs designed to help the first-time homebuyer.

But your greatest asset is the knowledge that you can buy a house, town house, or condominium without even involving a bank. You can buy directly from the seller, and you can have the seller carry the loan himself on a land contract, a contract of sale, or a wraparound mortgage. There are many sellers who will agree to do just that—some to avoid tax problems, others to create a monthly cash flow during retirement—so don't let your financial problems keep you from looking for that new house!

Let me suggest a good program for you to follow. In fact, many students in my Creating Wealth seminars have taken just this approach in order to move out of their rental units and into a home of their own. (To find out more, visit www.robertallenrealestate.com.)

Most people aren't in a financial position to buy their dream house right off the bat. But the home you are about to buy can be a stepping-stone to a bigger and better house somewhere down the road. Don't let your pride get in the way. Each step you take, just like each step you take up a mountain, will bring you closer to your destination. Each time you buy a small house, you will be building up equity for that larger, more ideal house. Your goal should be to move up through several houses, hopefully making a significant profit on each move, until you are able to invest in your dream house—free and clear. It's well worth it.

One word of advice: As you begin to search for your first home, your best bet will be to deal with a competent real estate agent who knows all the ins and outs of the local market. A capable and trustworthy agent can help you in countless ways both with this home and with your real estate investments in the future. That agent, or a lending specialist at a local bank, can also advise you on the financial steps you may need to take before applying for a mortgage.

So, let's see how you should go about overcoming the first big challenge: qualifying for a mortgage to buy your own home. If you are in a marginal financial position, you can take steps to raise your income, put more money in the bank, or pay off your debts. These are the basic steps to improve your chances of qualifying for a loan.

Perhaps taking a part-time second job, even if it's temporary, will boost your income by just the right amount. Maybe your spouse or partner can contribute enough to increase your total household income. Or perhaps you can make a difference by paying off a car loan or reducing your credit card balance.

You should be aware when applying for a home mortgage that having too much credit is almost as bad as having a bad credit rating. Lenders are worried that you might overspend your monthly budget on credit card purchases, leaving you without enough to cover the mortgage. So if you have any unused credit cards lying around, you might want to cancel those accounts. And it's always a good idea to postpone any major purchases, such as a car, home theater system, or European vacation until after you buy your house.

As a potential borrower, you will likely be faced with a wide variety of mortgage options: fifteen years or thirty years? Fixed rate or adjustable? A convertible loan or a balloon payment plan? Be sure to ask your lender about all your options, and be sure you understand the differences. Compare the different options based on where you are now, and what's likely to occur in the future. And don't forget to consider the safety factor—what loan would be best if you or your spouse lost a job or otherwise suffered a serious loss of income.

In my experience, qualifying for a loan and choosing the right mortgage for your specific circumstances can be time-consuming issues. But when you explore more creative approaches to buying your home, the challenges of matching your income and debt with a mortgage company's specific criteria tend to fade away. That's because you may well be able to buy that first home without involving a bank or mortgage company at all.

If you have absolutely no down payment to work with, see if you can find a real estate agent who is willing to receive his commission from the sale in the form of a note from you, the new owner. Many won't agree to do that; if you can't find one who is willing to help, try to learn as much about real estate as you can, and find a home that's for sale by the owner, known in the trade as a FSBO.

Try to find a don't-wanter—someone who will be flexible in the terms of the sale, someone who will agree to carry a loan instead of insisting on a large cash down payment. Especially look for people who are managing properties from out of state; they're usually the ones who are weary of the management hassle and will agree to your terms.

Another suggestion: Look for properties where the seller is facing foreclosure or is behind on two or three mortgage payments. These sellers are often flexible in their terms.

Don't despair. Finding the right combination—a don't-wanter, a property that suits your needs perfectly, and terms that fit your budget—takes time. Don't give up; the house you are looking for may be just around the corner. Keep looking until you find it.

If you find a good bargain with a seller who is willing to be flexible but who insists on some cash as a down payment, and if you don't have that cash, consider bringing in a partner. Your partner provides the down payment. You agree to make the mortgage payments, keep the property in top condition, and even make improvements while you live there. Then, when you sell the house, you'll split any profit with your partner. Convincing a partner that his investment is safe might take some effective talking, but you'll probably be able to show him or her a respectable return on that investment. Use all of your knowledge of real estate to persuade the partner to help with the cash outlay.

You might try the earnest money option: Find a property that's a good bargain, tie it up with an Earnest Money Receipt, find another buyer immediately, and resell the property for a profit. You've just earned your down payment for a home of your own!

If you belong to a credit union, you might consider borrowing the down payment. This might mean that your payments are higher until you repay the loan, but it is better than waiting to save for a down payment—something that usually never happens! You might have to hang on by your fingernails until you get that loan paid off, but if you find a property that starts to grow in value, your purchase will pay you back many times over.

Here's another proven technique. Search for a house that is up for lease; persuade the seller to give you an option to buy within a certain period of time. This technique locks in the price and gives you the opportunity to buy the home later on. If you have negotiated a hard bargain, you could even turn around and resell the home to a third party for a market price that is well above your option price. Again, you've just earned a down payment for the next purchase!

As a last resort, you could find an individual with a strong financial statement who is willing to cosign on your loan. That could be a family member or business associate who has a stake in your future success.

Any of these techniques—as well as the more sophisticated approaches we'll discuss later—can be used to come up with the down payment.

You should also be aware of special loan programs available to first-time homebuyers and would-be buyers with limited income. Fannie Mae, a private company that buys mortgages on the "secondary market" from other lenders, offers a wide array of programs in partnership with local lenders. Visit Fannie Mae's Web site (www.fanniemae.com) for an up-to-date list and description of their home ownership programs. Since 1968, Fannie Mae has helped more than 50 million families achieve the American dream; you could be next!

Another good source for loans is the Federal Housing Authority (FHA), a division of the U.S. Department of Housing and Urban Development (HUD) that guarantees loans for people who don't have large down payments. Under FHA loans, which can be obtained through most banks and mortgage companies, you could obtain a loan with virtually no down payment. You can even buy an older home and renovate it using an FHA-guaranteed loan. The interest rate is generally lower than it is when borrowing with any other arrangement. There are a few disadvantages: The loans take longer to obtain, and the appraisals are usually low, which can cause problems at closing. But FHA loans remain an important resource for buyers. (Visit www.hud.gov for more information.)

The U.S. Veterans Administration (VA) also sponsors a program for veterans; if you've served in the armed forces, you can buy a home with no down payment. You will have to be prepared to pay closing costs, however. Go to www.va.gov for more information.

Many state and local governments have become involved in helping renters become homeowners. One common approach is to offer tax-free bonds to generate funds for low-interest-rate loans to low- and middle-income residents. These funds often go begging because few people know about the various government programs.

Again, a good real estate agent or mortgage specialist can walk you through the many loan programs that may help you become a homeowner with almost nothing down.

So, quit gazing in despair at the balance in your checking account. There is a house, a town house, or a condominium out there just waiting for you to move in. Take a good look at your next paycheck and set something aside for tomorrow. Study the principles outlined in these chapters, and a few months from now you might be pruning your own fruit trees while your spouse drinks lemonade on your own back porch!

CHAPTER 16

Funds from the Philistines: Short-Term Funds from Hard-Money Lenders

"After learning about buying with nothing down, I fell in love with a house that I just had to buy. So I found a mortgage broker who was not afraid of being creative and trying new ways of financing. I was able to purchase my dream home with nothing down."

—LYNA FARKAS

If you think it's tough talking to your local bank or lending company about a loan to buy your own home, just wait until you try to get a loan on an income-producing property. You might say it's like trying to get funds from the Philistines!

But if you're going to be successful in building a fortune in real estate using other people's money, you'll need to know how to deal with commercial bankers, mortgage brokers (who can help you find the best source of funds), and mortgage companies (both in your hometown and on the Internet) that specialize in funding purchases just like the ones you're about to make.

There's a reason why bankers and mortgage companies are known as "hard-money lenders." In general, hard-money lenders offer you hard terms: a loan with a relatively high interest rate, a short payback period, and higher monthly payments than you might

131

expect. In addition, hard-money lenders always try to secure the loan by using a piece of property as collateral.

There's another good reason for calling them "hard-money lenders." If your income is low, your monthly obligations are high, or you are self-employed, these loans are harder to get! Hard-money lenders are wary of a borrower who is planning on investing borrowed funds in real estate. After all, every lending institution wants to keep its risk at a minimum.

In general, you should turn to hard-money lenders only after you have exhausted all other potential sources of funds. But if you have a great deal ready to go and you are equipped with the knowledge from this book, you can make banks and other lending institutions work for you.

First, you should be aware that there are several kinds of hard-money lenders: commercial banks, mortgage banks, mortgage brokers, finance companies, credit unions, and online lending companies. Each has its particular lending guidelines, and each has different goals and objectives. Let's take a closer look at the major kinds of hard-money lenders.

Commercial Banks

Virtually every community in the United States and Canada has at least one downtown commercial bank, and often many more in the suburbs. Most commercial banks generate significant profits by making loans to small, mid-size, and large businesses, including commercial real estate builders and developers. Most banks operate real estate lending subsidiaries that are a major source of mortgage funds. If you're a real estate investor with a solid proposal, they will want to talk with you.

Commercial banks offer three-, six-, or nine-month commercial notes that do not carry monthly payment obligations. But you should *always* be prepared to come up with the lump sum when the loan comes due either by taking out another loan or by converting that *balloon payment* into a monthly payment until you are able to pay the loan in full.

Mortgage Companies

Unlike commercial banks, mortgage companies focus entirely on the real estate finance industry, making both residential and commercial loans. Many former savings and loan institutions or "thrifts" became "mortgage banks" after the collapse of that industry in the late 1980s. More than 2,700 companies are members of the national Mortgage Bankers Association. Again, if you're interested in real estate deals, you should get to know a mortgage company in your area.

Mortgage Brokers

Mortgage brokers make their living by connecting potential borrowers with lending institutions, private investors, and other sources of funds for real estate transactions. The brokers typically charge the lender a fee equal to a certain percentage of the loans they arrange. A good mortgage broker should be able to contact several different lending institutions to find you the best rate and terms on a mortgage.

Finance Companies

These financial institutions specialize in loans for cars, boats, trailers, and other consumer items. They usually charge high rates for their loans and require a monthly repayment plan. In general, they should be avoided, but if you find yourself just short of the funds you need to complete a purchase, you might go to a finance company for a loan secured by your car or boat. If you *do* use a finance company, ask for the terms that will give you the most flexibility.

Credit Unions

If you belong to a credit union, you have a very good chance of obtaining a loan at highly competitive rates. That's because credit unions are owned by their members, unlike a bank, whose shareholders are focused on making a profit. One of my Creating Wealth seminar graduates who did not have a high-salaried job applied for a loan from his credit union to use as a down payment on a fifteen-unit apartment building. His loan was approved, and he was able to arrange for repayment terms that did not strap him with negative monthly payments. If this is an option for you, consider becoming a member and establishing a good business relationship with one of the loan officers.

Online Lenders

The rise of the Internet has spawned a host of online lending companies, as well as scam artists seeking only to separate you from your hard-earned dollars. A legitimate online lender may be able to offer you a better rate or terms than your local bank or mortgage company. That's because they don't have the "bricks and mortar" investment in local offices or staffers. You will have to decide if the savings offered online are enough to compensate for your inability to build a personal relationship with a local lender in your community. If you opt for the online company, be sure to check references to make sure it's a legitimate operation and that any transfer of funds is done in a highly secure way. And never, never, never send a "loan application fee" or your credit card or social security number to someone who contacts you via email.

Whichever type of institution you decide to use, search for the lowest available loan rates and, if possible, do not get locked into inflexible monthly payments. If such payments are required, always negotiate for the longest possible payback period, since this will lower your monthly payments.

As you gain experience, you will find out which lender or lenders will provide the financial support you need to carry out your nothing-down strategy. Over the many years I've been investing in real estate, I have found that one of my local bankers has consistently given me the best service at the lowest rates. When I began investing in real estate, I took action to establish a strong credit rating so I could borrow large amounts of money quickly on an unsecured basis. I approached the banker who handled my checking account and explained my objective. I then began to borrow small amounts of money so I could establish a history of prompt repayment. My first loan back in the 1970s was for $500, and I soon worked my way up to an unsecured credit limit of $5,000—a reasonable amount at the time.

But that's when I ran into trouble. As soon as I reached $5,000, the loan committee at the bank was reluctant to lend me any more money on an unsecured basis. As a result, I promptly moved all of my accounts to another bank that was more flexible in its terms and more confident in my ability to repay large amounts of money. Since then I have deposited my money in several banks in order to be able to borrow tens of thousands of dollars from each one if necessary. And there are situations where I still use those lines of credit to move quickly on certain real estate investments.

My advice to you is to find a banker who is friendly and interested in helping you establish a strong credit rating through borrow-

NOTHING DOWN FOR THE 2000s

ing small amounts of money. There are undoubtedly plenty of banks that serve your area, and lending is a keenly competitive business, so don't be afraid to get up and walk out of a bank that is not responsive to your needs and wishes. Write letters to the officers of banks where you are treated poorly; let them know how you feel.

A second suggestion is to constantly cultivate your sources for funds by visiting with lenders on a regular basis, or at least staying in touch over the phone or through email. Learn how their business operates and get to know the managers in each office. You will soon realize that bank officers and lending specialists are ordinary human beings, not fiery dragons. And the more you know about borrowing, the more confident you will become about your ability to borrow money.

But before you sit down to discuss a loan for a particular purchase, try to understand your banker's overall objectives, because there is likely to be a conflict with your own investment goals. A banker will be concerned about high security, while you are trying to negotiate the highest possible leverage. He wants collateral; you would rather have an unsecured loan. He needs appraisals, credit checks, approval from loan committees, title policies, and a pile of other paperwork; you just want to borrow money in the simplest and most straightforward manner. Whenever possible, try to supply what your banker wants. But once you have proved your prompt repayment ability you should ask your banker to start doing business your way.

If you recognize that your personalities clash, go to another bank. Life is too short to waste your time dealing with someone who questions your integrity, points out all the weak spots in your financial situation, reduces you to begging in order to get the loan, and then makes you pay for the "privilege" of doing business with him. There are plenty of good bankers in your area. Go to them.

There's a good analogy that describes the banker-borrower relationship. When you go to the doctor for a checkup, he asks you to strip to your shorts, stick out your tongue, and cough at the appropriate time. A banker interviewing you for a loan asks you to strip to the shorts financially. But that's where the similarity ends. The banker is concerned with *his* security, not yours. Don't be fooled by all the advertising that portrays the friendly banker who is anxious to lend you money. Just remember: The people who are writing the ads aren't making the loans!

Try to locate a young, aggressive banker who has enough experience to understand your request, but who has not been around long enough to be influenced by the "lifers" on the loan committee. Ask your loan officer if she owns any real estate besides her own home. If she does, your chances of getting a loan for real estate ventures will be increased, because the loan officer will understand your goals.

Let a banker know that she is competing for your dollars. There are plenty of banks, and she should be trying to attract your business. Remember, *your* business is important to the bank, not the other way around. Adopt that attitude, and you will begin to have the upper hand.

Try to help your banker—and yourself. Be prepared with typed financial statements, income tax statements for the last two years, pictures of some of your properties, and other supporting documents. Try to present as stable a financial picture as you possibly can. For instance, you might consider putting all of your highly leveraged properties in your spouse's name to reduce the loan-to-debt ratio.

Be as realistic with your financial statement as possible. If you want your bank to believe your statement, be sure to enter the value of your car below the car's current market value; your banker can check values very easily with his used-car books. If he can see that you are realistic on the things he does understand, he will trust your values on the things (such as real estate holdings) he may not understand.

Critical questions that a banker will want answered are:

- How much money do you want or need?
- Why do you need to borrow it from me?
- Where is your bank account now?
- Why don't you borrow the money from your own bank?
- What are you going to use the money for?
- How will you pay the loan back?
- If you can't pay the loan back within the specified time limit, how can I be sure that I will be able to collect the money from you?

Be prepared with answers to all of these questions. Keep your requests simple, and don't go into full detail about your creative transactions. *A confused mind always says "no."* Don't confuse your

136

banker with a long explanation of a complicated real estate deal. Simply tell him how much money you need and how you intend to pay it back.

A banker's chance for promotion comes with his capacity to make good loans. That's why he's concerned about any highly leveraged position. Convince him that you are not a threat to his security, and that you offer him a chance to get ahead in his career. From time to time drop in to discuss your progress with him. Let him know that you are successful and that you are a person of integrity.

When you find a good banker, let everyone know about him. Promoting him and his bank is an ideal way to create a long-term winning financial partnership.

Short-Term Borrowing

Because mortgages typically have terms of fifteen, twenty, or thirty years, they are considered long-term loans. It doesn't matter that most borrowers pay them off much more quickly—especially during times of heavy refinancing. From the bank's perspective, they are still long-term loans, and therefore carry a greater risk than loans that are repaid more quickly.

From your perspective, it is important to master the techniques of borrowing short-term funds and repaying them promptly. That will help you establish a favorable credit rating and a good working relationship with several cooperative bankers. By demonstrating your fiscal responsibility with small, short-term loans, you are establishing the groundwork for obtaining ever-larger, long-term loans in the future.

As you begin to establish good relationships with bankers, jump at every chance to borrow money. By borrowing money and repaying it on schedule, you can establish a credit history that could be worth hundreds of thousands of dollars later. Do what you can now. You might borrow $1,000 from one bank and deposit it in a money market account at another institution. When the note comes due, you can pay it off by writing a check from the money market fund. The interest charges on the loan will be largely offset by the amount of interest accrued from the account—and in the meantime, your credit rating will get a boost.

Or you could deposit $5,000 in a savings account and then ask the same bank for a $5,000 loan secured by those same funds. You could then deposit the $5,000 loan in a savings account at another bank, where you would request another $5,000 loan on the same basis. You could do this in four or five different banks simultaneously, proving to several bankers that you are able to borrow money and to maintain a savings account. This method requires $5,000 initial capital plus paying the accrued interest for the term of the loans. But if you are starting out with a negative credit rating, or are young and have no credit rating to begin with, this strategy will put you in a much stronger financial position.

Why use so many banks? First, when you can borrow funds from any of several sources, you have increased your flexibility and your capacity to buy larger properties. Second, if you have a short-term loan of $5,000 due at one bank, you can always go to another bank in your system and borrow the $5,000 to repay the first bank. This way you could keep a $5,000 note floating forever, and the only cost would be the interest. All the time you would be improving your credit rating through prompt loan payments.

It is feasible for a person with a good credit history to be able to borrow up to $50,000 on an unsecured basis from one bank. If you were able to borrow this amount from five banks, you could secure up to $250,000 in cash in less than a week. Of course, that is most likely to happen if you already have a good income and a strong credit rating.

In the initial stages of your borrowing program, your banker will probably ask to secure your loans on a piece of property you own. This is normal procedure. But you should request that your loans be moved to an unsecured basis as soon as possible so that you do not encumber properties you might want to keep free for trading purposes.

CHAPTER 17

From Bankers to Crankers: Tapping the Equity in Your Home

"I bought my first home using the nothing-down technique. When the market took a quick turn upward, I refinanced to consolidate into one mortgage. The builder of a new property let me put my upside-down mortgage on top of the selling price of his new property and the bank let me get a new mortgage on the new property which took his loan off the books. The builder took possession of my old property and I took possession of his."

—DR. NINA CRAFT, PH.D.

If you're serious about investing in real estate, you have to learn how to walk before you can run. Now that you know something about hard-money loans from a bank or mortgage company, it's time to look at the many other sources of funds—starting with your own home.

If you have owned a house or condominium for the past few years, you've probably built up a rather substantial equity because of rising real estate values. Many homeowners who already have a mortgage on their property take out a second mortgage in order to finance a kitchen-remodeling project or add a bedroom. Let's say you have a $250,000 home with $125,000 remaining on your first mortgage. That gives you $125,000 equity in your home, and most lenders would let you borrow around $75,000 of that equity for a second mortgage. That's $75,000 right on your doorstep that could be used to purchase investment properties.

Another popular alternative is to apply for a home equity line of credit. This is more flexible than a second mortgage because you can borrow money up to a certain amount whenever you want some extra cash. However, the money you borrow is still secured by the equity in your home.

A third option for tapping the equity in your home is to refinance your current mortgage and take out a larger loan. In our example, the owner of the $250,000 home might apply for a new $200,000 mortgage; after paying off the old $125,000 loan, he would have $75,000 available for other purposes—and just one monthly payment to make.

Many homeowners have become successful real estate investors by leveraging their home equity with a second mortgage, line of credit, or refinanced loan. The lender is happy to give them the funds because the loan is secured by the home, significantly reducing their risks. And the investors are happy because they can turn around and buy an income-producing property without having to take money out of a bank account or sell their shares of stock.

There are two downsides to this strategy. First, your monthly mortgage payment is likely to go up—a situation that may not matter if your new investment is generating a strong flow of cash. Second, taking out a loan secured by your home creates a risk. But if the real estate purchased with the borrowed funds is well-selected and underpriced in relation to the market value, the risk is minimal. And sometimes you need to take a risk to improve your long-range financial situation.

As an example, consider a family that owns a home valued at $200,000; they have paid down their mortgage loan to a $100,000 balance. After checking with several financial institutions, the owner locates a company that will issue a ten-year $60,000 second mortgage at a rate of 7 percent with no closing costs. The monthly payments will be about $700.

The family has decided to invest in a duplex priced at $200,000, using the $60,000 second mortgage as a down payment. The seller agrees to carry the remaining $140,000 balance for ten years at a rate of 8 percent. The monthly payment to the seller would be about

$1,700. That means the family would face an additional monthly payment of $2,400 for the two loans.

However, this monthly payment will be fully covered by the tenants of the duplex. Each tenant pays $1,200 a month in rent for a total of $2,400 a month. If the family members can maintain the duplex themselves, they will have at least a break-even cash flow, as well as the tax advantages of an investment property, and the likelihood of increased appreciation over the years.

What will the family's picture look like in the long run? Let's suppose both the house and the duplex appreciate at the rate of only 5 percent annually for the next ten years. At the end of ten years, the value of both the home and the duplex will have appreciated to $325,000 each. With both loans on the duplex paid off, the family would now have an additional $325,000 in real estate assets—a direct result of that $60,000 second mortgage.

Using a second mortgage is an excellent technique to raise capital for an investment program. Under *no* circumstances should any of the funds from a second mortgage be spent on consumer items. Leave your homeowner's equity alone unless you plan to use it on a solid investment.

If you can't use the second-mortgage technique because you lack equity, try refinancing your car, boat, or trailer or use a piece of jewelry, an antique, or some other valuable item as collateral for a loan. The monthly payments may be higher using this approach, but it provides a ready source of cash if the need arises.

Remember that whatever route you take to finance your real estate investment, you need to be flexible. Settle only for terms you are comfortable with, and don't get trapped into a bad situation. The money is there for the borrowing; take what steps you can to get established so that the money will be there for you.

The Second Mortgage Crank

So far, we've been looking at first and second mortgages on property you own. Now we'll examine how you can use a second mortgage on property you *don't* own in order to add it to your portfolio.

I call this the second mortgage crank because it allows you to "crank" the required down payment out of the property you want to buy through a refinancing done by the seller. This technique can also be called "subordination." When mortgage money is loose, this can be the most powerful technique in your arsenal. The first time I ever tried to use it, I held my breath during the whole transaction. I just couldn't believe it was going to work. But it did!

I called the out-of-state owner of a twelve-unit apartment building located near a large local university in Provo, Utah, to see if he wanted to sell his property. I had a real estate license and was farming the area for listings. He wasn't interested.

Several months later he decided that since he lived so far away from his property, he wanted to sell it and invest his money closer to his home. We listed the property for $315,000 with a 5 percent commission to be paid to me if I sold the property.

I did a thorough analysis of the property and determined that the net operating income was about $28,000 per year. Because the building was located in a good area, it was easily rented out to college students. I listed the property, turned the listing over to a colleague, and went to Europe for two months.

When I returned, the unit had not been sold, and no buyers were in sight. Suddenly I realized that I was a better buyer than a seller. I knew that the property was a great buy. I knew that I wanted it badly. But I also knew that I had no money with which to buy it.

When the listing expired I began to get imaginative. One day I received a telephone call from the seller in San Jose, California. He told me that he had an offer of $295,000 from a neighbor, but he felt an obligation to let me have the first crack. I told him that I would pay $300,000 and that I would fly there and meet with him that weekend.

When I hung up the phone I knew that I had committed myself. Until that telephone call, my ownership of the building was just wishful thinking. Now I had to produce. I had no idea how I'd do it.

Since the seller's equity was a whopping $220,000, I felt that he would be a little more flexible if I could give him most of his equity in cash. So I decided to go to a local lender and borrow 75 percent of the purchase price; in addition, I'd ask the seller to accept a second mortgage that would finance the remainder of the required 25 percent down payment. My proposal looked like the "After" drawing in the illustration on page 143.

When I arrived in San Jose, the seller and I sat in his living room to discuss my proposal. He went along with most of it, but insisted

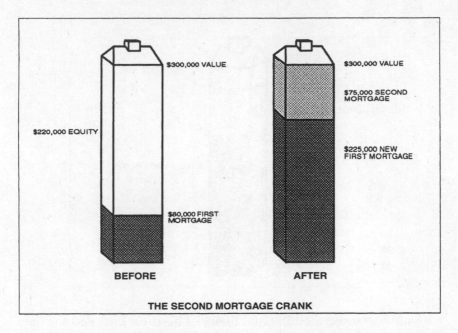

$300,000 VALUE

$220,000 EQUITY

$80,000 FIRST MORTGAGE

$300,000 VALUE

$75,000 SECOND MORTGAGE

$225,000 NEW FIRST MORTGAGE

BEFORE

AFTER

THE SECOND MORTGAGE CRANK

that he would accept only a $60,000 second mortgage, and he would have to have 12 percent interest. The most important motivating factor for the seller was the fact that he would be receiving $160,000 in cash, so he could afford to give me a break by lending me most of the necessary down payment.

There was one other problem: I had wanted to close six months from the date of our conversation, and he wanted to have all of his money by the first of the year. He feared that I would tie up his property for six months and then not be able to put the deal together. His worries were probably well founded: I was a young, single, basically inexperienced real estate agent. He wanted $5,000 earnest money.

I didn't have it. I finally persuaded him to let me have six months to try to put the deal together by offering him my duplex—and its $8,000 equity—with no strings attached if I defaulted at the end of six months.

I told him that if I *could* raise the money, he would receive $160,000 in cash plus a note for $60,000 earning 12 percent interest, and I would get my duplex back.

He accepted. We drew up our agreement on a napkin and we both signed. The financial picture is shown in the diagram on page 144.

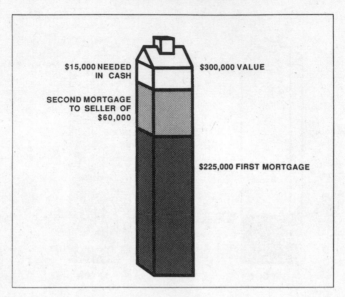

$15,000 NEEDED IN CASH

$300,000 VALUE

SECOND MORTGAGE TO SELLER OF $60,000

$225,000 FIRST MORTGAGE

I still had some monumental financial hurdles: I needed to come up with $15,000 in cash for the additional down payment. And I needed to be able to borrow $225,000 from my lending institution.

The first problem wasn't as bad as it seemed. As the new owner, I'd immediately receive approximately $15,000 in rents and deposits.

When tenants moved into the building, they were required to pay one month's rent in advance. As the new owner, I would also receive the rent and security deposits. This would be the source of my down payment.

To solve the second problem, I persuaded a good friend who had a strong financial statement to become my partner. He had the ability to get the money; I had the expertise. We applied for the loan together. He was the borrower and I was the co-borrower.

We were extremely lucky. Things fell into place. The money market was loose, the loan officer ignored any extraneous financing we were planning on making, and the building was appraised high enough to qualify for the loan because I convinced the appraiser with some of my own homework. There was only one remaining obstacle: the approximately $5,000 in closing costs.

Our luck held out. My partner and I were able to obtain a six-month loan for the $5,000 on our signatures.

Let's examine the financing:

Borrowed from lending institution	$225,000
First month's rent, deposits	15,000
Borrowed on signatures for closing costs	5,000
Seller's agreed second mortgage	60,000
Amount out of own pocket	-0-
Total	$305,000

Incidentally, three months later my partner offered to let me buy him out for $5,000 in cash. Instead, I persuaded him to take a recreational acre in a beautiful mountain location where I had $5,000 in equity.

So, the property became all mine—with nothing down.

Through this "second mortgage crank," I was able to *crank* out my down payment by borrowing it from the seller through a second mortgage. Essential ingredients for a successful cranker are:

- A motivated seller who has a very low mortgage balance and lots of equity
- A property in a good location
- A bank willing to loan up to 75 percent of the appraisal price, and
- A buyer who has a strong financial position or who can find a partner to provide the financial strength.

The illustration on page 146 shows what a potential "cranker" property might look like.

When you can persuade the seller to accept only a part of his equity in cash and carry a second mortgage for the balance, then you have the makings of a nothing-down transaction. In using a second-mortgage crank, it is essential for the seller and the lender to be fully aware of what you are doing. That is the only ethical and legal approach to take.

Now, let me point out that most banks will be reluctant to lend you the money for a mortgage if you have borrowed part of the down payment. However, there are some potential ways around this hurdle, especially if you've developed a relationship with your local lender who is willing to go out of his way to take care of you as a customer. Take a look at the following three examples of creative nothing-down thinking:

Moving the mortgage. Ask the seller to accept a second mortgage on another piece of property you already own. Use your other property as collateral to the seller until the refinancing is completed. If

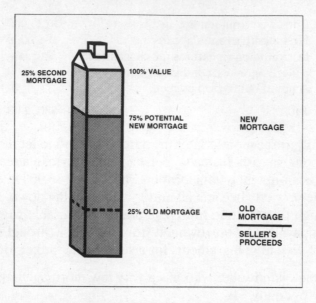

25% SECOND MORTGAGE

100% VALUE

75% POTENTIAL NEW MORTGAGE

NEW MORTGAGE

25% OLD MORTGAGE

OLD MORTGAGE

SELLER'S PROCEEDS

the bank officer requires proof that the down payment has been made, have the seller draft a letter stating that he has received the amount in the form of an *exchange* for other property or that he has already received "consideration" for his equity.

Uniform Real Estate Contract. Ask the seller to sell you the property on a Uniform Real Estate Contract with a $100 down payment. When you go to the bank, you will then be listed as the legal owner of the property, and the loan officer won't question you about a down payment. When the refinancing is complete, pay the seller the remainder of his equity and negotiate the terms of the second mortgage. In some instances the banker will require that you be the owner of record for at least six months before you can refinance. This limits your flexibility, but if the seller agrees to wait, it's an option that may work.

Seller refinance. If the seller refinances his own property before selling to you, the banker won't raise the question of your down payment. When the refinancing takes place, the seller deeds the property to you and you take over his payments on the new loan. He gets the cash from the refinancing plus a second mortgage from you for the rest of his equity. You get in for nothing down. In this case, you need to be sure that the seller's mortgage does not have a "due on sale" clause, otherwise the bank can call for repayment of that loan when the title on the property changes.

While using the second mortgage crank can at times be extremely complicated, the paperwork is worth it if you are able to invest in an excellent piece of property. And sometimes the returns are good. Looking back to my first deal using the second mortgage crank, I could have sold my $300,000 building one year later for $350,000. After discounting my closing costs and partnership costs, I could have pocketed more than $38,000—enough to get me started on my next deal! As it turned out, I held this property for several years, eventually earning more than a quarter of a million dollars.

CHAPTER 18

Some Great Tips on Buying Low, Refinancing High

"There are mortgage brokers that have programs for investors that can refinance up to 100 percent of the appraised value. In one recent year, I refinanced nine properties and pulled out $200,000 in cash."

—MIKE KOZLOWSKI

The second mortgage crank is just one of the many ways you can get the seller or the mortgage holder to help you complete a purchase for virtually nothing down. There are countless funding possibilities out there—almost as many as there are attractive income-producing properties for you to buy. Let's look at some of the other ways you can get to work on building your property portfolio.

The Overfinance Technique

Let's take a look at one of them, called the "overfinance" technique. This allows you to buy a property and in the process put cash in your pocket using the second mortgage crank technique with a little twist. Suppose we locate a $400,000 building that has a $100,000 existing mortgage. The seller wants some cash but is willing to be flexible with the balance of his equity, which totals $300,000. We know that we can obtain a new mortgage of $300,000 (75 percent of $400,000). However, we would much prefer not to make a $100,000 down payment; in fact, our goal is to pay nothing down—and walk away with extra cash in our pocket. Fortunately, the seller is highly motivated and understands the situation. He is willing to help us by carrying a second mortgage of $120,000 that does not have a "due on sale" clause. Once that mortgage is finalized, you can move ahead with the transaction, and the owner can receive the $180,000 balance of his equity in cash. The figure below shows how the transaction will look once the refinance is complete.

If you look closely you will note that the total amount of the two mortgages is $420,000 on a property valued at $400,000. Where did the other $20,000 go? Into your pocket!

Great?

No, not so great. While there is a place for this kind of deal, you need to consider the financial burden you assume by promising to repay all of the loans. Unless you have negotiated extremely good

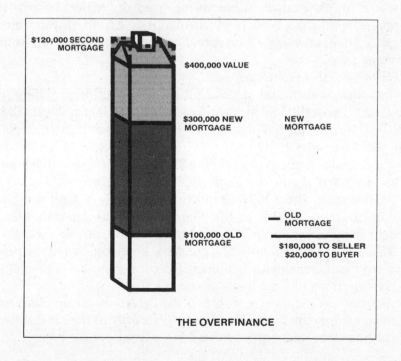

$120,000 SECOND MORTGAGE

$400,000 VALUE

$300,000 NEW MORTGAGE   NEW MORTGAGE

OLD MORTGAGE

$100,000 OLD MORTGAGE $180,000 TO SELLER
$20,000 TO BUYER

THE OVERFINANCE

terms, the property will probably generate a negative cash flow. You'll need to dig into your own pocket every month until the rents can be raised. The higher the overfinance, the more acute the problem becomes. You should only overfinance a property if you have an absolute profit-maker in which to invest the leftover funds. *Never* spend them on anything but another investment.

There is a more serious legal and ethical problem as well. If you decide to overfinance, you must *always* explain both the benefits and the risks to the seller, make sure that he understands the implications, and ask him to sign an affidavit agreeing to the overfinance. (One way to persuade him to agree to the overfinance is to offer him security on both his property and on another piece of property you own. You can remove the mortgage from your second piece of property once the seller is satisfied that you'll make payments promptly. This should take no longer than a year.)

Borrow from a Mortgage Holder

There is an alternative to borrowing from the seller: borrow the down payment from holders of existing first, second, or third mortgages, or people who sold on a real estate contract or wraparound mortgage.

How does this technique work?

Suppose you found a four-plex rental building selling for $250,000. The seller had an existing loan of $200,000 and wanted his $50,000 equity in cash if possible. If you don't have the $50,000, how can you come up with it?

First, find out about the existing $200,000 mortgage. To whom is it payable? Will the holder be flexible? Is a bank involved?

In our case, the $200,000 mortgage is really a Uniform Real Estate Contract payable to Mr. Garcia at $1,500 a month. Garcia bought the property from Mr. and Mrs. Peterson, and he owes them $100,000 at $1,000 a month. Mr. and Mrs. Peterson owned the property free and clear, with no mortgage on the home. The picture looks something like the figure on page 151.

Further investigation reveals that the Petersons are an older couple who are extremely nervous about the security of their investment. It's obvious they might be interested in a payout of their equity.

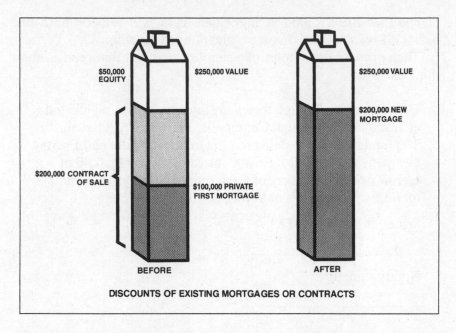

$50,000 EQUITY

$250,000 VALUE

$250,000 VALUE

$200,000 NEW MORTGAGE

$200,000 CONTRACT OF SALE

$100,000 PRIVATE FIRST MORTGAGE

BEFORE

AFTER

DISCOUNTS OF EXISTING MORTGAGES OR CONTRACTS

After Garcia purchased the property, he sold it to the current owners to create a monthly cash flow for himself. For the last four years he has enjoyed $500 a month net cash flow (the difference between the $1,500 he receives and the $1,000 he pays the Petersons). But his business has recently declined, and his wife has asked for a divorce. Garcia hasn't been able to raise enough money to settle with his wife, and he desperately needs extra cash. He doesn't think his mortgage in the building is salable, and he considers himself stuck.

Armed with this information, do you think it is possible to bargain with the Petersons, as holders of the underlying mortgage, buy out Garcia in cash, and still purchase the building with no cash investment?

The answer is yes.

First, you should approach each of the mortgage holders. Offer to pay Garcia $75,000 *cash* for his $100,000 mortgage; offer the Petersons $75,000 for their $100,000 mortgage.

Prepare for some moans and groans, but once the dust settles, remind the Petersons that they'd be much better off with $75,000 in cash than with their worries about future security and with the hassle of collecting a monthly check for the next fifteen years. Remind

Garcia that the $75,000 in immediate cash will remedy both his business losses and his divorce obligations to his wife.

Then prepare two copies of a simple document that reads something like this:

I, *[seller's name],* agree to sell my interest in a home located at 22556 Peacock Lane, Centerville, Va., for $75,000 cash. The funds should be delivered to Greenacre Title and Escrow Company, where this note and instructions will be held in escrow pending delivery of the required cash by *[your name] (or his/her assigns)* on or before (Date).

Signed this day (DATE).

_____

Notary signature

_____

Get Garcia and the Petersons to sign these documents. You just made $50,000.

"How?" you ask.

Approach your bank or mortgage lender about getting a new loan on the property. Since you paid $250,000 for it according to your agreement with the seller, apply for a 80 percent loan of $200,000. The banker will want to know where your down payment is coming from; just tell him that it is being held in escrow at Greenacre Title and Escrow Company and that the $200,000 mortgage money should be delivered to the title company for final dispersal.

Upon approval, your money will be delivered to the title company. The following events occur:

- The title company will pay $75,000 to Garcia for his $100,000 interest in the property.
- The title company will pay $75,000 to the Petersons for their $100,000 interest in the property.
- The $50,000 that remains will be paid to the seller as a $50,000 cash down payment on his $250,000 building.

You just purchased a $250,000 building for $200,000 (your mortgage loan), and the $50,000 equity you earned is clear profit.

The only loan you have to pay off is the $200,000 first mortgage. Of course, you will have to pay closing costs on the new loan plus title charges and other miscellaneous expenses, but most of these outlays can be covered by the rents and deposits that you will receive as a new owner. One more thing: There should be a steady, monthly cash flow from the rental units, which you can put into your pocket.

The holders of the underlying mortgages might not be as generous as you would like them to be. What happens if both the Petersons and Garcia decide to discount their mortgages by only $20,000 instead of $25,000? You'll be $10,000 short. But use your imagination and creativity, and try one of the following alternative plans.

Plan #1. Persuade the seller to receive only $25,000 in cash instead of $50,000, and have him take back a second mortgage of $25,000 as soon as the refinance is complete. See below for how this will look.

Plan #2. Persuade the Petersons or Garcia (or both) to receive $70,000 in cash and a $10,000 personal note for the rest of their equity. The results are as shown on page 154.

Plan #3. Persuade the seller to receive $25,000 in cash and a $25,000 note. Then negotiate with Garcia and the Petersons con-

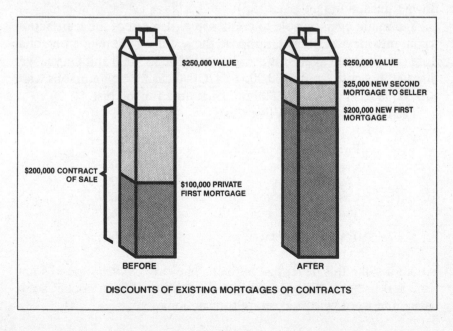

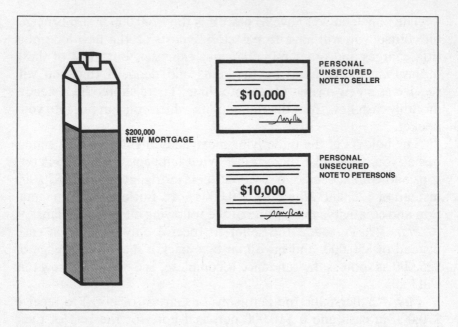

cerning who takes the discounts and the notes. Perhaps Garcia will take a $20,000 discount, but the Petersons will discount their note by only $5,000. You will still be able to accomplish your nothing-down transaction (see page 155).

You might even be able to crank some cash out of the transaction to put in your own pocket. Suppose the seller would take a personal note (not secured against the real estate) for $25,000 and Garcia will discount his note from $100,000 to $70,000 cash. The Petersons want $70,000 in cash with a $10,000 personal note for the rest.

The results would look like this:

First mortgage proceeds	$200,000
Cash to seller	25,000
Cash to Garcia	70,000
Cash to Petersons	70,000
Total cash paid out	165,000
Your net proceeds	$35,000

Situations like this never just happen. They are *created*. Spend some time and use some imagination, and you'll be able to pocket some cash on most of your real estate transactions.

154

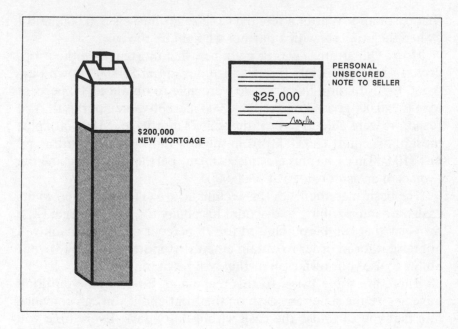

$200,000
NEW MORTGAGE

PERSONAL
UNSECURED
NOTE TO SELLER

$25,000

Buy Low, Refinance High

Of all the techniques we've discussed so far, this one is the easiest to use and the simplest to understand for both buyer and seller. In essence it consists of finding sellers who are willing to sell their properties immediately for a substantial discount and all cash.

Here's an example. One afternoon as I was talking with a broker friend, I asked if he had any property in exchange for a quick cash-out of his equity. He mentioned that he had recently taken on a house on a guaranteed-sale program, and he was ready to sell it for a great price.

A couple of weeks later his wife showed me through the house, and I was flabbergasted. The house had been newly painted and carpeted, and new drapes had been installed. The grounds were beautiful and well cared for. The place was immaculate. It took me about three seconds to make my mind up; a few minutes later I was in his office with an offer.

The property had a new loan on it for $180,000; the seller wanted a $250,000 price including $70,000 cash for his equity. I knew that the market price was at least $300,000 because I was in the process of building some new houses that didn't look as nice and

155

that cost more. Within a few days the seller had his $70,000, and I owned the property with a partner who put up the cash.

How? Our strategy was to get a new first mortgage on the property as soon as possible to refinance our initial $70,000 down payment. In a situation like this, we were able to obtain an 80 percent loan ($240,000) based on the $300,000 market-value appraisal. As a result, we were able to pay off the seller's mortgage ($180,000), plus most of his equity ($60,000) from the new mortgage. By putting up just $10,000 in cash (plus closing costs) my partner and I became the owners of an asset valued at $300,000.

The basic ingredients of this technique are (1) a seller who wants cash now and is willing to discount his equity for the privilege; (2) a property that can be purchased for 75 percent of what a bank will appraise it for in order to obtain a new first mortgage; and (3) your ability to use your own cash or that of a partner.

There are some twists to this technique. First of all, you don't have to give the seller any cash on the front end if you can convince him that you can raise the cash within thirty days. Every time you talk to a seller, ask him, "What is your lowest cash price if I give you all of your equity in cash within thirty days?" For example, suppose you found a small $150,000 condominium for $120,000 cash. Negotiate with the seller to pay him $120,000 cash in thirty days; then apply for a $120,000 loan from a local lending institution based upon its $150,000 appraisal. Your only investment is to cover closing costs—about $5,000 in this case. This sounds easier to do than it is. Most traditional lenders refuse to do these kinds of transactions. The better your relationship with your banker, the more easily these kinds of situations can be structured to your advantage.

Another twist is to find a property that, in its present condition, is only worth what the seller is asking but which, with some minor cosmetic repairs, would appraise for a lot higher. Buy the property from the seller at a low price, make some minor improvements, and refinance the higher-valued property for enough money to pay the seller and cover the expenses you incurred in fixing up the property.

Sometimes the sellers can't wait thirty days for you to refinance the property. They need their money now. How can you take advantage of a low price? You have to cultivate your cash sources well so that when a "steal" comes along, you will be able to come up with immediate cash. This is one of the main reasons I always keep my bank lines of communication open. If I need a quick $100,000 for six

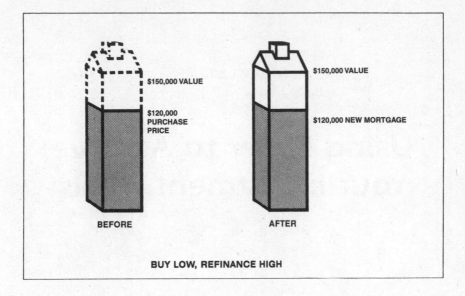

$150,000 VALUE

$120,000 PURCHASE PRICE

$150,000 VALUE

$120,000 NEW MORTGAGE

BEFORE

AFTER

BUY LOW, REFINANCE HIGH

months, I can get it. It also doesn't hurt to have a few partners who can come up with cash within forty-eight hours' notice.

Using the "buy low, refinance high" technique, you could take a $100,000 investment and use it over and over again—buying first one property and then refinancing your cash out again and repeating the process several times a year. You would not need extra capital, and each time you would end up owning a piece of property that had been purchased substantially under the market price.

When you buy real estate with small down payments and high leverage, you generally have to pay top dollar—retail prices. When a lot of cash is involved, the prices come down in a hurry. You can continue to spread your money into as many properties as possible, but if you have the resources, the "buy low, refinance high" technique can make you more "real" dollars in less time than any other method.

How do you raise cash to take advantage of the opportunities that exist all around you?

- Establish yourself with several lenders.
- Explain the program to a partner.
- Sell another piece of property to raise cash.

As you can see, there are all kinds of possibilities. I have a great deal of confidence in these "buy low, refinance high" techniques.

CHAPTER 19

Using Paper to Achieve Your Investment Goals

"Bob Allen taught me to look at more than just a few 'in the box' concepts to make almost any situation in real estate work. That has increased my profit margin by 100 percent, if not more."

—KRISTEN DOMINGUEZ

Now it's time to delve a little more deeply into the richly rewarding world of "paper."

Paper refers to mortgages or notes that may be *unsecured* (no strings attached) or *secured* by a piece of property or other collateral. *Hard paper* comes from a bank or other lending institution, such as a typical first mortgage. *Soft paper* is a note with lenient, flexible terms.

When you buy your first investment property with nothing down, the seller may take back 100 percent of the $400,000 purchase price using a *soft paper* note with flexible terms. When you borrowed $10,000 on your signature from your bank, you filled out a personal note that said you owed the bank $10,000; that note is *paper.* (The note would still be *paper* even it was secured against other property.)

Whenever you buy real estate with little or no down payment, there will be paper involved. The creative use of paper makes the difference between success and failure in those investments.

How can you make the best use of paper? Let's start with notes. Your obligation to pay a note (1) should be unsecured by collateral if possible, (2) should be negotiated at the lowest possible interest rate, (3) should be negotiated with the longest term acceptable to the seller, and (4) should not require monthly payments or should require only low monthly payments. These conditions are critical to success.

The key to borrowing money and making good use of paper is to incur debt by deferring the obligation to repay as far into the future as possible. This concept is against the seller's goals, which more often than not include the repayment of loans as soon as possible. The more the seller is a don't-wanter—and the more serious a don't-wanter he becomes as the negotiations proceed—the better your chances of working paper to your advantage.

The hierarchy of paper is clearly illustrated below:

High interest rate	Short-term payoff	High monthly payments
•	•	•
•	•	•
•	•	•
•	•	•
•	•	•
Low interest rate	Long-term payoff	Low monthly payments or no monthly payments

Always start at the bottom of each column in your negotiating, and work your way up slowly and carefully. Avoid the top of the hierarchy, as high monthly payments can kill your wallet.

Using paper to your benefit is *critical* to the success of any investment you make. Let's look at an investor who ignored the conditions that would have ensured his success.

John is just beginning to invest in real estate and wants to build up a portfolio for future retirement. He has little money saved, and has about $250 extra cash flow a month to invest.

John locates a fairly sound three-unit apartment building selling for a bargain-priced $150,000. The seller is a don't-wanter, but he needs $10,000 in cash. The seller's existing first mortgage of $125,000 is payable at $1,000 a month; the seller wants to receive the balance of his $15,000 equity over a seven-year period at 7 percent interest, secured by a second trust deed (mortgage) on the property.

159

John is so excited about what seems to be a great deal that he ceases to negotiate and hurriedly signs the Earnest Money Receipt. He arranges for a personal loan of $10,000 from his credit union, a balloon note that is due and payable in six months, with an interest rate of 9 percent.

The closing date arrives and John becomes the proud owner of an "alligator." John hasn't done his homework. The seller had told him rents were $800 per unit and that monthly expenses were about $800. But the first few months are a revelation. Two of the units are rented out for $600; the other one is rented for $550. Expenses during the summer do run about $800 a month, but during the winter, when gas bills are higher, monthly expenses go as high as $1,500.

John took possession in September. Financial details were:

Monthly gross rents ·	$1,750
September expenses	($900)
First mortgage payment	($1,000)
Second mortgage payment to seller	($225)
Monthly negative cash flow	($375)

Even though John really only has $250 to spare each month, he can probably manage to come up with the extra $125 needed to feed his alligator. (And John is lucky; if a major repair had been needed or a unit went vacant, he really would have been in trouble.)

Then suddenly it's winter and the monthly costs rise dramatically. John is starting to feel the pinch. What's worse, his six-month note is coming due soon.

John has learned the hard way what happens with a "short fuse" note: It explodes. He doesn't want to sell the building, so what are his alternatives? Probably his best bet is to try to convert the credit union loan to a bank loan with a monthly payment. That payment would be about $200 over a five-year period at 8 percent interest.

But now, instead of having $250 extra income each month, John has a negative cash flow of $575 per month (the new loan plus the costs of operating the building), and that outflow of cash speeds up during the winter months.

John becomes a serious don't-wanter. He has learned that when you don't feed your alligator, it eats you. And a person who is being eaten alive by an alligator is the most desperate don't-wanter of all.

As a real estate investor, you must be on the lookout for alliga-

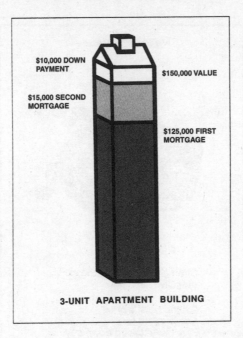

$10,000 DOWN PAYMENT

$150,000 VALUE

$15,000 SECOND MORTGAGE

$125,000 FIRST MORTGAGE

3-UNIT APARTMENT BUILDING

tors every time you negotiate to buy a piece of real estate. The lower the down payment, the more probable the creation of an alligator. You must learn how to cage the alligator from the very start. See the illustration on page 162, prepared by my brother Richard J. Allen.

Ways to Cage the Alligator

There are several surefire ways to avoid negative-cash-flow properties and "cage the alligator," as shown in the illustration.

The first and most effective technique is to cut the seller's price. If this is not possible, then you should analyze the rents and expenses to see if there is room for improvement. How long will it take to increase rents to a level at which there will be no negative cash flow? Can you afford to feed this property until the rents break even? If the answers to these questions are not satisfactory, then you may consider giving a larger down payment, thus lowering the mortgage payment.

If none of the above solutions seems to solve the problem, then you have only one avenue left to you: structuring the mortgage payments to meet your cash-flow needs. This must be done in your negotiating with the seller from the very beginning. That's why it is

ALLIGATOR CAGES

Strategies for caging the alligator
(negative cash flow)

Cut the seller's price
Ask for more rent
Give more toward down payment
Eliminate more expenses
Structure the mortgage payments

so important to know as much as you can about the property you are trying to buy before you enter formal negotiations. Once you have bought the property it is impossible to go back and ask the seller to accept a different payout schedule.

Let's rework John's situation so there is some comfortable leeway. Consider these solutions:

Paper Formula #1. Structure the seller's note to seasonal demands.

In John's situation, monthly expenses were $800 for the six warm months and $1,500 for the colder six months. Yearly total was $13,800. If the seller is really anxious to sell, he should agree to receive payments on his note that coincide with your payment schedule. Suggest that during the summer months he will receive $425 ($200 a month more than originally negotiated) and during the six lean months of winter his monthly payment will be only $100 ($125 less than normal). Such a payment plan will give you extra money when you need it and structure extra payments when you have extra money to spend.

Remember, note payments are not sacred. Play with the numbers so they come out to your advantage.

Paper Formula #2. Structure a balloon mortgage.

Rather than giving the seller monthly payments, throw a balloon mortgage at him. A balloon mortgage is any type of note that has a lump-sum payment due at the end of the life of the note.

If John had wanted to apply a balloon payment in his situation, he would have offered the seller a $15,000 mortgage secured against his property with no monthly or yearly payments. The interest on the note would accrue from year to year, and the entire balance would be due in one lump sum or "balloon" at the end of seven years. (If a seller balks at this situation, calculate for him what his balloon payment will be in seven years—the $15,000 will have grown to nearly $25,000. The figure may have some influence on the seller who is considering retirement and will need something to live on.)

Having no monthly payments relieves you of an additional burden, and the obligation to pay is deferred. But don't forget that you *do* have an obligation to pay. Your extra cash flow should be reinvested into something else that will be used to help defray the large future obligation. The property itself will be one of the best sources for repaying this obligation. If the building is worth $150,000 when you buy it, it could be worth more than $200,000 at the end of seven years if it appreciates at an average rate of 5 percent per year. You could then refinance the building and come up with the necessary money.

This method sounds easy, but there are cautions. It is always a good idea to protect yourself against the future possibility that it will be impossible to refinance the property. What if mortgage money is tight and you can't find a lender who will make you a loan? Ask the holder of the note for a grace period if mortgage money is impossible to find. And let the holder of the note do his own checking; he might be able to find a source of financing *for* you.

Paper Formula #3. Try reverse paper.

This is sometimes called "walking the paper backward." Rather than agreeing to pay the seller $225 a month, John could have agreed to make only a $100 monthly payment. Although this amount is not enough to cover the interest charges (thus the name "reverse"), it will at least help the seller in his cash-flow situation and will reduce the final amount owing. Of course, the note will still continue to grow, but not at as great a rate.

Paper Formula #4. Increase the length of the amortization with a lump-sum payment (or balloon payment).

This formula is successful because sellers usually like to receive a monthly payment on their notes but would like to receive their cash as soon as possible. Have the seller accept the monthly payment of his note *as if* the note were going to be paid over a period of twenty-five or thirty years. At the end of seven years, make a balloon payment for the remaining balance to the seller. For example, if you owed $15,000 on the down payment and it was set up on a thirty-year amortization at 7 percent, the monthly payments would be only about $100. That's less than $250 and might give you some breathing room. In seven years the remaining balance on the note will be about $13,300, and you will have to pay it in one lump sum. Again, consider cashing in on the increased property value. The chart below shows some different amortization schedules.

The longer the amortization without a balloon payment, the better. Balloon payments are not good except when the property they

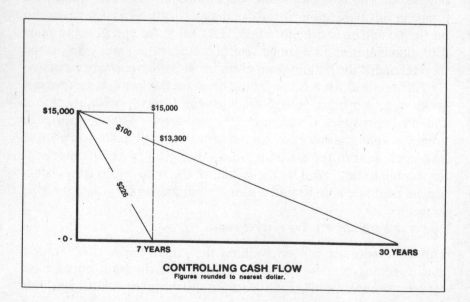

CONTROLLING CASH FLOW
Figures rounded to nearest dollar.

are used on has such an excellent price it is hard to pass up—then use a balloon only if you feel confident that you will be able to obtain the money at the end of the period.

Paper Formula #5. Increase the interest rate.

Depending on his motivation, you might be able to convince the seller that you will have a rough time making payments under the stringent terms he demands. You may ask for the interest on the $15,000 note to be just 2 percent for the first year, and for it to increase a percentage point each year on the remaining balance. With this formula your initial payments would be lower, escalating in line with your increasing ability to pay.

Paper Formula #6. Pay interest only.

Rather than amortizing the loan, negotiate a semiannual or annual interest-only payment. This situation relieves the constant monthly burden of a fully amortized loan over a short period of time and allows John a full year (or half a year) to obtain the needed money. However, this approach works best when interest rates are high; in a low-rate investing climate the difference between paying interest only and paying the fully amortized amount is likely to be small.

Paper Formula #7. Moratorium on interest payments until cash flow increases.

If John had done his homework, he would have realized that he would be experiencing a substantial negative cash flow during part of the year. Until he had a chance to raise the rents to a level that would cover all of his expenses, he should have negotiated a note with the seller that did not have any payments for the first twenty-four months, but that converted to an amortizing loan at that time with higher monthly payments at that point.

Paper Formula #8. Convert any balloon notes to amortizing notes when they are due.

Whenever possible, defer payments until you have a chance to become comfortable with your situation. John should have negotiated with the credit union on his due date to have the $10,000 balloon note converted into a monthly amortizing loan; in fact, he should have written that into the note at the beginning of the arrangement. John could have raised rents enough in a six-month period (perhaps $50 to $100 an apartment) to cover the added cash flow needed to amortize the new monthly payment.

These first seven formulas work well to increase your flexibility when you've written a note.

But what about mortgages?

Most people mistakenly believe that once a mortgage is placed on a property it cannot be removed unless it is paid off in cash. While banks and lending institutions are rather rigid about creative maneuvers with mortgages, you *can* be creative with mortgages assumed from private persons.

Mortgages are not riveted to a property once a property is mortgaged. A mortgage is nothing more or less than a note for the repayment of a debt and a collateral agreement in case the note is not repaid. If you understand that, you can work all kinds of creative twists in your purchases.

Paper Formula #9. Move the mortgage.

If you are buying a piece of property from a seller who is going to carry back a second mortgage (or trust deed) for part of his equity, tell the seller you want to move the mortgage to your home (or some other piece of property you own). He might question you. Explain that his mortgage will be just as secure against your own home as against the purchased property—in fact, it might be more secure because you don't intend to lose your own home to foreclosure. Since a mortgage is simply a security arrangement anyway, he may feel secure enough with what you are offering.

Moving a mortgage has several advantages. If you don't want to sell your home, another mortgage on it shouldn't bother you. Transferring the loan to your own home frees you to sell (or trade) the newly purchased property at any time and to collect all of the equity instead of paying part of it to the previous owner. It leaves you with greater flexibility.

Several years ago I advised a client who had a six-unit apartment building and wanted to trade up to a sixteen-unit building I had found for him. He began to arrange for a sale of his six-unit building that would give him $100,000 in cash for his equity, but he still lacked enough for the necessary down payment of $200,000. He

approached the holder of a $100,000 note against his six-unit build-
ing and asked if the note could be secured instead against the
sixteen-unit building. The note holder gave the go-ahead. When the
sale of the smaller apartment building was completed, my client collected the $200,000 in cash and used it as a down payment on the
sixteen-unit building. The holder of the note transferred his note to
the new property. Everyone was satisfied. Without this technique,
my client would have had to seek a $100,000 loan from a conven-
tional lender, and might have been denied. The transaction may not
have taken place. The diagram below tells how it worked.

How can you convince the holder of a second mortgage to move
it to another piece of collateral? Following a few guidelines will help
you convince him that he will be protected.

Give him the right to refuse the move if he feels his security is
inadequate. Let him inspect the new building and feel comfortable
about the move.

As an inducement to move the mortgage, offer the seller one of
the following alternatives: (1) an increase in position from a third to
a second mortgage or from a second to a first (use only as a last
resort); (2) an increase in interest rate after the move (a good way

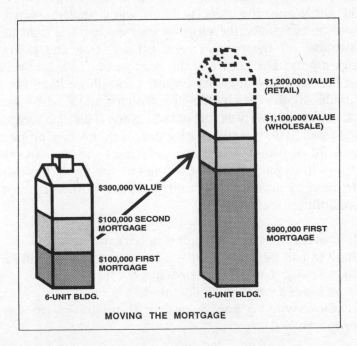

$1,200,000 VALUE
(RETAIL)

$1,100,000 VALUE
(WHOLESALE)

$300,000 VALUE

$100,000 SECOND
MORTGAGE

$900,000 FIRST
MORTGAGE

$100,000 FIRST
MORTGAGE

6-UNIT BLDG.   16-UNIT BLDG.

MOVING THE MORTGAGE

to give him something without giving up much yourself); (3) an improvement of the value of the collateral with more equity or a larger building; (4) payment of a portion of the note in the move, a technique that will give him some cash and shorten the length of your obligation to him; or (5) agree to increase the monthly payment without paying any immediate cash (with this offer he will have more cash to spend monthly).

Try to include the "move of the mortgage" concept in all notes secured by your property, because you will need greater flexibility as you progress into your investment program.

The legal terminology of moving the mortgage is called "the substitution of collateral." In other words, the seller agrees to accept a different form of collateral for security on the note you owe him. In the note, you will want your title company to include a clause such as: "The seller agrees to accept a substitution of collateral for this note at any time in the future as long as the seller has the opportunity to inspect the new property and can feel comfortable that his note is adequately secured. Of course, this approval will not be unreasonably withheld by the seller."

As another example, I had title to a sixty-acre piece of property in a sparsely inhabited region of Utah back in the 1970s. There was a $12,000 note against the property. There was virtually no way I could have sold or exchanged the property unless I had the right to move the mortgage off the property and offer it free and clear as an exchange equity. The holder of the note was flexible and willing to remove the mortgage any time I wanted to sell the land. So, whenever I made an offer on a building I always included a sixty-acre tract of *free and clear* property as part of the equity. If a seller accepted my offer, all I had to do was transfer the note onto my new property.

This kind of transaction is also referred to as *definancing*—the process of either paying off an existing indebtedness or moving the indebtedness to another collateral location. With this technique, your possibilities are endless!

- It allows you to borrow against unborrowable assets.
- It gives you flexibility to fix up new property and sell for cash to raise cash for buying property.
- It provides a pyramiding potential.
- It allows you to borrow cash without having to sell your property.

Paper Formula #10. Use the security blanket.

The security blanket is used very successfully when the seller balks at one of your creative financing formulas. Consider, for example, 100 percent financing. The seller's first concern is: "Where is my security for the note you owe me? How do I know that you won't trick me out of my money?" The seller is obviously insecure. Play on that insecurity—give him more security than he bargained for. For example, if the seller of a three-unit building was concerned about a $75,000 note against the property (since you will be highly leveraged and might not be able to make your payments), offer him a "blanket mortgage" that gives him additional collateral in the form of equities in other properties you own and don't intend to sell in the near future.

You can also use the blanket-mortgage technique simultaneously with the moving-the-mortgage technique to placate a dubious note holder. Don't make the blanket mortgage permanent—you don't want to tie yourself up for the length of the note—but make it long enough to satisfy the seller that you will make your payments and that they'll be made on time. Then renegotiate the mortgage and free up your properties. Use a blanket mortgage as a last resort, but remember that it is extremely effective. Many of the sellers who are initially reluctant to accept your original offer will be agreeable to a blanket mortgage.

If the seller is still concerned about his security, buy a life insurance policy (term, of course) with a face value equivalent to the mortgage, in this case, $75,000. If you die, the policy will be paid to the holder of the note (since he is the beneficiary of the life insurance policy), and the mortgages will be removed. A term life insurance policy for $75,000 is a small price to pay for something that might ensure your long-range success. (There's an additional benefit in this technique: If you do die, your family will be better off financially because they will be clear of the mortgage in question.)

Paper Formula #11. Create paper.

As long as you own the property, you can create paper against it to use as down payments on other property. Consider this example:

Let's say you find a don't-wanter apartment building owner who is extremely flexible. Offer to buy his $200,000 rental property; give him a $20,000 note for his equity and assume his $180,000 loan. You'll need to offer him collateral for his note, so suggest he take a $20,000 mortgage on your home. At 7 percent on a ten-year note, the monthly payments would be just $232 until the mortgage is paid in full.

You just created a note out of thin air and attached it to a property you already owned. Now you can create a note against the equity in the $200,000 rental building and use it to buy another property. Whenever a bank turns you down, use this technique to finance your down payments.

In essence, the power of the creation-of-paper technique lies in allowing an investor to borrow 100 percent of his equity in the real estate holdings. He can structure the repayment schedule on the "created" note to fit his personal situation. All it takes is to find a don't-wanter who would rather have a note than his property. For the nothing-down investor, the benefits are multiplied: no qualifying for bank loans, no complicated loan papers to fill out, no high interest charges, no high monthly payments, no credit checks.

Take this technique a step further: "Create" an unsecured note against your future earnings. Write out a note on a standard promissory note form attainable at any stationery store. A highly motivated don't-wanter would be happier with a note secured against your future earnings than he would be with his property. Very few buyers

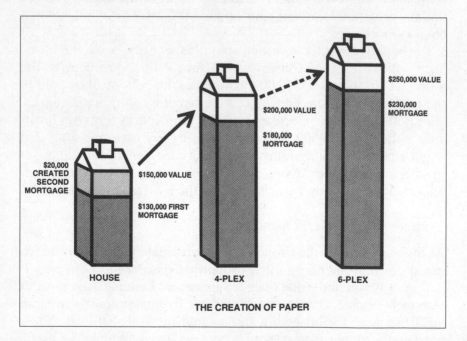

THE CREATION OF PAPER

170

will accept a proposal like this, but you'll never know unless you ask. I've found several. Remember that it's worth a try.

Paper Formula #12. Trade discounted paper for the down payment.

Try buying an existing second mortgage at a substantial discount from someone who wants cash now. Then trade off the note at full face value and pick up your profit going in. In our previous example, the seller was expecting a $20,000 note secured by his own building. If he is a real don't-wanter he won't care if the note is secured by another piece of property. Your seller doesn't have to know that you paid $8,000 cash for the $15,000 note only two weeks earlier. Just sit back and enjoy your $7,000 profit!

Paper Formula #13. Use subordination.

The technique of subordination is widely used in land development, but it has application in any field of real estate. Don't, however, use the actual word "subordination." Attorneys cringe when they hear it. Why? To subordinate means to allow someone to put a new loan on the property and to have the seller's equity subordinated to the first mortgage loan.

In other words, if something goes wrong, the first mortgage holder is paid off first from the foreclosure sale. Whatever is left over is paid to the person who subordinated his or her interest. Sometimes there is not enough money to pay all the lien holders.

While subordination is used widely in the land-development business, it can also be used in transactions involving already-developed property. Let's take an example based on the experience of one of my students. Mr. Smith, who owned an eight-unit apartment building, wanted to sell my student a piece of ground suitable for construction of a new four-unit apartment building. Mr. Smith didn't want much cash for his $25,000 equity in the land, so my student offered him a cash down payment of $5,000 if he would accept a third mortgage against the eight-unit apartment building. Mr. Smith accepted. My student received the lot free and clear of mortgages, and Mr. Smith got $5,000 in cash plus a third mortgage on another piece of property. With the free-and-clear lot, my student was able to obtain adequate financing to build a new four-unit building without investing additional funds.

Paper Formula #14. Keep the payment constant, lower the interest rate, increase the principal amount.

If you have a $25,000 note payable at 9 percent interest over a fifteen-year period, the monthly payments are $253. By keeping the payment at $253 and lowering the interest rate from 9 percent to 6 percent, it is possible to amortize a larger loan—$30,000 to be exact. In other words, by lowering the interest rate you can increase the amount of loan you can pay back.

Perhaps you can even pay more for a property than what it is listed for by negotiating for a lower interest rate on the mortgage. A greedy seller may agree to accept a larger purchase price and let you have a lower down payment. By creating this situation you will make real estate more attractive to future buyers because of the low interest rate.

Paper Formula #15. Reduce your mortgage payment period by half.

If you can't imagine using any of the previous paper techniques, there is one method that any homeowner can use to pay off a mortgage sooner. Did you know that the mortgage payment you make on your home is not fixed? You probably can't make a smaller-than-normal payment, but you *can* make a larger one. A small increase in your monthly mortgage payment can have a drastic effect on your mortgage balance.

If you were to make an extra $100 payment each month on your loan, your total interest costs would plummet, and you could likely pay back your loan several years early. It's also a fast way to build up equity, which you could use for other investments.

Make sure you check with your mortgage company to verify that the extra payment is applied to the principal each month. Each company has different rules about extra payments.

Study these paper formulas. Apply them when you invest in real estate. There are limitless combinations and variations; tailor them to meet your specific needs. You'll find they can bring success and enhance the final negotiation process.

CHAPTER 20

Nothing Down:
Five Wealth-Building
Stratagems

"Lack of money never killed a deal. It's the way you THINK about money that makes or breaks the deal."

—ROBERT LYNN

As you continue to learn more about investing, you need to remain continually focused on your primary goal: buying real estate with nothing down. "Nothing down" does not mean that the seller receives no down payment. It means that the down payment comes from somewhere else. It means that *the down payment rarely comes out of your pocket.*

As you seek out nothing-down deals, study the sample solutions I've listed in this chapter. Use one alone or combine them to increase your effectiveness.

You can learn a great deal from the types of deals the students in my Creating Wealth seminars encounter every day, and the strategies they use to close the sale using as few of their own dollars as possible. (For more information, call 801-852-8711 or visit www. robertallenrealestate.com.)

Here's just one of hundreds of examples. Let's say my student, Harold, found a fourteen-unit building in a small town. It had been advertised for several months in our local newspaper. At first glance the potential transaction did not seem very promising. The seller required too much down payment. The units were too small and the rent was too low.

But my student took it a step further and found a wonderful opportunity to jump into real estate investment. Harold went back to the property and invited the seller to lunch. They had a friendly and productive discussion that opened the door for Harold to practice the techniques he had learned in my seminar. Because the building had been on the market for several months, the seller had become a serious don't-wanter, and Harold realized that the seller would be willing to be a little creative in the terms of the sale.

Here are the facts pertaining to the property. Let's see if you can be as creative as my student was:

Description of property: 14 one-bedroom units (a converted home and motel)

Listed price: $600,000

Mortgage information: $450,000 remaining balance on a 30-year term at 8 percent interest

Monthly payments on mortgage: $3,300

Down payment: Seller would like $75,000

Average monthly rent collection: 14 units @ $750 = $10,500 (Rents were all too low.)

Tenants' deposits: $750 per unit = $10,500

Real estate agent's commission: 6 percent of sales price = $36,000 (based on $600,000 price)

Reason seller needs to sell: Financial obligations turned him into a don't-wanter

Seller's other outstanding obligations: $30,000 in other debts at hardware stores, lumberyard, and so on

Make a guess! How much cash out of your own pocket will you need to buy this property? How will you come up with it?

The first thing Harold did was to offer less—$550,000. As a don't-wanter, the seller accepted that price immediately. Now Harold had to solve the problem of the $100,000 down payment. As it eventually turned out, Harold only had to come up with $7,000 in cash to close the deal. To get that cash, he formed a partnership with his father, and his father funded the venture. In addition to forming a partnership, Harold used five fundamental creative ways to lower the amount of the down payment. Let's look at them one by one.

1. Use of Rents and Deposits

Harold learned early in the negotiation process that rents were due on the first of each month. Because of this, he knew that barring any major vacancies before the closing, there would be $10,500 in rents and $10,500 in security deposits that would become the property of the buyer on the closing day. He also knew that the first mortgage payment would not be due for thirty days following the closing date, so he negotiated the closing date to coincide with the day the rents were due. He also made sure that his first regular mortgage payment to the seller would fall due thirty days after the apartment building had been purchased. Harold ended up collecting $10,500 in rent at the closing; after taking care of some minor operational expenses, Harold could apply what remained to the down payment. When the thirty days were up, Harold just collected the next month's rent and applied it to the mortgage payment. This step alone provided him with more than $20,000 toward the $100,000 down payment

Harold also used security deposits (amounting to $10,500) toward the down payment. But don't deposits belong to the tenants, and don't they have to be returned to the tenants when they move out? Yes. But when one tenant moves out, another moves in—and the deposit from the new tenant can be given as a refund to the old tenant. In some states, deposits can be held together (commingled) in the bank account of the building owner; in other states the law requires the funds to be held in a separate escrow account that cannot be touched. Make sure you know the law and obey it; if you are allowed to hold the money in your account, you can apply it to down payments instead of taking money out of your own pocket.

2. Time Payment of the Real Estate Agent's Commission

One of the seller's first obligations on completion of the sale is to pay the real estate agent his commission. In our example, the real estate agent's fee was 6 percent of $550,000 or $33,000. That amounted to a large share of the required down payment. Harold approached the real estate agent about lending him some of the commission; in return, Harold gave the real estate agent a personal note guaranteeing to pay the money in two payments: $5,000 in cash and the balance—$28,000—on a note due in three years. The seller wasn't involved in the transaction or the negotiation—he didn't need to know what happened to the commission.

Not all real estate agents will agree to lend you part of the commission, but the ones who do will probably not charge you a high interest rate, will not require credit checks or extensive paperwork, and may not ask you to secure the note against any property. You should be able to negotiate some excellent terms. One way to convince the real estate agent to take a note is to tell him that if he doesn't help you out, you can't buy the property—then there will be no sale and no commission at all. If necessary and if you can handle it, give him a small monthly payment.

It will be much more difficult for you to arrange this kind of loan if the real estate agent is not his own broker. If the real estate agent works for another broker, he must share any commissions he earns—sometimes up to 50 percent of the commission will go to the broker. This leaves a real estate agent little to live on, let alone to lend out. Try to deal with the listing agents or brokers if you plan on borrowing commissions. The more people involved in the commissions split, the less you will be able to borrow. Try always to deal with the listing agent on a large piece of property. If he can list and sell a property at the same time, he earns so much that he thinks he can afford to lend you some of it. In Harold's case, the lister, seller, and broker were the same person. The situation was ideal.

3. Assumption of the Seller's Obligations

The seller's major reason for dumping his property was to relieve himself of some financial obligations. Harold sensed the seller's motivation and agreed to transfer part of the seller's obligations to his own name. This offer appealed to the seller, so Harold contacted all of the seller's creditors to explain that he, not the seller, was going to pay the notes off. Harold was able to extend the notes' due dates and in some cases he was able to get a discount by paying cash. Harold then subtracted the amount of the obligations, totaling $30,000, from the down payment he would make to the seller.

You could arrange something like this in several ways. One seller had not paid his bills for several months. An astute buyer entered the picture and visited each of the seller's creditors (who had understandably become quite anxious) and negotiated to pay them off in cash if they would accept fifty cents on the dollar for their outstanding notes. Many took him up on his offer, and he was able to substantially lower both the price of the property and the amount of required down payment.

4. Prepaid Rent as Part of the Down Payment

Harold discovered early in the negotiation period that the seller and his family, who lived in the apartment building Harold was buying, would have to find somewhere to live while looking for a house to buy. Harold offered to let the seller and his family live in his apartment until he found a new home or for at least six months. The rent of $750 a month would be applied toward Harold's down payment. In this case, the six months' rent prepaid was $4,500, which reduced the amount of down payment Harold had to take out of his own pocket.

5. Satisfaction of Seller's Needs

Harold learned from his conversation that the seller needed to buy some appliances and furniture for a home he was building. Harold talked about the situation with the seller, and then bought $10,000 worth of needed items using his own credit cards and store credit. This $10,000 package, which Harold didn't have to pay for several months, became another part of the down payment, substantially reducing the amount of immediate cash required to buy the building.

By using these five nothing-down techniques, Harold was able to accumulate $103,000 in credits toward the purchase:

Rents and deposits	$30,500
Real estate agent's fees borrowed	28,000
Seller's obligations assumed	30,000
Prepaid rents to seller	4,500
Seller's furniture bought on credit	10,000
Total credits	$103,000

Of course, Harold still had to pay out some cash debits at the closing:

Real estate agent's cash	$ 5,000
Closing costs	5,000
Seller's down payment	100,000
Total debits	$110,000

But the bottom line for Harold was that he didn't have to pay the $100,000 down payment—not even close! The total amount of cash needed to close this transaction was only $7,000 (the difference between the debits and the credits). Harold was able to borrow that amount from his father. As a result, Harold took *nothing* out of his own pocket toward the down payment; he virtually purchased the building for *nothing down*.

Two things will make you successful in your efforts to reduce a down payment. First, talk to the seller. Find out his needs, his obligations; try to determine why he is selling. Such information can give you clues to a workable approach. Second, use the techniques listed simultaneously in creative combinations. Look at what Harold did with all five.

So far, we have already covered more than two dozen ways to reduce the size of a cash down payment, but that's only scratching the surface. In the next few chapters, you will learn many more nothing-down techniques that you can apply tomorrow. All it takes is courage, and a little creative imagination.

CHAPTER 21

Seven More Nothing-Down Techniques

"A woman who was tired of dealing with renters wanted $95,000 for selling a half duplex, which came with a $65,000 assumable mortgage. When asked about her plans for the cash, she replied, 'Put it in the bank, I guess.' My son Derek suggested that she might want to loan the money to us and carry a second mortgage as collateral. He insisted that she go home, think about it, and talk it over with her husband. The next morning they met and both agreed to lend us $30,000 for five years. We paid her $500 cash. Shortly after, we sold a half share to a joint venture partner for $11,000."

—JOHN PEACOCK

As you learn more about reducing your down payment, understand that as far as a down payment is concerned, the seller is your best friend. Talk to him. Learn what you can about his situation. Let him tell you (without knowing it) which of these techniques will bring a favorable response:

1. The Ultimate Paper-Out

Not long ago, one of my students, we'll call her Sharon, wanted to invest in more real estate as a way of improving her tax position, but she didn't have any cash to use for an investment.

A neighbor of mine owned a ten-unit apartment building but lacked the time to handle the management. In a conversation with me, he mentioned that he would gladly sell his building for nothing down. He was a serious don't-wanter. He had all the symptoms: a rational decision to sell with totally irrational terms, the motivation to act immediately, and the willingness to be as flexible as necessary.

I considered buying the property myself, but my time was spread too thin, and I soon would have been a don't-wanter for the same reason my friend was. But the property was perfect for Sharon. Within two weeks, we had the property signed over into her name. Here are some of the financial details:

Sale price	$500,000
First mortgage	375,000
Second mortgage	100,000
Third mortgage	25,000
Required down payment	0

The seller arranged for a second mortgage of $100,000 through a lending institution he worked for. He paid the loan fees and interest fees to set up the new loan. Sharon assumed both the first and second mortgage loans. The remaining $25,000 of the seller's equity was put in the form of a note secured by a third trust deed against the property. While interest accrued on the note for the first three years, there were *no monthly payments!* At the end of the first three years the note would begin a monthly schedule for a payout over a ten-year period.

A quick look at the cash-flow situation revealed that the income from the rents was not enough to cover expenses and mortgage payments on both the first and second mortgages. Sharon would have to come up with an additional $1,000 a month!

Wasn't it a crazy move to make? Shouldn't income from rental properties cover mortgage payments? Isn't it wrong to invest in something like this?

In Sharon's case, the answer was no. Remember, she wanted to improve her tax situation. Paying out the extra $1,000 a month did just that—and didn't alter her lifestyle because of an adequate cash flow from other sources.

After Sharon had owned the property for a year, she placed the following ad in the local newspaper:

Apartment building for sale by owner.
$600,000
Call Sharon, 555-555-1234

Three days later, she sold the property for her asking price—$600,000 cash. The original owner received his $25,000 (third mortgage) from the sale, and Sharon received $575,000 in cash.

Sharon's down payment was nothing at the time of the purchase, but she had to make a "deferred down payment" of $1,000 negative cash flow each month. That amounted to about $12,000 during the year she owned the building, and was her only out-of-pocket cost. The bottom line: In one year of ownership, the property's market value rose by $100,000. Subtracting the $25,000 note to the seller and the $12,000 in the deferred down payment, Sharon netted $63,000 in her year of ownership.

Sharon's nothing-down deal is not an isolated example. This kind of transaction happens every day in every major city of our country. It might as well start happening to you. The technique is called the "paper-out formula" because the seller actually takes his equity in the form of paper or mortgages. No cash is transferred. The buyer gives his promise to pay the seller's equity over a specified period of time. The buyer has 100 percent leverage. Total leverage almost always results in a negative cash flow.

What about negative cash flows? Don't be scared of a negative cash flow *if* you have the money to cover it. *If* you can eventually raise the rents to cover it, or *if* you plan on keeping the property only a short while and expect to sell it for a substantial profit.

One word of caution: Be deadly accurate in your projection of the expenses. Most owners with negative cash flow end up in trouble because they didn't project accurately enough what the expenses would be, and the negative cash flow gets greater and greater. Soon the alligator eats them. Do your homework carefully before you buy something that appears to be a marginal property.

2. The Balloon Down Payment

In this transaction the buyer gives the seller part of the down payment in cash and then negotiates to pay the rest in several "balloon payments." For instance, on a down payment of $30,000 the buyer might pay $6,000 at the time of the sale, $12,000 six months later, and $12,000 a year after the sale.

181

This approach is really quite logical. The seller, who must have a majority of his equity in cash, and who therefore requires a cash down payment, may be persuaded to sell his property if he received a portion of the down payment immediately and the rest in a relatively short period of time. You can take possession of the property with a relatively small down payment and a promise to pay the rest.

This is a gutsy technique, but it gives you some breathing room, some time in which to search for the remaining down payment. You may just want to fix the property up and put it back on the market for a quick profit. Your new buyer would provide you with the money to cover the balloon payment. A word of caution: Have other sources to bail you out in case you can't sell quickly enough.

It is common practice for a seller to accept part of a down payment in cash and the rest in the form of a second or third mortgage.

"Taking out a second mortgage" does *not* mean that you go to the bank and borrow the money secured on a second mortgage. Banks are not involved in any way in the process; it's a transaction you work out with the seller.

Let's look at an example.

Upon graduating from college I began looking for properties to invest in. The first newspaper I picked up ran an ad in the income-property section of the classified ads that went something like this:

Income property, duplex close to campus reasonable down payment. Seller anxious. Call Terry at 555-4321.

I called immediately and got an appointment to visit the property that afternoon.

The property was rather run-down in appearance but was well built, and the location was excellent. The sellers, a mother-and-son partnership, had been trying to sell for some time. The son was attending college and didn't have time to manage the duplex. The mother needed money to pay the tuition, and they were don't-wanters who were growing desperate. A real estate firm had tried for months with no success to sell the property at $26,500—a high price in the mid-1970s. In desperation the owners had canceled the listing and had begun to advertise the property themselves for $25,500. Their loan was $19,000 and they wanted to cash out.

After examining the property "thoroughly" (at the time I didn't really know what to look for), I called up the least expensive appraiser in the Yellow Pages and had him do a quick appraisal. He estimated that the duplex was worth $22,500 without the furniture, which was probably worth $1,000.

That wasn't much consolation. I went to visit the seller at his apartment so I could assess the situation. After several hours of talking, we reached a solution. They would accept a price of $25,000. I would assume his loan of $19,000 at the bank. The remaining $6,000 equity would be paid as follows: (1) $1,500 upon closing, (2) $1,000 in two months, (3) an additional $1,000 in another two months, and (4) the remaining $2,500 in equal monthly installments of $75 until paid in full (about four years). The $75-a-month payment was secured by a second mortgage on the duplex.

Four days after I bought this property for $25,000 with a $1,500 down payment, a neighbor approached me and offered me $28,000 for the property. He had been in Mexico and had not known the property was on the market. He agreed to continue to make the balloon payments I had negotiated with the seller. And he paid me back my original $1,500 down payment plus the $3,000 profit.

3. Using Talent, Not Cash

You may be able to trade the seller some of your valuable services as part of the down payment. If you are an accountant or an attorney, you could give your seller credits toward the use of your services—for instance, offer to do his taxes for the next ten years. I once offered a building contractor a partial equity in a building lot I owned in exchange for the use of his labor on my own personal residence. He agreed to do all the carpentry work on my home for free in exchange for my equity in a $14,000 building lot upon which he could build himself a home. We both came out ahead—and happy.

Take advantage of any services you have that can be traded in part for real estate equities. One of my students was in the business of selling air conditioners. He could buy the merchandise at dealer's cost and trade it for full retail value as equity in a rental apartment building. Let your imagination run wild.

4. High Monthly Down Payments

If you are blessed with a high monthly surplus cash flow, but don't want to wait to save for the down payment, consider offering the seller his equity in the form of a very high monthly payment. For example, suppose a seller wanted to sell his $160,000 home with a $20,000 equity. Offer to buy his home with no down payment, assume his existing loan of $140,000, and make him a $500 monthly payment, including interest, on his remaining equity. An anxious seller may bite because he knows that he can get his full price this way rather than a lesser price and an all-cash offer.

This technique offers you the flexibility of having at least thirty days to find another buyer if you are going to sell the property for quick profit. It also acts as a forced savings plan: At the end of the twelve months you will have been forced to pay more than $6,000 cash to buy the property, but the property will probably have appreciated during that period of time. If the property appreciates in value by only 5 percent, you could sell it yourself for $168,000. That would give you a net profit of $2,000, or a 33 percent return on your $6,000 investment.

5. Raising the Price, Lowering the Terms

If you determine that the seller is more concerned about his price than about what he receives in the form of cash, appeal to his sense of greed. Using the numbers from the previous example, offer him the full price of $160,000 if he will sell the building to you with no-down or low-down terms. Tell him he can choose: $145,000 all cash or $160,000 with no cash down. The real estate industry operates under one universal rule: The more cash involved in the sale, the lower the price. The converse is also true: The lower the cash, the higher the price and profit to the seller. *It may be to your advantage to offer a higher price for a lower down payment.*

6. Splitting the Property

This is another creative way to get into a real estate purchase. One of my students purchased a sixteen-unit apartment building with a small two-bedroom home on the same piece of property included in the deal. Since the property was commercially zoned and located near the city's downtown section, she simply split the home out of the legal description of the original property. After paying $820,000 for the combined property, she was able to sell the sixteen-unit building for $800,000, and the small home to another buyer for $210,000. Her profit was about $190,000 after owning the property for eighteen months.

Another one of my students came across the same sort of situation a few years ago. He and his wife had been looking for property ever since they had mortgaged their home to buy a fifteen-unit building. The wife made an offer on three duplexes; they asked me if there was a way for them to buy all three units without using any of their own cash. We decided they should sell two of the units for a higher price; the profit they earned would give them some cash to pay the owner of three units. They had negotiated a three-month closing date. The properties were substantially underpriced, so they went looking for someone who would pay a high price on two of the units before the closing date arrived. Then they would have sold the two units to the new buyer in a simultaneous closing that would have given them enough profit to be able to buy the third unit without investing any of their own cash. This technique is discussed in more detail in the chapter on options. As it turned out, my students located a man who was willing to lend them the money for the down payments on the three units, and they decided to buy the properties and keep them.

Here's another example of the splitting technique. A friend purchased an older, thirty-unit apartment building that had a large amount of antique furniture in it. He removed the furniture and sold it to an antiques dealer for $20,000. This helped him with the down payment he had negotiated, since he had given himself ample time to sell the furniture for cash.

Other splits? Several years back I bought a house that had a very deep, weed-covered back lot. The neighbor around the corner approached me before I closed on the sale and asked if I was interested in selling the back lot to him. I agreed to sell it to him at a price that not only covered my down payment but allowed me to put some extra cash in my pocket. Of course, to accomplish the sale of the back lot I had to have it released from the mortgage with a lending institution. This required a new survey, a new appraisal, a new title policy, and some paperwork. But it was well worth it!

7. Deferring the Down Payment with No Mortgage Payments

My students are always teaching me new techniques. At one of my Creating Wealth seminars, one of my repeat students related this story to me. I thought it was creative enough to include as part of the arsenal of nothing-down techniques.

After having taken my seminar, this student went out into the marketplace to find some property to buy. He located an older six-unit building that the seller owned free and clear of any mortgages. The property was in an excellent location and was priced right. There was only one problem. The seller was willing to hold the mortgage for my student, but he wanted a $10,000 down payment. Unfortunately, my student did not have that much cash at the time. He began to use his head instead of his pocketbook and came up with the following solution. He knew that the seller had other sources of income and didn't have to rely on a mortgage payment from the buyer.

So my student proposed that the seller turn over the property to him with no down payment and *no mortgage payments* for six months. Interest would accrue on the mortgage for six months; at the end of this period, normal monthly payments would commence and continue for the next twenty-five years until paid in full. The seller reluctantly agreed, since he was able to obtain his full asking price and terms with the small exception of the six-month delay in the down payment.

As soon as the buyer took over the property, he was able to collect the rents and the security deposits and put them in his bank account. And as each month rolled around he collected the rents and let them accrue in his bank account. He paid out only necessary expenses and did all of the maintenance work himself to save money. As you can guess by now, since he did not have a mortgage payment to make, the majority of the income he collected went right into savings, and during the next six months he was able to save enough money to come up with almost all the required $10,000 down payment. In effect, the buyer borrowed the down payment from the seller, who let him repay it over the next twenty-five years. Not bad.

CHAPTER 22

Options Can Help You Make Your First Million

"This is the best business in the world! All it takes to 'Create Wealth' is to use a little creative thinking. I was able to use an option to control a property for just $10, and assign my position to another party for a $37,000 profit in less than sixty days!"

—SCOTT D. MILES

When you were a child, did you ever sit on the scorching cement on a sweltering July afternoon, patiently hold a magnifying glass over a scrap of last night's newspaper, and stay motionless until the edges of the paper began to blaze? You learned that by concentrating the sun's rays into a limited area, you increased their power significantly.

The same principle applies in real estate. If you concentrate all of your energies and abilities in one limited area of real estate investment, you will increase your power significantly. One such specialty is options.

An option is the greatest form of leverage available to the real estate investor today. It is a simple agreement between the seller and the prospective buyer that says the seller will sell his property to the buyer at a fixed price in the future. In exchange for this "right to buy," the prospective buyer gives the seller an agreed-upon amount of money.

For example, I give you $5,000 for the right to buy your duplex for $350,000 within two years; if I come up with $350,000 to pay you anytime within the two-year period, you *must* sell me the duplex even if you changed your mind in the interim.

Why would you give me an option to buy your duplex on such terms? There are three very good reasons:

1. Your property may be worth only $275,000 on today's market, and you might think its value could never increase to $350,000 in the two-year period of time, a figure that would represent a 9 percent annual increase. If you planned on keeping the duplex for at least two years, taking my $5,000 option would just be gravy.
2. The $5,000 option money is not taxable until the year the option is exercised. This means that you could take my money and spend it as you wished without reporting it on your income tax statement. If I exercised the option, you would simply include the $5,000 as part of the down payment and pay the tax accordingly. If the option was not exercised, you would pay capital gains tax on the option money received. It is like receiving tax-free dollars.
3. The innate greed in each of us yearns for an outlet—and the outlet is the option. If you feel the value of your property can never increase to as high as the option price, you lose nothing by gambling on me. You are actually hoping that I succeed in paying such a price for the property. It's like having your cake and eating it, too. You get to use my $5,000 for two years tax free, and your chances of getting an outrageously high price for your property are also high. In essence, we make a bet with each other: I am betting $5,000 that your property will be worth more than $350,000 in two years. You are betting the imaginary profit that I am wrong.

So why in the world would I want to take an option to buy your property? Obviously, I don't want to gamble $5,000 of my money on an option unless I am absolutely sure the property I am buying will be worth *more* than the option price at the end of the option. But suppose I know that your duplex is located across the street from a

OPTION

In consideration of $.., ...
and .... of .... County, State of ....,
Optionor....., grant.... to.. and ....,
Optionee....., the option to purchase the hereinafter described property for the purchase price of $................,
to be exercised by giving written notice thereof to Optionor..... at ...., County of
...., State of............................., at any time on or before............................,
19........, at................ o'clock .... M. If this Option is exercised, then after receiving written notice thereof,
Optionor..... will furnish Optionee..... with an abstract of title brought up to the date of exercise of the Option or
a policy of title insurance in the amount of the purchase price and, upon payment of the purchase price due,
will deliver to Optionee..... a good and sufficient...................................deed conveying marketable fee simple
title to the hereinafter described property, free and clear of all encumbrances except as herein mentioned. The
consideration paid for this Option shall........... be credited on the purchase price.

DESCRIPTION OF PROPERTY

_____
_____
_____
_____
_____

ENCUMBRANCES

_____
_____

Dated at... this................
day of.., 19..........

_____

_____
Optionor.....

STATE OF................................. } ss.
COUNTY OF.............................
On the................day of..., 19........., personally appeared before
me.. and ...., the
signers of the above and foregoing instrument, who duly acknowledged to me that they executed the same.

_____
Notary Public

My Commission Expires: Residing at...

_____

FORM 119 - OPTION - KELLY CO., 55 WEST 900 SOUTH, SALT LAKE CITY , UTAH vacant parcel of ground that has just been rezoned commercial for a regional shopping mall. Your property might be worth twice as much as commercial office or retail space instead of a duplex. I decide it's worth a gamble. And sure enough, the mall goes in, I pay the $350,000 option price, sell for $400,000—and pocket a tidy profit.

To pull this off you must be comfortable with several assumptions:

- The property must be optioned at the right price; you must know the market value.
- The property has potential for a significant increase in value.

There are advantages to options besides profit. The holder of an option does not have to manage the property during the option period, nor is it necessary for him to pay taxes, insurance, or any other expenses. Since the liability of the option holder is limited to the extent of his option money, he does not have to be bothered with large debts or mortgage payments. If at the end of the option period, the option holder decides not to purchase the property, he simply loses his initial option money. He has no legal problems that would have resulted if he had contracted to buy the property. The biggest benefit of all is that the option holder does not have to pay interest.

All in all, the option is simple, easy to use, and very profitable if used correctly. It requires very little money and involves very little risk. Let me share with you a success story that illustrates how the use of options can be extremely valuable to the high-leverage investor.

Elizabeth, a good friend of mine, decided to do some investing in real estate on her own without partners. She discovered a six-unit apartment building the owner wanted to sell for $325,000—definitely under the market price at that time. Elizabeth contacted the owner of the building and offered to buy his building in four months for $325,000 cash. To bind the transaction, he gave her an option to buy the building at the agreed price. She then gave the seller $3,000 option money and placed this ad in the classified section of the newspaper:

Six-plex for sale by owner
$350,000
Call Elizabeth, 555-555-1235

Within three days she had a buyer who came up with cash. Elizabeth walked away from the transaction less than three months later with $25,000 in her pocket.

A short-term option like this can be used only if you are absolutely sure that the property optioned is substantially underpriced, and if you are absolutely sure that a strong market exists that will enable you to sell quickly. Long-term options involve much less risk.

Another friend of mine did the same thing with a piece of development ground that he optioned for a mere $100 and sold within a few weeks for a substantial profit.

In my travels to various seminars I have had conversations with several investors who spend their entire time studying the values of land in their respective areas and then paying for options on the ground or buildings that seemed to offer the greatest potential for appreciation. They do not purchase any property at all; they just option it. It is a full-time occupation and very lucrative. A very astute real estate agent in my area optioned a large tract of agricultural land from a local farmer for what seemed to be an outlandish price. After nailing down the property, the real estate agent went to the town planning commission, had the property rezoned for commercial shopping space, and resold the package to a developer for a $3 million profit—on just one transaction. Ironically enough, the developer who bought the land soon resold part of the parcel for an even greater profit. Here's a case where everyone made money.

1. Equity for Options

If you don't have any money to work with and you would like to use options as a tool to increase your net worth, you could offer the property owner your own personal property as an option payment instead of cash. I once offered my duplex as an option payment for a large twelve-unit apartment building. If I had not come up with the cash to buy his building within six months, the seller could have kept my duplex. Needless to say, I hurried. If you have a recreational lot somewhere in the arid reaches of this planet that you bought while you were half-crocked, you could always offer it to a seller as an option on his property. Any equity that you have is usable as an option on another piece of property. If the seller balks at the idea of using your property as an option, convince him that you will cash him out at the end of the option period.

Shouldn't an option involve the least amount of cash possible? Not always. If it causes the seller to balk at your offer, you may be better off raising a larger amount of cash as an initial option deposit in exchange for more lenient terms for exercising the option. A payment of $4,000 to $5,000 may be necessary to convince the owner that you are serious. Once the seller agrees to the terms of the option, he cannot change his mind later on, so construct the option to give yourself as much flexibility as possible. You should always try to structure the option so that the terms will be enticing to a new buyer if you need to sell your position to someone else during the term of the option.

What happens if you don't have the money to cash out the seller when the option comes due? You need to provide for this eventuality in the original option by negotiating a *rolling option:* State in the option agreement that the option can be extended for another year by the additional payment of $10,000 (or some amount agreeable to the seller). If you really want the property, it would be easier for you to come up with an additional $10,000 than to have to come up with the entire purchase price. In addition, you'll have an additional year to come up with the necessary money. Negotiate two or three such terms of extension if the seller is agreeable.

The rolling option is also used extensively in land transactions when a developer does not want to buy a large piece of ground all at once. The interest charges on a large piece of undeveloped property would eat a developer alive within a short period of time. Instead, a developer can negotiate to buy a smaller portion of the ground for cash and option the remainder at higher prices for later on. If the project does not go as well as the developer had hoped, he can drop the options, lose a small amount of money, and go on to another project. But if the project is a success, he can option the remaining ground as the need arises. In effect, he rolls his option from one piece of ground to the next until the entire property is purchased and developed.

There are two especially creative ideas that use the option philosophy:

2. The "Earnest Money" Option or "Offer to Purchase" Option

Whenever you purchase a piece of property, you normally use a standard Earnest Money Receipt or Offer to Purchase signed by you and the seller to bind the transaction. The earnest money agreement establishes the terms of the sale and the completion date, which is usually thirty to sixty days in the future. If someone should come along within this period and offer you more money for the property than you had committed to pay for it, is there any reason you could not sell him your interest in the earnest money agreement for a profit?

Suppose you found a twelve-unit apartment building that was priced $75,000 under the current market rate for such units. If you could find a buyer willing to pay the market price for the building, that would give you a $75,000 profit before the closing date. And there is no reason why you could not go through with this deal. It is totally legal and honest. You have given the seller a check for earnest money that will be forfeited if you are unable to complete the transaction according to terms. If the seller gets his terms, it doesn't matter *who* ends up with the property.

Whenever you find a property that is substantially undervalued, make an offer on it subject to an earnest money agreement to perform within sixty to ninety days. Then you have two or three months to convince someone else that the property is a good buy, and you can pick up extra cash by selling your interest in an earnest money agreement.

The first time I used this technique, I did not hesitate. I found a choice apartment building for sale offered on excellent terms and for an excellent price. I prepared an earnest money option to purchase the building, and the sellers accepted my $500 check. The closing date was scheduled seven weeks later. I immediately contacted a client and convinced him that the property was an excellent buy—for $7,000 more than I had agreed to buy it for. He checked with his advisors and verified my claims. When the original closing date rolled around, he gave me the money to close the transaction in my name. As soon as I legally owned the building, I sold it to my client for a nice $7,000 profit.

Note some important factors about this deal. First, I did not have the $50,000 needed for the down payment that the seller had wanted originally. But I *had* given $500 to the seller, which I would have forfeited if the deal had fallen through. You don't have to have a lot of cash in your pocket in order to tie up property. Use the earnest money option technique.

I could have avoided the hassle of closing this transaction in my name if I had written the original Earnest Money Receipt or Offer to Purchase correctly. I had agreed to close in my name in the original offer to purchase. However, if I had written that I "or my assigns" would close, then I would have been able to let my client come in with the down payment on closing day. He would have bought the property with the written understanding that as soon as he received title to the building he would transfer the $7,000 profit to my account. This kind of transaction can be accomplished without ever having to notify the seller of your intentions. The seller does not have to know that you are immediately reselling his property for a profit, and the new buyer does not have to know that you don't own the property he is buying (you merely control it with an earnest money option).

This is best accomplished by setting up separate accounts at two different title companies. In the first title company, you deposit your earnest money check and your earnest money agreement or offer to purchase. You give instructions to the closing officer that you will be depositing the down payment for the closing on or before the day of closing and that the money will be coming from another title company.

At the second title company, you instruct your new buyer to deposit his down payment (which is enough to cover the down payment you negotiated with the seller of the property and a little extra to cover the profit you wish to make on the transaction). The buyer does not need to know that you are making a quick profit. He just expects that when he deposits his down payment, you will be transferring to him the title to the property. In actuality, the closing officers of the two title companies confer on the phone about how the title is to be transferred from the seller to you to the new buyer. This is called a "simultaneous closing," or a "double escrow." The result of the double escrow is that the money from your new buyer is used to pay off the seller and you keep whatever profit you earned for putting the two people together. The mechanics of the double escrow are well known to title companies in your area. If you have any questions about how this works, you might give one of these companies a call before you use the earnest money option technique.

I read about a couple in Texas who began optioning ground a few years ago and made more than $5 million in just a few years. How did they do it? They copied from the county records the names and addresses of all property owners who lived out of state. They reasoned that these people would be less likely to have kept track of the rising values of their property. They were right. They sent out form letters to hundreds of out-of-state owners offering to buy their property for cash with a 90- to 120-day closing. A large percentage of the owners offered to sell at prices well below current land values.

Once an affirmative letter was returned, the couple would go inspect the ground to see if it really was worth buying. If they felt that a profit was probable, they would send a $500 earnest money check to the owners and would have them sign the agreement binding the transaction. Then they would place ads in the local newspapers announcing a sale of the property. They tried to price the property just under current market prices to ensure a good response. As soon as a buyer was located for the higher-priced land, they closed the transaction, using a double escrow, and kept the difference as profit. As an example, suppose the couple found eighty acres below the market at $6,000 per acre. If the going market price was $8,000 per acre, they could tie up the property and advertise it for $7,000 an acre. It would not take long to sell the property for cash at such a good price. Their profit would be $1,000 per acre—a total of $80,000 for just one eighty-acre transaction. You can generate the same results if you know your marketplace.

Another strategy is to find a seller who does not realize the value of his property and who is willing to give you a longer than normal time period for closing the transaction. In one of my seminars, I discussed the use of the earnest money option, and two of my students took my techniques to heart. One father-and-son partnership began researching the county records in a sparsely populated county of Utah, and to their surprise they found hundreds of properties belonging to out-of-state landowners who had held their land for years without realizing its value. They have made tens of thousands of dollars buying land from out-of-state owners and selling the property in smaller pieces to in-state owners on good terms.

Another law student used the same idea and reviewed the county records that showed the out-of-state owners of improved property. He wrote thirty-five letters, received eight replies, and affirmed two offers to sell. A lady called him long-distance to tell him that she had owned a triplex for several years and wanted to sell at a price and terms that he could dictate within reason. This young student didn't have any money, but he did have a good idea, and it paid off for him.

Here's another example: A group of real estate agents recognized the potential of a particular parcel of land and approached the seller with an option to buy. They requested a closing date nine months in the future to give them time to come up with the money. The seller agreed and accepted $1,000 as a deposit. In the next nine months these enterprising men had the property rezoned from agricultural to multiple residential dwelling land. They took an architect in with them who drew up plans for a beautiful condominium project. With these plans, the city gave them preliminary approval for the development. Then they found a local building contractor who showed an interest in the property and sold the ground to him for $500,000 more than they had agreed to pay the original seller. They did this without ever having to own the property physically—they just controlled the eventual sales price with an offer to purchase. When the time rolled around to close with the original seller, the new owner, who was the building contractor, simply completed the transaction in the place of the real estate agents. Obviously, this is a powerful technique.

3. Lease with an Option to Purchase

Another creative way to use the option technique to lower your down-payment requirements is to use the "lease with option to purchase" technique. Let's look at an example that shows the benefit of such a technique.

While searching for property to buy, you find a man who has a house up for rent. It is a four-bedroom house located in a decent neighborhood. It is worth $150,000. The owner is trying to rent it because his home sat on the market for six months, priced at $170,000 with no takers. Since the owner had already bought a new house and had moved into it, assuming the additional mortgage payment and all other homeowner bills, he decided to put the house up for rent or lease rather than go into the hole every month to pay the $1,000 per month on the existing $90,000 mortgage.

Obviously, the owner doesn't need a lot of cash, since he has already purchased his new house and has already adjusted to making a higher mortgage payment. But he is definitely concerned about having to hand over an extra $1,000 a month until his old home is leased or sold. This seller is a special kind of don't-wanter. He doesn't want the hassle of managing his own property, and he wants to save himself from a negative-cash-flow situation.

Offer him a solution to his problems and create an advantage for yourself. Offer to lease his home from him for five years for $1,100 a month. Tell him that you will handle all maintenance and that he will never get a call from you, only a regular monthly check. In return, ask him for an option to buy his house from him in five years at a price of $215,000, which is an increase of about 5 percent a year on a $170,000 price. You should also require that at least 25 percent of the lease payment be applied to the eventual purchase price. In this case that 25 percent would amount to $16,500 and would lower your option price from $215,000 to $198,500.

Suppose the seller decided to accept your offer of a firm price of $215,000 within five years but with no lease credit. If property values increase at an annual rate of between 5 and 10 percent as they have been over the past few years, then the house will be worth between $215,000 and $274,000 by the time the option is ready to be exercised. The seller can sell the house to anyone he wants to in the meantime, but the option will remain in force, and the new owner will have to honor the contract that the seller had with you.

The only investment you will have in the option is time. Once you have negotiated your option, you will have to find a renter so that you don't have to make the $1,100 monthly payments on the lease. As soon as you locate a renter, your only responsibility will be to make sure the renter treats the property carefully and that the property always stays rented.

As the second and third year roll around, you will be able to increase the monthly lease payments by as much as $100 a month. Every time a new renter moves in, the rent can be increased. If you have five or more "lease/option" properties, your monthly cash flow could easily be more than $1,000 after only two years of operation.

You're probably wondering where to find people who will lease their property with an option to buy. Think about it for a second. If you were in the same situation, what would you do? Advertise! Look at your favorite FSBO (for sale by owner) websites in your community and send them an email. Turn to the "Homes for Rent or Lease" section of your daily newspaper's classified ads and see how many ads are there. Call every person listed in the ads and ask "Are you interested in giving an option to buy your property if I

RESIDENTIAL LEASE WITH OPTION TO PURCHASE

RECEIVED FROM _____

the sum of $ _____ (_____, hereinafter referred to as Tenant,

evidenced by _____ DOLLARS),

_____ as a deposit which, upon acceptance of this Lease, the Owner

of the premises, hereinafter referred to as Owner, shall apply said deposit as follows:

	DEPOSIT RECEIVED	BALANCE OWING PRIOR TO OCCUPANCY
Non-refundable option consideration	$ _____	$ _____
Rent for the period from _____ to _____	$ _____	$ _____
Security deposit	$ _____	$ _____
Other	$ _____	$ _____
TOTAL	$ _____	$ _____

In the event that this agreement is not accepted by the Owner or his authorized agent, within _____ days, the total deposit received shall be refunded.

Tenant hereby offers to lease from the Owner the premises situated in the City of _____, County of _____

State of _____, described as _____

_____

and consisting of _____

upon the following TERMS and CONDITIONS:

1. **TERM:** The term hereof shall commence on _____ , 19_____ , and continue for a period of _____ months thereafter.

2. **RENT:** Rent shall be $ _____ per month, payable in advance, on the _____ day of each calendar month to Owner or his authorized agent, at the following address: _____ or at such other places as may be designated by Owner from time to time. In the event rent is not paid within five (5) days after due date, Tenant agrees to pay a late charge of $ _____ plus interest at _____% per annum on the delinquent amount. Tenant further agrees to pay $ _____ for each dishonored bank check.

3. **UTILITIES:** Tenant shall be responsible for the payment of all utilities and services, except: _____ which shall be paid by Owner.

4. **USE:** The premises shall be used as a residence with no more than _____ adults and _____ children, and for no other purpose, without the written prior consent of the Owner.

5. **PETS:** No pets shall be brought on the premises without the prior consent of the Owner.

6. **ORDINANCES AND STATUTES:** Tenant shall comply with all statutes, ordinances and requirements of all municipal, state and federal authorities now in force, or which may hereafter be in force, pertaining to the use of the premises.

7. **ASSIGNMENT AND SUBLETTING:** Tenant shall not assign this agreement or sublet any portion of the premises without prior written consent of the Owner which may not be unreasonably withheld.

8. **MAINTENANCE, REPAIRS, OR ALTERATIONS:** Tenant acknowledges that the premises are in good order and repair, unless otherwise indicated herein. Owner may at any time give Tenant a written inventory of furniture and furnishings on the premises and Tenant shall be deemed to have possession of all said furniture and furnishings in good condition and repair, unless he objects thereto in writing within five (5) days after receipt of such inventory. Tenant shall, at his own expense, and at all times, maintain the premises in a clean and sanitary manner including all equipment, appliances, furniture and furnishings therein and shall surrender the same, at termination hereof, in as good condition as received, normal wear and tear excepted. Tenant shall be responsible for damages caused by his negligence and that of his family or invitees and guests. Tenant shall not paint, paper or otherwise decorate or make alterations to the premises without the prior written consent of the Owner. Tenant shall irrigate and maintain any surrounding grounds, including lawns and shrubbery, and keep the same clear of rubbish or weeds, if such grounds are a part of the premises and are exclusively for the use of the Tenant.

9. **ENTRY AND INSPECTION:** Tenant shall permit Owner or Owner's agents to enter the premises at reasonable times and upon reasonable notice for the purpose of making necessary or convenient repairs, or to show the premises to prospective tenants, purchasers, or mortgagees.

10. **INDEMNIFICATION:** Owner shall not be liable for any damage or injury to Tenant, or any other person, or to any property, occurring on the premises or any part thereof, or in common areas thereof, unless such damage is the proximate result of the negligence or unlawful act of Owner, his agents, or his employees. Tenant agrees to hold Owner harmless from any claims for damages, no matter how caused, except for injury or damages for which Owner is legally responsible.

11. **PHYSICAL POSSESSION:** If Owner is unable to deliver possession of the premises at the commencement hereof, Owner shall not be liable for any damage caused thereby, nor shall this agreement be void or voidable, but Tenant shall not be liable for any rent until possession is delivered. Tenant may terminate this agreement if possession is not delivered within _____ days of the commencement of the term hereof.

12. **DEFAULT:** If Tenant shall fail to pay rent when due, or perform any term hereof, after not less than three (3) days written notice of such default given in the manner required by law, the Owner, at his option, may terminate all rights of Tenant hereunder, unless Tenant, within said time, shall cure such default. If Tenant abandons or vacates the property, while in default of the payment of rent, Owner may consider any property left on the premises to be abandoned and may dispose of the same in any manner allowed by law. In the event the Owner reasonably believes that such abandoned property has no value, it may be discarded. All property on the premises is hereby subject to a lien in favor of Owner for the payment of all sums due hereunder, to the maximum extent allowed by law.

    In the event of a default by Tenant, Owner may elect to (a) continue the lease in effect and enforce all his rights and remedies hereunder, including the right to recover the rent as it becomes due, or (b) at any time, terminate all of Tenant's rights hereunder and recover from Tenant all damages he may incur by reason of the breach of the lease, including the cost of recovering the premises, and including the worth at the time of such termination, or at the time of an award if suit be instituted to enforce this provision, of the amount by which the unpaid rent for the balance of the term exceeds the amount of such rental loss which the Tenant proves could be reasonably avoided.

13. **SECURITY:** The security deposit set forth above, if any, shall secure the performance of Tenant's obligations hereunder. Owner may, but shall not be obligated to, apply all portions of said deposit on account of Tenant's obligations hereunder. Any balance remaining upon termination shall be returned to Tenant.

14. **DEPOSIT REFUNDS:** The balance of all deposits shall be refunded within two weeks from date possession is delivered to Owner or his Authorized Agent, together with a statement showing any charges made against such deposits by Owner.

15. **ATTORNEY'S FEES:** In the event that Owner is required to employ an attorney to enforce the terms and conditions of this agreement or to recover possession of the premises from Tenant, Tenant shall pay to Owner a reasonable attorney's fee whether or not a legal action is filed or a judgement is obtained.

16. **WAIVERS:** No failure of Owner to enforce any term hereof shall be deemed a waiver, nor shall any acceptance of a partial payment of rent be deemed a waiver of Owner's right to the full amount thereof.

17. **NOTICES:** Any notice which either party may or is required to give, may be given by mailing the same, postage prepaid, to Tenant at the premises or to Owner at the address shown below or at such other places as may be designated by the parties from time to time.

18. **HEIRS, ASSIGNS, SUCCESSORS:** This lease is binding upon and inures to the benefit of the heirs, assigns and successors in interest to the parties.

19. **TIME:** Time is of the essence of this agreement.

20. **HOLDING OVER:** Any holding over after expiration hereof, with the consent of Owner, shall be construed as a month-to-month tenancy in accordance with the terms hereof, as applicable. No such holding over or extension of this lease shall extend the time for the exercise of the option unless agreed upon in writing by Owner.

21. **PEST CONTROL INSPECTION:** The main building and all attached structures to be inspected by a licensed structural pest control operator prior to delivery of physical possession. Owner to pay for (1) Elimination of infestation and ¹ or infection of wood-destroying pests or organisms, (2) For repair of damage caused by such infestation and or infection or by excessive moisture, (3) For correction of conditions which caused said damage and (4) For repair of plumbing and other leaks affecting wood members, including repair of leaking stall showers, in accordance with said structural pest control operator's report.

    Owner shall not be responsible for any work recommended to correct conditions usually deemed likely to lead to infestation or infection of wood destroying pests or organisms, but where no evidence of active infestation is found with respect to such conditions.

    If the inspecting structural pest control operator shall recommend further inspection of inaccessible areas, Tenant may require that said areas be inspected. If any infestation or infection shall be discovered by such inspection, the additional required work shall be paid by Owner. If no such infestation or infection is discovered, the additional cost of inspecting such inaccessible areas shall be paid by Tenant.

    As soon as the same are available, copies of the report, and any certification or other proof of completion of the work shall be delivered to the agents of Tenant and Owner who are authorized to receive the same on behalf of their principals.

    Funds for work to be done at Owner's expense shall be held in escrow and disbursed by escrow holder to a licensed structural pest control operator upon receipt of Notice of Work Completed, certifying that the property is free of infestation or infection.

22. OPTION: So long as Tenant is not in substantial default in the performance of any term of this lease, Tenant shall have the option to purchase the real property described herein for a PURCHASE PRICE OF $_____ (_____ DOLLARS), upon the following TERMS and CONDITIONS:

_____
_____
_____
_____
_____
_____
_____
_____
_____
_____
_____
_____
_____
_____
_____
_____
_____
_____
_____
_____
_____
_____
_____
_____
_____
_____

23. DISCLAIMER: The parties acknowledge that speculation of availability of financing, purchase costs, and lender's prepayment penalties is impossible. Therefore, the parties agree that these items shall not be conditions of performance of this agreement and the parties agree they have not relied upon any other representations or warranties by brokers, sellers, or other parties.

24. FIXTURES: All improvements, fixtures, attached floor coverings, draperies including hardware, shades, blinds, window and door screens, storm sash, combination doors, awnings, outdoor plants potted or otherwise, trees, and items permanently attached to the real property shall be included, free of liens, unless specifically excluded.

25. PERSONAL PROPERTY: The following personal property, on the premises when inspected by Tenant, shall be included in the purchase price and shall be transferred by a Warranty Bill of Sale at close of escrow.

26. ENCUMBRANCES: In addition to any encumbrances referred to above, Tenant shall take title to the property subject to: (1) Real Estate Taxes not yet due and (2) Covenants, conditions, restrictions, reservations, rights, rights of way and easements of record, if any, which do not materially affect the value or intended use of the property. The amount of any bond or assessment which is a lien shall be ☐ paid, ☐ assumed by _____

27. EXAMINATION OF TITLE: Fifteen (15) days from date of exercise of this option are allowed the Tenant to examine the title to the property and to report in writing any valid objections thereto. Any exceptions to the title which would be disclosed by examination of the records shall be deemed to have been accepted unless reported in writing **within said fifteen (15) days.** If Tenant objects to any exceptions to the title, Owner shall use all due diligence to remove such exceptions at his own expense **within sixty (60) days thereafter.** But if such exceptions cannot be removed **within the sixty (60) days allowed,** all rights and obligations hereunder may, at the election of the Tenant, terminate and end, unless he elects to purchase the property subject to such exceptions.

28. EVIDENCE OF TITLE: Evidence of Title shall be in the form of ☐ a policy of _____ title insurance, ☐ other: _____ to be paid for by _____

29. CLOSING COSTS: Escrow fees, if any, and other closing costs shall be paid in accordance with local custom, except as otherwise provided herein.

30. CLOSE OF ESCROW: Within _____ days from exercise of the option, or upon removal of any exceptions to the title by the Owner, as provided above, whichever is later, both parties shall deposit with an authorized escrow holder, to be selected by the Tenant, all funds and instruments necessary to complete the sale in accordance with the terms and conditions hereof. The representations and warranties herein shall not be terminated by conveyance of the property.

31. PRORATIONS: Rents taxes, premiums on insurance acceptable to Tenant, interest and other expenses of the property to be prorated as of recordation of deed. Security deposits, advance rentals or considerations involving future lease credits shall be credited to Tenant.

32. EXPIRATION OF OPTION: This option may be exercised at any time after _____, 19____, and shall expire at midnight _____, 19____, unless exercised prior thereto. Upon expiration Owner shall be released from all obligations hereunder and all of Tenants' rights hereunder, legal or equitable, shall cease.

33. EXERCISE OF OPTION: The option shall be exercised by mailing or delivering written notice to the Owner prior to the expiration of this option and by an additional payment, on account of the purchase price, in the amount of:
$_____ (_____ DOLLARS)
for account of Owner to the authorized escrow holder referred to above, prior to the expiration of this option.
Notice, if mailed, shall be by certified mail, postage prepaid, to the Owner at the address set forth below, and shall be deemed to have been given upon the day following the day shown on the postmark of the envelope in which such notice is mailed.
In the event the option is exercised, the consideration paid for the option and _____ percent from the rent paid hereunder prior to the exercise of the option shall be credited upon the purchase price.

The undersigned Tenant hereby acknowledges receipt of a copy hereof.

_____ Tenant's Broker   Dated: _____ Time: _____

By: _____ Agent   _____ Tenant

Broker's Initials: _____ Dated: _____   _____ Tenant

_____ Address   _____ Address

_____ Phone   _____ Phone

ACCEPTANCE

The undersigned Owner accepts the foregoing offer.

BROKERAGE FEE: Upon execution hereof the Owner agrees to pay to _____, The Agent in this transaction, _____ % of the option consideration for securing said option plus the sum of $_____ (_____ DOLLARS)
for leasing services rendered and authorizes Agent to deduct said sum from the deposit received from Tenant. In the event the option is exercised, the Owner agrees to pay Agent the additional sum of $_____ (_____ DOLLARS).
This agreement shall not limit the rights of Agent provided for in any listing or other agreement which may be in effect between Owner and Agent. In the event legal action is instituted to collect this fee, or any portion thereof, the Owner agrees to pay the Agent a reasonable attorney's fee and all costs in connection with such action.

The undersigned Owner hereby acknowledges receipt of a copy hereof.

          Dated: _____ Time: _____

_____ Owner's Broker   _____ Owner

By: _____ Agent   _____ Owner

FORM 106(a) (5-90)   COPYRIGHT © 1983, BY PROFESSIONAL PUBLISHING CORP. 122 PAUL DR. SAN RAFAEL, CA 94903 (415) 472-1964   **PROFESSIONAL PUBLISHING**

lease your house?" Don't forget to ask if some of your monthly rental can be applied toward the eventual option price.

Most people won't be interested. Don't get discouraged. This is a numbers game. You may have to send out dozens of emails or call every night for a month or more. You'll soon be able to recognize the old ads and save time. Of the people who are interested in your offer of a lease option, only a small percentage will finally agree to let you have a long-term lease of up to five years. Of those who accept the long-term lease, only a few will agree with the option price necessary for you to make a profit. Some people will be well aware of the increasing values of local real estate, and will insist that the option price be determined by evaluating the current market value of the house (perhaps determined by appraisal) and increasing this value by 10 percent or more per year until the option date. Forget this kind of seller. You won't see a penny of profit, so why should you handle maintenance and find renters for someone else?

Even though it's hard to find a good lease/option property, it is well worth the search. What are the benefits of this lease/option wealth blueprint?

1. It lets you become a future owner of real estate now without the outlay of a large amount of cash.
2. It provides a growing cash flow as the market rents increase. Depending on the number of homes you have leased/optioned, you can have thousands of dollars of positive cash flow from property you don't even own!
3. You don't have to fight the constantly increasing tax and insurance costs—those are the owner's responsibility. Your lease should be for a constant sum for a five-year period. If you negotiate otherwise, be sure there are enough benefits in the property (such as a low option price or the ability to apply lease payments toward option price) to ensure that you will benefit in the long run.
4. Usually, people who are lease/optioning their property are trying to avoid a constant mortgage payment. This figure will often be much lower than the property rental value. The difference can be $250 a month or more. Thus, you avoid having to charge higher rental rates that would render you less competitive.
5. You have locked in a price based on a future value. If the

property is well selected, you may make much greater returns than normal, especially if the property can be converted to a different use, such as commercial or office space. The option can be sold at any time for as much as you can negotiate. It could provide a handsome cash flow to you as you sell off your options to other investors.

But there are some negatives. You cannot retain any tax advantages from such optioned properties. The seller still owns the property; you have just negotiated a future sale. You will have to spend hours managing your properties and leasing them to new tenants. You will also have to be responsible for all major repairs and minor maintenance unless you specify otherwise in your lease agreement.

Here are some general guidelines to follow in the lease/option game:

1. Don't lease a property unless you can get a long enough lease to make it worth your while—preferably three to five years. Always begin with a five-year option, and don't come down unless your other benefits are great.
2. Make sure that the future option price allows you enough room to make a profit. I usually try to keep the eventual price less than 5 percent per year compounded increase. You can lower the option price by having the seller credit part of your monthly lease payment toward the eventual option price, a technique that can defray the bite of a large future option price.
3. Option only properties that are in good neighborhoods and have potential for a steady increase in value. If the neighborhood is deteriorating, you will be working for nothing. Also, choose properties that are easily maintained, such as those constructed of brick or stucco.
4. Call your local rental agency and offer to pay a finder's fee for every property you eventually lease with an option to buy, based on the firm's referral. Try placing an ad in the newspaper requesting "a lease with an option to buy." Keep at it and you'll eventually get results.

Investing in real estate through options is a five-year retirement plan that is feasible and possible with determined effort. Don't be discouraged if people are not thrilled to lease their properties for five years. Start out with a few shorter-term options, and look for the kind of a don't-wanter who will let you write the terms of the lease/option to suit yourself. Your knowledge and confidence will grow as you become more familiar with the option technique. I'll wager that five years from now your hobby of buying with options will be a full-time one, and you'll be well on your way to achieving your financial goals.

CHAPTER 23

Greed and Need:
Using Partners

"Because my credit is not established, I asked my mother-in-law to put my first investment property under her name. I can refinance the property after a year and become the owner. This also gives me a leverage of looking for another property since the first one is not in my name yet."

—JOSEPH PAZCOGUIN

Ice cream magnates Ben and Jerry, cartoon characters Garfield and Odie, and superheroes Batman and Robin all have something in common. They are all famous partners. One wouldn't be the same without the other.

The same thing can happen for you in real estate investment. If you need more money than you can get alone in order to purchase that perfect property, consider letting a partner come up with the cash. You'll have to give your partner half the profits, but remember: Half a pie is better than no pie at all!

My first experience with partners took place many years ago when I purchased an option on a very valuable piece of apartment ground. At the time I didn't have much experience and was naive enough to think I could do anything. I found a three-and-a-half-acre parcel of land in an excellent location that was ripe for development. It belonged to a church organization whose agent was trying to sell it.

I contacted the agent and established a friendly relationship with him. He had offers on the property for $150,000, but he thought it was worth more. I offered to buy the property from him in a year for $200,000; I agreed to give him $2,500 as option money. He accepted. I was bound to keep my part of the bargain.

The deal was a good one. There was only one problem: I didn't have $2,500. At the time, I hadn't established sufficient credit to borrow even as little as $500 from my bank. This was back in the 1970s when $500 was a lot of money to loan! I approached a good friend who had a growing dental practice and drove him over to the property. I convinced him that it was worth the gamble. He had the cash and was easily able to contribute the $2,500 for the option.

Once we had the property tied up, I began looking for a buyer. I had one year. To make a profit I needed to find someone who would buy the property for more than $200,000.

About eight months later we were approached by a builder who was looking for ground; we negotiated a purchase price of $275,000. When the sale was completed I took a check for $10,800 to my dentist partner—his share of the profits and a 400 percent return on his initial investment. The rest of the money was split with my real estate broker.

The ingredients for success in this story are simple. I found a piece of property that had potential, and I persuaded a partner to finance the property. Without the partner I would never have seen any of the $30,000 I eventually put in my pocket.

Start cultivating partner relationships now. Try to have at least three or four partners in the wings to use when you need them. If you are careful you will never have to use your own capital for any real estate venture again. You will always be able to rely on other people to provide all the investment capital you will ever need.

There are two main motivations that bring people together to form a partnership. It's usually your need for money and his greed and desire to earn more than 10 percent on his invested dollars. If you treat your partners fairly, you will never lack for people who will be willing to lend you money for your investing. It will also get around if you return good profits—the word spreads fast. But if you burn anyone, word about that will get around, too.

There are a number of people who have sizable amounts of money sitting in CDs, money market funds, and even old-fashioned passbook savings accounts. Your job is to convince them that the returns will be much greater if they will join with you and invest in real estate. Let's look at the ways to influence partners and to form partnerships, and how to treat partners as far as profit is concerned and how to dissolve a partnership when the time comes.

There are some good basic rules concerning partnerships.

1. Don't ever form a partnership unless you absolutely need to.

It's too expensive. If you have adequate funds, adequate experience, adequate time, and adequate fortitude to do it yourself, do so. If you're weak in any of those areas, the partnership is probably a good idea.

2. At the beginning of the relationship, define exactly what each person will contribute to the partnership.

For example, your partner's responsibility might be to provide the money; your responsibility would be to negotiate, deliver the earnest money receipt, and complete closing procedures. Obvious contributions that a partner would make include cash, equity in other property, the ability to borrow money readily, strong credit history, and good connections in the right places. Obvious contributions you could make include your time, your knowledge, and your fortitude. Whatever you decide on, get it down in writing and make it specific so there will be no misunderstandings.

One interesting way you can use a partner is to buy his financial statement—in other words, if he's got a good financial statement and a strong relationship with a progressive banker, have him refinance a piece of property. As soon as the refinance is completed, have him give you a quit-claim deed transferring all rights, title, and interest to you, even though his name is on the mortgage and stays there until you are able to assume it. You might pay him for the service. It's well worth it.

By the same token, you could make it worthwhile for a seller to take out a loan against his own property and in turn lend you the proceeds. Secure the loan on another piece of property you own, and pay a good rate of interest. The possibilities are limitless.

ROBERT G. ALLEN

3. Maintain maximum control of the relationship.

If you feel in any way that a partner is limiting your freedom, end the partnership as soon as possible. Don't waste valuable time with a partner who does not trust you or who does not understand a good deal when he sees one. A good relationship sometimes takes time to establish, and the best thing you can have on your side is a good track record of making profit for both yourself and your partners. When you have established a good track record you will be able to call one of your former partners and say, "I've found a great buy on a ten-unit building. The required down payment is $75,000. Do you want in or don't you?" It will be that simple. If partners have made money with you before, they will find a way to say yes.

4. Keep each partnership on a property-by-property basis.

Each project should be evaluated on its own merits, the profits should be split when the property is sold, and the partnership should be dissolved. This practice allows you to be more flexible when other opportunities arise. For instance, if you have an agreement to buy properties with a partner and he runs out of money, you should be free to look elsewhere for another partner if you run across a good deal. It should be clear from the very beginning that your partnership is temporary.

5. Decide from the outset what procedure you will follow if one of the partners decides to sell out to the other.

Establishing this early will prevent misunderstandings if one partner does decide to sell out.

6. Decide early how you'll divide profits.

Try to negotiate the best arrangements you can for yourself while still making it attractive enough for the partner who is putting up the money. Here are some ideas to incorporate.

If you're sure that your project is going to be a winner, don't give large percentages of the profit to your partner. Offer instead to pay your partner 25 percent return on his money or 25 percent of the profits, whichever is less. That's still many times what he'd earn in a bank. Today, most people are very satisfied with 6 to 12 percent yields on their investment.

If your partner is financially established, he will probably wish to forgo your offer of a guaranteed percentage return and will opt instead for your less-guaranteed program of a percentage of the profit. The harder the bargain you drive with your partner, the better off you will be when it comes time to divvy up the profits. I never give away more than 50 percent of the profit to anyone in a partnership, and I try to retain as much as I can for myself. You may say that your partner's dollars are the first to be returned upon the sale of the property, after which all remaining profits are to be split 60 percent to you and 40 percent to your partner. Or you may decide that a 50/50 relationship is best for both parties. Whatever you decide, get it in writing! And whatever happens, guarantee that the partner will at least get his original investment back. And then stand behind your guarantee. A partner should understand (and should be guaranteed) that he would not lose one penny of his original investment, regardless of whether or not he makes a profit.

If you plan on being a nothing-down investor, you've got to begin living a borrower's life. The key to maximum leverage is OPM— other people's money! You have to learn how to overcome your reluctance to ask people for money. From now on, every person you meet is a potential partner. You are looking for people who will trust you with their money—it's as simple as that.

Let's look at the various sources of investor capital.

1. Relatives

Most people find it very difficult to borrow from a relative. Granted, it has its drawbacks, and could cause serious problems if anything negative happened, but there are also obvious benefits. Relatives are more likely to lend you money because they know you.

2. Friends and Business Associates

Word travels fast when you know what you are doing and you prove it by making money for yourself and others. Talk up your latest adventures with every crowd you have a chance to talk to; someone there will want to spend a little money for a profitable cause. Just make sure you are selective and careful.

3. The Seller

The seller ends up lending money to the buyer in many of the real estate transactions I am familiar with by agreeing to let the buyer pay him a portion of the remaining equity over a period of time. The borrowed equity is secured by a mortgage on the property purchased, a mortgage on other property, or a personal note. Whenever a seller takes back a second or third mortgage he is, in essence, lending his money to the buyer.

Some methods of dealing with partners will help ensure a successful experience:

1. Choose your partners carefully, make sure all the terms of partnership are in writing, and stand behind your investments. You'll find that teaming up can provide a good solution to an otherwise troublesome money crunch.
2. If necessary, give a partner some added security by placing the property in the name of the money partner. Retain a written agreement with him that whenever the property is sold—and since the property is in his name, he alone can make the decision on when to sell—the profits will be split according to your written agreement. It can be a simple agreement drafted in mutually satisfactory language and signed by both of you, or you can ask your attorney to formulate an agreement. The simple, do-it-yourself method can work just as well and be legally binding, but using a competent attorney is the best route.
3. Agree to pay the partner his profit and invested capital first after the sale of the property. He will thus know that your profit is subordinated to his and that you will probably work harder to see that things happen as you say they will.
4. Do not get mixed up in limited partnerships. These are not for the investor who likes to have any control over the situation. The fewer the partners, the better. If you don't have the time to do your own looking for properties, visit a real estate agent who specializes in commercial properties. They will give you professional counsel and help you determine the best route for you to take in real estate.
5. If at all possible, avoid investing your own dollars into a partnership. In lieu of cash, give your partner confidence in your

ability to raise cash from other sources. Remember, your contribution to any partnership is the talent, the intangible experience that makes the whole partnership have life and meaning.

6. Don't be discouraged by those who aren't interested in being your partner. You may have to talk to twenty people before you form your first partnership. Once you prove yourself, however, you will find people beating a path to your door to lend you money.

7. When you find yourself in a bad partnership, get out as soon as possible. Learn your lesson and don't make the same mistake again.

Let me challenge you to find five people in the next two years who will be willing to lend you $50,000 each. Think of the tremendous financial resources you would have at your disposal using the $250,000 you borrowed from your partners. And your partners would love you for it because you would be doing something for them that they could not do for themselves.

How do you overcome your fear of asking other people (perhaps even total strangers) for money? Easy! Go out into the real estate market and locate a fabulous property that could be bought for below market value if you could only raise the cash. Then we'll see how shy you are. At that point you have a very important decision to make. Either you get up the courage to ask someone to join you in making a tidy profit or you let your fear cost you thousands of dollars. It's up to you. Whenever I talk to a group of people about real estate investing, I ask for a show of hands of those who either have $50,000 in the bank or who could get $50,000 in thirty days if I would double it for them. Generally, over three quarters of the people raise their hands. It's amazing how fast people come up with money when they smell a profit. This same principle can work for you. If you don't have the money, somebody in your city does—and he or she is just waiting for you to ask for it. Show them how they can make a profit and you'll all laugh all the way to the bank. And you'll have friends for life.

Of course, as soon as you can afford to, get out on your own. Partnerships are great, but if you can afford a whole pie, why should you give half of it away? Until the day that you can go it alone, I challenge you to find five partners who would lend you $50,000 each for real estate investing. I think you could find five partners easily within a two-year period of time if you use the techniques outlined in this chapter. Just think of what you could buy if you had $250,000 cash in your wallet!

CHAPTER 24

Creating "Born-Again Property" Through Conversions

"Critical thinkers find problems; creative thinkers find solutions."
—JOHN MCCLUNG

Remember what we said about land earlier: "They're just not making any more of it." While that is clearly true, it's not the whole story. You can change how a parcel of land is used through a process known as conversion—another way to dramatically increase your return on a real estate investment.

The number of conversions has increased rapidly in the past few years because many metropolitan areas have run out of suburban land to continue growing. Natural barriers, antigrowth amendments, and ever-longer commutes have stopped or slowed the expansion in a number of large and mid-size cities. Another factor fueling the conversion boom is the desire by many types of people to live in a downtown environment, close to jobs, museums, clubs, and restaurants. Young professionals may enjoy a loft residence near their jobs; an older couple whose kids have gone off to college might prefer a luxurious condominium within walking distance of their favorite shops and restaurants.

What do these trends mean for you as a real estate investor? For one thing, they create opportunities to earn a great deal of money by converting a current building, which may not be in the best condition, into an attractive income-producing property. Because of the complexity of these conversion transactions, you may need to bring in a partner or two, and hire experts to assist in the process. But the potential profits from conversions are extremely lucrative, so you shouldn't let the challenges keep you from exploring these opportunities in your market.

Everywhere you look you will see buildings that are functioning in a completely different capacity from that for which they were designed. "Big box" retail stores have been converted into telephone call centers with hundreds of office workers. Old apartment buildings have been converted into luxury condominiums. Gas stations have become retail stores. Farmland is now prime residential and commercial ground in many parts of the country.

Property conversions are simply changing one land use to another. This is done for several reasons:

1. A building or piece of land has outlived its original intended use.
2. A building or piece of land has failed in its originally intended use. For instance, a gas station can't compete with the other two gas stations on the block, so it is converted into a retail store.
3. It has become economically unfeasible to operate the property as was originally intended. Maybe a farmer is not able to return enough money from his crops, so he sells to a commercial developer who builds a shopping mall on the site of the old farm.
4. Demand for a certain use, such as downtown lofts or condominiums, has increased beyond the supply of available land.
5. A builder, developer, or investor recognizes the possibility of a significant profit by changing the use.

Conversions provide limitless possibilities for the creative real estate investor.

Look at the relative values of a typical acre of ground under different uses. Let's say that in your part of the country, a typical acre of undeveloped land or land used for agricultural purposes sells for $5,000. The actual price will vary a great deal by location—an acre in the middle of nowhere might be worth much less than that, while an acre next to a fast-growing city might sell for a hundred times that price.

But regardless of the actual numbers, the important thing is to look at what happens when that acre is developed. If this land were converted to subdivision lots, it could sell for $50,000 to $500,000, again depending on location.

If the subdivision land could be used instead for apartment ground, the seller could reap more than $750,000 an acre in some locations.

The highest-priced ground is land used to building shopping centers and office buildings—land that might sell for $1 million per acre and more.

The graph below shows the relative values of each of the different types of property.

For a fantastic profit opportunity, all you need to do is convert land from one use to another. Unfortunately, this is not easy to do in the conventional real estate market. To convert vacant unused land to farming ground takes ingenuity and guts. Several years ago one of my closest friends hired a full-time legal legman to file claims with the Idaho state government to homestead vast unusable tracts of desert. Once the ground was in his name—perhaps five thousand acres at a time that he acquired for little or nothing—he purchased one of those massive circular sprinkling systems. He filed for a well

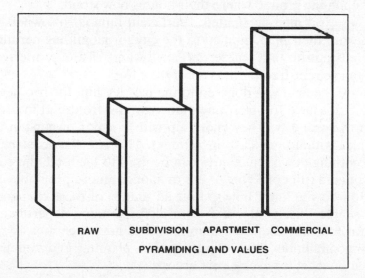

RAW SUBDIVISION APARTMENT COMMERCIAL

PYRAMIDING LAND VALUES

permit and proceeded to irrigate the property until it became suitable farm ground. By converting only a thousand acres a year at great prices for the buyers, he increased his income to more than $1 million annually. Not many people are doing this; not many people have the guts or the creativity. But it only has to happen once to put you over the hump.

Converting farmland to subdivisions is a little easier. In most parts of the country, any ground within a two- to five-mile limit of town is fair game for a future subdivision. If you can acquire the ground at "farm" prices and resell it to a builder, you will turn a tidy profit, multiplied by the number of acres you buy—even if you have to hold the land and pay taxes for a few years until the city grows out to your land.

Urban areas may offer excellent profit opportunities for an apartment building developer looking for new ground for his next project. If you can purchase contiguous houses at low prices, you might be able to assemble a package of ground large enough for a good-size apartment complex. The houses can be torn down, making way for a beautiful project.

I heard of two investors who approached the owners of old, run-down houses in an area zoned for apartments. Most of the owners were widows who could not take adequate care of the property; the investors offered them a brand-new apartment for a home and an ownership position in the new apartment complex, which would be built upon the ground where their houses now stood.

These two men persuaded a sufficient number of owners to go along with their plan, applied to the city for a building permit, and built a beautiful unit where the new owners of the property were able to live rent-free for the rest of their lives.

Since the land was donated to the partnership, the two developers did not have to invest any money on the front end in order to build the property. They ended up with a major ownership in the complex without any cash investment. This is a classic example of how nothing-down techniques can be used to facilitate the conversion of land from one type of use to another, more profitable one.

How do you know how to take advantage of these changes? It's very simple. Just go down to your city's planning department and ask for a zoning map; the map indicates how each area is zoned. Many communities are now putting their planning and zoning maps on the Internet for even easier access.

214

Apartments are usually zoned into one specific area, commercial space into another. Any property that is in an area zoned for different properties can be converted. For example, any house along a major artery leading into a major shopping district has potential as either an office or a shopping space. Of course, the property must be in an area that is zoned for commercial use, or you'll have to apply for a zoning change—something that is difficult and time-consuming to obtain. But if it were easy, everybody would be doing it. A little hard work can pay off big.

Another potential opportunity exists when one property is adjacent to another zone of higher use. When an older apartment building is directly next to an office zone, for example, there is the possibility that the apartment building could be converted to offices.

Let's look more closely at some conversion possibilities.

1. Conversion of an Apartment Building to an Office Complex

One of my first major purchases was a beautiful fifty-year-old, twelve-unit apartment building in the center of my city, population 60,000. It was a classic building with a brick veneer and stately white balconies in an excellent location, directly across from the county courthouse. It cost me $141,000 back in the mid-1970s.

I kept the building for six years. It never generated much income and appreciated only modestly. I avoided spending a lot of money on it because I always wanted to convert these units to office space for my corporate headquarters. In 1981 the time came to make a major decision. The units needed at least $25,000 in repairs. It was time to ask some hard questions.

How many square feet were usable as office space on each floor? Approximately three thousand square feet each on three floors.

Was there adequate parking for office space? Checking with the city, I learned I would need one parking space for each five hundred square feet of office space. I would therefore need eighteen spaces. I had thirteen spaces already, and I could rent an additional five spaces from a neighboring office building.

Was the property zoned for the intended change? The city master plan showed that my building was in a professional office zone. The city planner indicated that there would be no problem with the proposed conversion, but I would have to submit my plans to the city council for its approval.

Was there an adequate market for office space if I didn't take up all of the space with my own operations? I called one of the county commissioners and found out that they needed extra space for some of their county offices. In fact, they had recently purchased some buildings across the street from my apartments for some badly needed office space. One of the tenants in the buildings the county bought needed a new office and asked about my rates. Others also expressed interest. Signed leases from future tenants would give me added borrowing power at the bank.

What about costs? I hired a local architect to make a study of the kinds of improvements that would have to be made to the building; his cost estimate was $150,000 for major renovation.

What about the bank? Would it lend the money? By now I had enough clout at the bank to show the loan officers the benefits of a construction loan to convert the building.

What would it be worth after conversion? I estimated rents on similar office space and saw that I could turn my old $200,000 apartment building into a brand-new office building worth perhaps $500,000—with a substantially larger equity.

The diagram below shows how the building looks before and after the proposed conversion.

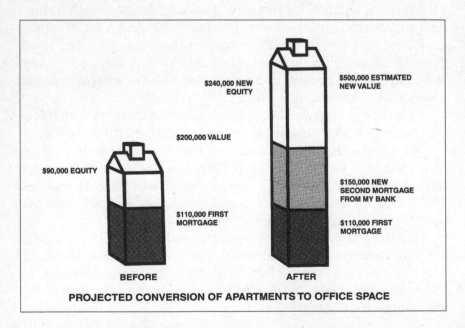

PROJECTED CONVERSION OF APARTMENTS TO OFFICE SPACE

And what about the cash-flow picture? As an apartment building, it generated a break-even cash flow at best when you consider all the repairs needed to keep the fifty-year-old shell patched together. But I estimated that even after I had incurred $150,000 in new debt, the income from the new office building (when I made adjustments for the fact that I would be a major tenant) would be a positive cash flow.

I decided, finally, that the only logical alternative was to start the conversion process.

And so we began—and immediately ran into all kinds of unanticipated problems. Let me summarize by saying that the total bill came in at about $350,000—only a slight $200,000 miscalculation by the architect. But the extra money spent turned the project into one of the top-notch office buildings in the city. An appraisal ordered by my banker put the value at $735,000 (I had guessed low!), and based on this appraisal the bank advanced the necessary money. Since it is such a prime location and has such fine amenities, we have no trouble charging top dollar for office rent.

In the final analysis, the conversion of this apartment building to an office building was a profitable one, although I had my doubts there for a while. The building became worth more than $700,000 with loans of about $450,000.

So, as you can see, conversions can be sweet, if you're careful.

2. Condominium Conversions

My first positive experience with condominium conversions took place in 1978. It provides an excellent example of how you can profit from this change of use, even though prices today are probably about ten times higher than the ones in this example!

My partner and I were able to locate a choice ten-unit building in an excellent location. Four of the units were being rented out as commercial office space. The remaining six units were apartments, each containing about a thousand square feet of space with two bedrooms. We negotiated a purchase price of $208,000 with a down payment of $30,000 and a land sales contract of $178,000, with monthly payments of $1,524.36 until paid in full. Once we owned the building we contacted our attorney and had him prepare the necessary documents for the conversion of the ten rental units into ten condominiums.

217

ROBERT G. ALLEN

In order to accomplish this, certain items had to be taken care of. First of all, the city had to give authorization for the change in use. Our attorney met with the city planners to explain what we intended to do. They asked to see our condominium documents and a new survey of the property. Once they were satisfied that the papers were in order, permission was granted to sell the individual units on the market for a price of $32,000 per unit. All the units were sold quickly because of our easy financing; we agreed to accept a $5,000 down payment and to carry the financing ourselves for the balance of the $27,000 owing. Here is our profit picture:

Sale of ten units @ $32,000	$320,000
LESS:	
Commissions	$ 20,000
Survey	1,000
Attorneys' fees	2,500
Miscellaneous sales costs	1,500
	$(25,000)
Net sales proceeds	295,000
Less cost of building	208,000
Profit	$ 87,000

The interesting part of the story is yet to come. We required a down payment of $5,000 per unit, bringing the total cash down payment to $50,000. When we deducted our $25,000 costs of conversion (commissions, attorneys' fees, etc.) from the total down payment, we came away with $25,000 in cash. This covered almost all of our original down payment of $30,000 on the property.

Then where is our benefit for converting the units to condominiums? As you remember, our monthly payment on the property when we bought it was $1,524.36. By selling the units as condominiums and carrying back the paper ourselves, we created a situation whereby the new owners made a total monthly payment of approximately $2,500 per month. With this money we made the payments of $1,524.36 and kept the difference of almost $1,000 a month.

In summary, we bought the building with a $30,000 down payment, sold the units as condominiums, got back $25,000 in cash at closing, and had a monthly cash flow of approximately $1,000 a month for twenty-five years. We did not have to make any extensive improvements in the property—we simply sold the units "as is." The attorney did most of the work for us. The real estate company took care of the sales. All that was necessary for us to do was to come up with the idea in the first place and to delegate the details to the professionals. Profit was created because we knew that people would pay more for a condominium than they would for a rental apartment unit. If you're like me, you'll be looking for an apartment building just waiting to be converted.

3. Residential Subdivisions

Another form of conversion from one use to another is converting land that has been kept vacant for farming or other reasons into a residential subdivision. Your land is a prime candidate if it is near a growing metropolis. The increase in price from one use to the other can be dramatic.

Let's look at a ten-acre parcel of ground that has been used for raising corn. The farmer is getting older and wants to retire; he has watched the sprawling city slowly encroach and almost completely surround his small farm. Since his livelihood has been derived in part from his land, he has resisted the offers of previous land subdividers; now, with retirement in sight, he begins to contemplate selling his property so he can enjoy the life he has always wanted.

Along comes a creative real estate investor—we'll call her Jennifer, a cash-poor, but creative investor. Since Jennifer has done her homework, she knows that farm ground this close to the city limits has recently sold for $100,000 an acre. The farmer has kept close track of the higher land price sales, and he wants at least $100,000 an acre for his ground. He must have $100,000 or nothing at all.

When Jennifer begins to negotiate, she must have all of the facts at her fingertips. She checks with the city to determine the difficulty of obtaining building permits on any subdivision lots that would be created. Is there adequate water, sewer, and fire protection? What are the fees that must be paid to the city or county? Will there be any problems when a final plan of the subdivision is submitted to the planning department for approval? Is the land properly surveyed? Is there a market for property in this area? What size lots can be sold and at what prices?

Jennifer checks with a reputable land surveying company and asks the owner these questions; he has most of the answers.

In the case of the ten-acre parcel, all of the signs are "go." Building lots have sold for as high as $60,000 a lot within the last three months. The surveyor draws up an inexpensive preliminary subdivision plan showing that once roads and sidewalks are accounted for, there will be about thirty lots ready for sale.

Jennifer is able to obtain a firm bid from a local contracting outfit (recommended by the surveyor), which has agreed to do the improvements on the property such as roads, sewer, water lines, and sidewalks. Here is the financial picture:

Cost of the land	$1,000,000
Cost of the improvements (at $12,000 per lot)	360,000
Sales costs at $5,000 per lot	150,000
Total costs	1,510,000
Gross sales of 30 lots at $60,000	1,800,000
Less total costs	1,510,000
Total profits	$290,000

The profit picture is very good for such a small piece of ground and a year's work. You would also be wise to sell the lots on a wholesale basis to a local builder who needs the land for his next home subdivision. You may be able to sell the whole thirty-lot package for $50,000 per lot, avoiding sales costs, and end up with a similar profit. When you have a choice, always pick the quick profit over the long-term method. Better to make a fast nickel than a slow dime.

What about financing the land in the first place? Use the subordination technique discussed earlier. The seller is going to have a tremendous tax consequence if he receives all of his $1 million in one year. Convince him that he should accept only 25 percent of the money during the first year of sale. Thus, by structuring the receipt of cash in several tax years, the tax consequences are greatly reduced. A 25 percent down payment amounts to $250,000; the rest ($750,000) should be subordinated to a construction loan that you obtain to make improvements on the property. Since the improvements will cost about $360,000, you will need to find a bank that will give you a development loan; some will lend up to 75 percent of the value of the developed building lot.

Every year thousands of homes are being built, and land is desperately needed by growing building companies. You can fill a need by bird-dogging the land for them and reap a profit in the process!

Keep your eyes open. Make conversions like this one and the others we've discussed work for you.

CHAPTER 25

Overcoming the Ten Biggest Roadblocks to Your Success

"Eighty percent of success is changing your internal psychology so that you create your life, rather than reacting to what life gives you. The rest is just making your internal visions manifest in the real world."

—JASUN LIGHT

What are the roadblocks to investment success? This question nagged at my brother, Richard, who helped me organize this material into seminar format. He designed a questionnaire for the thousands of our seminar graduates nationwide. I thought you might be interested in knowing what the top ten barriers are. Here they are in order of greatest concern:

1. Negative cash flows and balloons
2. Lack of capital resources
3. Tax and estate aspects
4. Lack of time
5. Difficulty getting partners
6. Lack of equity resources
7. Lack of specific goals
8. Difficulty finding don't-wanters

9. Difficulty in negotiation
10. Ignorance of creative acquisition techniques

Since there seems to be such concern about how to overcome these barriers, I would like to analyze each of these barriers, and show you how I solve these problems.

But before I do, let me tell you my attitude toward perceived barriers like these. Those of you who are inordinately concerned with the obstacles confronting you are not thinking creatively. In a real sense, almost of all of these barriers are merely figments of our imagination—they are simply excuses that we create to give us an "out" for not doing what we know we have to do. As far as I am concerned, there are no barriers. *None.* In my mind, there are no excuses. When I look at myself in the mirror every morning I can truly say to myself that the only person standing in the way of my ultimate success is me. That may sound too simple, but it is true. Now, with that in mind, let's talk about some solutions.

1. Negative Cash Flows and Balloons

Interestingly enough, according to our analysis, there are two major reasons people give for why they become don't-wanters: negative cash flows and balloon mortgages. In other words, the greatest barriers to getting into real estate and the greatest reasons for getting out of real estate are the same. So what do you do about it? First of all, be very careful when you buy. Don't buy without doing a careful analysis first, and be able to afford your negatives if you are buying a property with reverse cash flow.

In order to be conservative, I also recommend the following rules:

a. *Never* buy a property that has a balloon mortgage of less than five years unless the price is *at least* 10 percent below market the day you buy it. Don't buy it unless you are planning on reselling the property quickly for a short-term profit and are certain that you can find a buyer. If you are buying for the long run, you want to avoid balloons. In this way you train yourself not to speculate.

b. *Never* buy a property that has a high negative cash flow unless the price is *at least* 10 percent below market the day you buy it. Force yourself to get out of the speculators' fever and think

223

ROBERT G. ALLEN

rationally about every property you buy. If the seller will not cut his price, then ask for more flexible terms. Ask the seller to carry second and third mortgages *with no monthly payments* and zero interest for a period of time. Will a seller accept such terms? Sometimes, yes, most often no. But we keep on asking, unafraid of rejection, until we find exactly what we need. Unfortunately, there is a dilemma we all face in buying property. Sometimes, in order to avoid negative cash flows (or to buy creatively), we need to create balloon mortgages. There are trade-offs that each of us needs to analyze when buying. Would I rather have a negative cash flow and avoid balloons? Or would I rather have no negative cash flows and negotiate for seller carry-back notes or mortgages with short-term balloons? This is a decision that you must make for yourself.

c. Whenever you do agree to a balloon mortgage, no matter how far in the future, you should always negotiate for a twelve-month extension beyond the balloon due date just in case you can't solve the problem in time. You agree to pay a nonrefundable fee of $1,000 or more for the privilege of extending. This gives you twelve extra months of breathing room and can sometimes spell the difference between success and failure.

For those of you who can't afford negative cash flows and who want to avoid balloon mortgages, there is another solution. Sell a half interest in your properties either to an investor partner or to the tenant who plans on living long-term in the property. A partner is easy to find to cover the negatives if a nothing-down deal is offered. In one of the recent seminars I taught, a student stood up and offered to take over up to a $500 monthly negative in exchange for half of the ownership of the property. Advertise in the paper. Your ad might look something like this:

NOTHING DOWN

Need partner to pay $500 per month negative cash flow on my excellent investment property in exchange for half ownership and no management hassles.

It is better to own half of something than all of nothing.

Of course, the ultimate way to avoid negative cash flows *and* balloons at the same time is to buy wholesale. Nothing down

224

doesn't always mean that there is no cash involved in the transaction. It means that the cash doesn't have to be yours. You should be looking for partners with lots of cash (if you are blessed with fat bank accounts, so much the better). These partners will use their cash, with your urging, to invest in the rare property that is sold 20 to 40 percent below market but requires immediate, large chunks of cash. The seller doesn't want to carry paper; he wants cash and is willing to discount for the privilege of getting it fast. In these instances you can assume low-interest-rate mortgages with low monthly payments—and, of course, no balloon payments. How you handle your partner and the repayment of his invested cash depends on your relationship. You may decide to just sell the property and claim the profit and move on to the next deal. Or you may refinance the property, pay your partner back, and keep it for the long haul.

2. Lack of Capital Resources

Most Americans are confused on this issue. They think they need to have money in order to make money. Not so. They only need to know how to find the money. But what is even more important is that they learn how to find bargain properties. Then, once they have found an excellent bargain property, they can concentrate on how to bring in the necessary financial resources to solve the problem. This might mean using their own cash or that of a partner.

You should know that the motto of all creative investors should be *"If I don't have it, somebody else does."* This is the essence of leverage: using other people's strengths. By combining one person's strengths with another's weaknesses you can create a winning team. If you don't have the capital assets to get the ball rolling, you must look for those who do but don't have the time or the expertise to use them. I am reminded of a story of one of our very successful graduates who works with a wealthy attorney in buying properties. In the beginning this student had no money or assets. He approached an attorney who had both money and expertise in the foreclosure area but no time to look for property. They worked together marvelously because each could not live without the other.

So, the major solution to the problem of capital assets is to borrow some, either from your friendly banker or from a partner. Remember, if you don't have what you need, someone else does.

And you can probably convince that person in a win/win way to lend you what you need in exchange for some of the benefits of real estate.

3. Tax and Estate Aspects

Why are these barriers? Real estate can offer significant tax benefits. Because tax laws tend to change frequently, I suggest you do as I do: hire a competent accountant and tax planner. It is not cheap, but they can advise you on the best tax strategy for your specific situation, and perhaps save you tens of thousands of dollars in the long run. If you are worried about paying too much in taxes, the simple answer is: Buy as much property to depreciate as you can.

As for estate matters, I recommend that you align yourself with a competent estate attorney. He can help you arrange your affairs so that you can sleep at night knowing that your family is well taken care of.

How do you find these competent professionals? I find that word of mouth is the best method. Ask your friends and business associates. Who does your work? Is she good? How much does she charge? Usually the more a professional charges, the better they are. Pay twice as much and get it done right the first time.

4. Lack of Time

I can just hear you saying, "I'm so busy at my job I don't have time to look for property." Yes, most people are so busy earning a living that they don't have the time to make any real money. But each of us has the same twenty-four hours to live each day. Why is it that some of us are far more productive than others? Is it luck? Is it brains? No, I think it's just that the most successful people have developed their own unique system for managing their time more efficiently. They are in the habit of a daily routine, and as the saying goes, "Routine brings perfection within the grasp of mediocrity." In other words, even a mediocre person with a modest daily self-improvement routine will outperform a disorganized genius ninety-nine times out of a hundred.

The first step in organizing time is to set goals. Then, set priorities on your activities so that the most important tasks get done first. Most of us spend our time on the least important activities because they are easy to accomplish and give us a good feeling as we cross them off our to-do list. It is much more important to work on difficult but important tasks, because these move us toward our long-range goals.

The next step is to set aside a regular time, if possible just before you go to bed, when you review the activities for the upcoming day and block out times for their accomplishment. During the night your subconscious mind can be processing the information while you sleep. Having done this, when you wake up you will be miles ahead of the competition.

Then, arise an hour earlier in the morning than you usually do. This is important. The average person gets up at the last minute, gets ready, eats breakfast on the run, and arrives at work in total chaos. What a way to prepare for the day! You need to be different. Get up a bit early. In the quiet, peaceful hours of the morning, before anyone else is up, take thirty to sixty minutes to read books and articles that are related to your long-term goals. One by one, as the lights come on in your neighbors' houses, and the world starts to groan into activity, you will feel a sense of power in knowing that you are different. Normal people don't do such things—that's why they're normal. But you are special. You have the courage to change your life a little bit at a time. Slowly, day by day, you are growing. Great things are not accomplished in a day but are the result of small sacrifices taken regularly over a long period of time. Close your eyes, take a deep breath, and realize that you have overcome yourself. Meditate, pray, or just give thanks for another day to discover the purpose of your life. Open your eyes and you're ready to take whatever the world has to dish out.

Using just these simple steps, anyone should be able to budget two to five hours a week for property acquisition. It should be a regular time. Involve your family—your spouse or children. Delegate the finding of excellent buys to creative real estate agents. I'm sure there are plenty of real estate agents in your area who would be happy to find property for you and to handle many of the time-consuming details. Look for those who have read *Nothing Down* or taken my Creating Wealth seminar (call 801-852-8711 or visit www.robertallenrealestate.com). It's nice if the real estate agents you use already speak the language of creative financing. Use them. Their commission is well earned.

I think I can say that no one is too busy to buy real estate successfully.

5. Difficulty Getting Partners

How do you find partners? The chapter on partners discusses several sources. Relatives. Friends and business associates. And the seller himself. I feel that for many people the problem is not finding potential partners but getting up the courage to ask someone to join with you in making in the best investment in the world. For me, the best approach has always been to work backward. Find the deal first. Locate property that has enormous benefits that you know you will have no trouble discussing with a partner. Once you have found the great deal, your desire to own it will force you to find someone to help you accomplish your goal. I have often asked seminar graduates the following question: "If I could find you a great property that could be bought with nothing down, no negative cash flow, and no management hassles, would you let me use your credit to obtain a new loan and give me 50 percent of the deal?" I never have a problem finding a taker. The answer, then, is not to wait to find a partner (if this is what is stopping you), but to get out there in the marketplace and find a property that any partner would be happy to own with you.

Once you have the "bird in the hand," you can begin by calling your friends and explaining the deal to them. Always ask them if they know of someone who might be interested in a great deal. If they aren't interested, they can bow out gracefully by giving you a referral. Then you can tell the referral that you were "sent" by someone. Approach the well-to-do people in your neighborhood or in your social and church groups. Don't be embarrassed. If the deal is really all that good, you'll be doing both of you a favor by mentioning it. If you have run out of acquaintances, you might try contacting real estate offices looking for solid-money partners. Try accountants and attorneys who represent affluent clients. It takes imagination and courage, but the fruits are sweet.

6. Lack of Equity Resources

I think this falls under the category of partners. Remember our motto: "If I don't have it, somebody else does." And that somebody may be sitting next to you at this very moment. Have you asked?

7. Lack of Specific Goals

Everyone should have the goal of buying at least one property per year. That's a minimum goal. But there are some who can't seem to get up the courage to set even a minimum goal. Are you one of those fence-sitters? Go back to the chapter on goals and reread it. At the end of the chapter is a goal-setting form for you to fill out and commit to. Set your goals! Put them in writing! Display them in a prominent place in your home and read them daily! And then let your subconscious mind work out the best way for your goals to become a reality.

8. Difficulty Finding Don't-Wanters

This can be a sticky problem, but there are easy solutions. One fellow wrote recently that he had called thirty-seven people without any positive results, and he was a bit discouraged. Remember that we all have feasts and famines, and you may be in a famine for a while. I have them all of the time. I think the best way of finding don't-wanters is in the following order:

a. Place your own ad in the paper. Have you thought about a billboard? Maybe ten of you should go together and rent an outdoor sign and share the leads. It's a thought.

b. You need to let people know that you are in the market. Have you visited ten real estate offices lately and told them that you are in the market? Until you have, you can't gripe about a dearth of don't-wanters. It takes time.

c. Use the Internet to seek out don't-wanters quickly and efficiently. Start compiling a list of the email addresses of real estate agents in your area, and drop them a note from time to time. Find a website where local owners advertise their properties without an agent (the FSBOs we discussed earlier). Take a look at the photos and descriptions of the property, and if the price looks interesting, arrange a tour. You can do that very quickly and efficiently using email.

d. Look for attractive listings in your market. Go to the website of a local real estate broker who has access to all the for-sale properties in the local Multiple Listing Service (MLS). Look for the clues in the remarks section of each advertised property. Try to determine how flexible the seller might be. Work with a good, flexible real estate agent to help you in this process.

e. The newspaper is an excellent source of don't-wanters. Learn how to recognize the clues that lead to nothing-down deals. It is a gold mine of information.

Finding don't-wanters is like prospecting for gold. It's not easy but it's well worth the effort. Keep talking to people. Use the Internet. Ask and ye shall receive.

9. Difficulty in Negotiation

There are two good chapters in this book on negotiating. Reread them. But as you do, I want you to remember the win/win philosophy of negotiating. It may seem to you that I am not looking out for the best interests of the seller when I negotiate. Not so. The best and most satisfying negotiations to both parties are those in which we try to understand the needs of the seller, and then try to structure our offers to meet these needs. It is only when we understand the seller's problem and try to help him that the trust that is vital in creative transactions is built. We are not trying to create adversaries in our negotiations; we are trying to build friendships! And how could you take advantage of a friend? You can't! Instead, try to put yourself in the shoes of the seller. You ask yourself, "How can he win by this offer?" and then you practice, practice, practice.

10. Ignorance of Creative Acquisition Techniques

There are literally thousands of techniques for putting together buyers and sellers in creative ways. Rather than provide you with a long encyclopedia of methods, I have concentrated on the most basic and useful techniques.

I think the reason why many of my graduates feel there's a barrier here is that they want to understand everything perfectly before they act. And this is nothing more than the age-old problem of procrastination—though in different clothing. You learn how to use the techniques by trying them out, not by studying them.

Some people know what to do. Others do what they know. I hope these ten barriers are not stopping you from doing what you know you must do.

CHAPTER 26

What Should You Do When You Become the Don't-Wanter?

"You cannot have a great day without a few bad days along the way."
—PETE SILVA

From the tone of this book, you might think calling someone a "don't-wanter" is a put-down, a bad word, perhaps. Well, if that is the way you feel, I think you've missed the point. And this is the point: *We all become don't-wanters sooner or later!* That's right. Sooner or later, if you are in the marketplace buying (as you should be), you are bound to buy a lemon. That is the nature of risk. You should see some of the properties I have bought over the years! In reality, you win some (most) and you lose some (a few). You have to have the attitude "I knew it would happen; sooner or later I had to slip up and buy a property I had no business buying."

Now what do you do when you end up with a bad situation? Notice that I didn't say "bad property," because there are no bad properties. It is your ownership and what you do that determines your success or failure. Let me give you a few principles to follow when this inevitable problem arises.

231

1. Do your homework before you buy.

An ounce of prevention is worth a pound of cure. Be careful of negative cash flow and balloons. If you follow just this one bit of advice it will eliminate most of the don't-wanteritis down the road.

2. Diversify into different real estate properties.

When you buy several properties, this reduces the risk to your overall portfolio if one of your properties should have problems. That is one reason I like single-family houses. Buy several smaller properties rather than a few large ones because if one of your properties should cause you trouble, it represents only a minor portion of your entire portfolio. You can dump it without ruining your program. On the other hand, suppose you owned a large fifty-unit apartment building and the neighborhood deteriorated or rent controls were introduced. You would be left holding a huge white elephant with not much marketability. If you own ten properties and one of them goes sour, you can sell the bad apple and concentrate on the rest without losing much sleep.

3. Cut your losses and run with your winners.

This is an old stock market adage that holds true in real estate, too. A neophyte investor tends to hold on to her precious real estate, troubles and all, either hoping for a miracle or burying her head into the sand of neglect. I see so much of this, and those of you who specialize in foreclosures can agree with me that people are emotional and irrational when it comes to unloading a problem property. I recommend that you "Get rid of your bad situations!" They only drag you down emotionally. Salvage as much as you can and get out. You can't be positive and aggressive and creative when you are being eaten alive by a don't-wanter property. Learn from your mistakes, determine never to make the same mistake again, and get back out in the marketplace with renewed wisdom and confidence.

4. Be creative in disposing of your properties.

Let's suppose that you are examining your portfolio of properties and find one that never really measured up to your expectations. It was just wishful thinking from the start. This is an apartment building that has a negative cash flow because your projections were too optimistic. It is a headache at best. In retrospect, you would have done better to have never laid eyes on it. It's time to cut your losses. Some more details:

Purchase price:	$300,000
Loans:	$290,000 (You had a balloon come due and had to refinance with a short-term, higher-rate loan. Closing costs and deferred interest ate up most of the appreciated equity.)
Appraisal:	$310,000
Fair price:	$305,000
Fair equity:	$ 15,000
Loan payments:	$ 3,000 monthly
Rents (minus operating expenses):	$ 2,500 monthly
Minimum negative:	$ 500
Location:	Marginal
Appreciation potential:	Marginal

Diagnosis: Get rid of this turkey!

Seven-Step Property Disposal Plan

Here's a systematic way to dispose of a property—just like the one above—when you become a don't-wanter. Following this plan step-by-step will help cut your losses, because you will be less likely to make a decision based on pure emotion.

1. Get an appraisal on the property.

Get a local appraiser to do a realistic appraisal on your property. You need to get a feeling for what your property is worth. If the appraisal is more than you expected, you can use this in your marketing efforts. If the appraisal is much lower than you expected, you can either adjust your expectations or get a second opinion from another appraiser. Try to get the best written appraisal possible. That will help you negotiate with potential buyers.

2. Decide what you want from the sale of your property.

Depending on the circumstances, you may just want to get rid of this property at all costs and as soon as possible—the true don't-wanter—or you may wish to test the market for the best price and terms with no specific time pressures. In either case, you need to be realistic about what you expect to get. If you're a don't-wanter, don't let your pride get in the way. Be as flexible as you can. The more flexible you can be, the easier it will be to sell. Don't be afraid to sell with nothing down as long as you protect yourself with solid buyers and additional collateral. In our case study, the property is a turkey that we want to move quickly. The questions in your mind should be: "How can I structure the sale of this property so that the buyer gets a good deal and I come out okay?" Think creative finance. Can I accept a monthly payment instead of cash? Can I sell the paper I carry at a discount for cash? Can I trade the paper I carry to another don't-wanter in the next twelve months and thereby move through the paper to a better property? Am I willing to pay someone to take this property off my hands? Am I willing to accept a loss in order to move this property quickly?

Come to terms with your bottom line—that is, what you need, not what you want. Be realistic.

In our example, we have decided that a fair price will be $305,000 with a $15,000 equity. We decide that we will accept anything from $15,000 in cash to a free-and-clear office computer system with all the bells and whistles. In short, we want out.

3. Write an ad that reflects your flexibility.

You need to attract buyers . . . fast. The more buyers attracted by your ad, the more likely you are to find a taker. That's true whether you post your ad in the local newspaper or at an online FSBO website. You have a lot of competition in the market, so you will need to differentiate yourself from all the other sellers. The best way to attract buyers is to let them know that they are going to get a good deal. That is where the appraisal comes in. Hopefully, your ad can indicate that the buyer is getting a good deal as far as either the price or terms are concerned. Some possible advertising phrases: "You make

$5,000 the day you move in! Professional appraisal $310k. Your price only $305k." Or, "Why go to a bank when I can give you a better rate." Or, "Nothing Down." Or, "I don't need cash. What have you got to trade for my house?" Or, "No qualifying" (in the case of an assumable FHA or VA loan). Or, "I want out! I don't need cash. Make me a creative offer."

A few years ago, in selling my own personal residence, I decided to use a nothing-down technique. I knew that it would take months to sell in the soft market at that time, so I sold it with nothing down and an eighteen-month balloon payment, which, incidentally, was paid on time. Sellers of property around my home were not as flexible as I was. They held out for cash, and as a result they sat on their properties for over a year, all the time making mortgage payments and subjecting themselves to many more months of the emotional stress that goes with selling a house.

Writing the ad is very important. Try to make it stand out from the rest. Put a box around it. I still remember one ad in a Salt Lake City paper a while ago that stood out like a sore thumb. It read, "I'm down. Kick me!" Now *that's* flexibility!

Start to run your ad in the local paper. Or post it online tonight.

4. Prepare a flyer on your property with pertinent details and a picture.

Indicate all the benefits the buyer will be acquiring by buying your property. Make one flyer for investors and another for prospective buyers. Pass the flyer out when you go to the bank, the dry cleaners, or your local Starbucks. It's like farming. You've got to plant a lot of seeds.

5. Talk to everyone you know who might be in the market for a bargain property.

Call up the tenants you have in your other properties. Talk to people at work. If you have employees, let them have first crack at the property. I sold one of my single-family houses recently to one of my employees. Of course, it was nothing down. But I was happy to do it. It might have been difficult for him to qualify for a new loan, and he was very grateful. The prime candidate for an investment home is someone who is now living in an apartment or a mobile home. Leave flyers at some of the apartment complexes showing the residents just how easy it will be for them to afford your property.

6. If the numbers permit, involve a creative real estate agent.

In our example, it will be difficult to involve a real estate agent because the fee will be at least $15,000—all of your $15,000 equity—and after closing costs you will end up losing money. Also, the real estate agent's fee often has to be paid in cash, and this may negate some of the creative financing you are trying so hard to make available to your buyer. But if you have enough equity in the property and you want a quick sale, a real estate agent can be invaluable. The local multiple-listing services is a great tool and exposes your property to every real estate agent in your city—a marketing strength that can't be overlooked.

If you have room in your pricing to include a real estate agent's commission, you should search out a creative one. I like to deal with those real estate agents who have been educated in creative financing through my own Creating Wealth program (call 801-852-8711 or visit www.robertallenrealestate.com).

Once you have found a worthy real estate agent, work with him or her to write creative newspaper ads, get some attractive digital photos and prepare a write-up for the multiple-listing service and the agent's website. Most listings do not indicate financial flexibility, so make sure that your listing stands out. I have often agreed to pay higher commission on the listing in order to attract the attention of more real estate agents.

7. If the above steps don't produce results, change your ads, meet more people, or get more flexible or creative until you do get some results.

If you are willing to be more flexible, you may consider running the following ad in your paper:

I'll pay you $3,000 to move into my house!

Using our case study as an example, you would offer to sell the house for $310,000—the full-appraised price. The buyer assumes the underlying $290,000 loan. And you carry back a $20,000 second mortgage with negotiated payments; the buyer gets $3,000 from you at closing as a buying bonus. Check out the buyer thoroughly, of course. Your money and your property are at risk, but this just might flush out a qualified buyer.

If you are suffering from an unbearable negative cash flow, perhaps you can solve your don't-wanter problem without even selling your property. Maybe you should sell only half of it. This is what you call "syndicating the negative." (Wasn't there an old song about this? "Accentuate the positive, eliminate the negative"?) Do you think you would have any trouble selling one-half ownership in a property for nothing down if you required your partner to pay all the negative cash flow? The answer, as you should have guessed, is *absolutely not!* There are thousands of people out there who would love to partner with you for a share of the benefits. In essence, you make the down payment and they make the monthly payments. It's a win/win partnership.

As a final solution, you can do what more than one innovative seller has done recently to get rid of a don't-wanter property. Faced with a tough sale on their new $150,000 home, one Midwest couple held a lottery and raffled off their house! Wouldn't you pay $100 for a good chance to own a new $150,000 home? They printed up sixteen hundred tickets, including a few extras to cover their advertising expenses, and sold out in just two weeks. As soon as the last ticket was sold, they drew the winner's name—and walked away from their don't-wanter property.

Now that is what I call creative. Remember, the odds are that you will be a don't-wanter yourself someday. When that happens, don't despair. It's only a small barrier. Cross over it and be on your way to financial independence. There is no other way.

CHAPTER 27

Different Strokes for Different Folks: Variations on the Nothing-Down Theme

"Finding suitable financing to close my deals were my biggest challenge, and the mortgage brokers I was dealing with only made my challenges bigger. Since I couldn't beat them, I joined them! Now the financing process no longer intimidates me, working as a professional with the professionals. The possibilities are endless!"

—OSEYE COHEN

Real estate is a multifaceted investment, a miracle of flexibility. It will do for you financially just about anything you want it to. If you want appreciation, tax shelter, equity buildup, or cash flow, or any combination of these, you can find a formula that will solve your needs. But you have to be specific. If you want appreciation, choose formulas that are suited for appreciation. If you want cash flow, you need to use cash-flow formulas. The mistake most investors make is using appreciation formulas when what they really need is cash flow.

The Cash-Poor Investor

Take, for example, the case of a beginning cash-poor investor. He can barely keep his nose above water, couldn't even think of handling a negative cash flow, and would be devastated by any unexpected expenditure such as a major roof repair. And despite these strikes against him, he buys big chunks of real estate hoping for the big long-term bucks when it is those short-term bucks that hold the key to his success or failure. He doesn't need $1 million in five years. He needs an extra $500 per month now. And when he has *this* problem solved, maybe he will be in the right frame of mind to think about the future.

Perhaps a better approach is for a cash-poor investor to take things one step at a time. Rather than marching out into the cold, cruel world of investments to make a quick fortune, he should look upon his real estate operations as a sort of part-time job with a goal to have his real estate activities generate monthly cash flow. (You'll notice I didn't say "investments.") Generally, this person wants a comfortable cushion of monthly cash flow plus a few small chunks of cash to be used later in his investment program. The primary goal is to generate cash or cash flow to enhance the financial strength and stability of the investor (I really should say "employee").

I am trying to make the distinction between "investor" and "employee" to reinforce the fact that real estate is technically not an investment; it is a business. And those who treat it like an active hands-on business generally prosper, while those who treat it like a passive armchair investment are the ones who moan and groan the loudest about how lousy real estate is as an investment. It is lousy as an investment, but it is simply marvelous as a business. (I hope that doesn't confuse anyone.)

Therefore, let me catalog a few of the many cash-flow-generating techniques and formulas that are available. Go for the cash flow first, then build up a cash pool, and when you are ready you can go for the capital gains.

To make this a little more realistic and useful to you, let's assume that you are a cash-poor investor (who isn't?) with a steady job and fairly good credit rating. You are living from paycheck to paycheck. You want to invest in real estate, but don't dare because you don't have much margin for error. You would feel more comfortable if you had $10,000 in cash and $400 or $500 per month surplus income.

Question: How could you use your knowledge of real estate investing to help you reach your comfortable cash-flow goals within a six-month period of time?

Let's try it.

ROBERT G. ALLEN

The first step is to write down our goals. Let's get the subconscious mind on our side.

Second, devise a plan. There are five major ways to squeeze cash or cash flow from real estate:

1. Buy it right and lease it out.
2. Buy it right and sell it.
3. Lease it right and sublet it.
4. Option it right and sell the option.
5. Buy discounted paper right and sell it.

The essence of all of these cash-flow-generating categories is becoming an expert in finding bargains, wholesale situations, and remarketing those bargains to the public at retail. That's what free enterprises is all about.

Let's examine each one in turn.

1. Buy it right and lease it out.

What do I mean by "buy it right"? In order for you to buy a home, for instance, and have a positive cash flow of at least $500 per month, you would need a perfect combination of the following ingredients:

- Low price
- Low interest rates on mortgages, and or
- Deferred payments on mortgages
- High rent-to-value ratio

What is the probability that you will find an inexpensive home that you can buy for sixty cents on the dollar with nothing down that has a low-interest-rate, long-term assumable loan? Not very great. And this probability is reduced even further if you live in a city where housing prices have climbed through the roof (sorry for those of you living in cities like San Francisco, New York, Washington, D.C., Honolulu, etc.).

But this doesn't mean that finding a good buy is impossible. If you have chosen to buy wholesale properties and rent them out for cash flow (and you happen to live in areas of the country where this is more feasible), then you should gear up a program that will increase

240

the probability that you will be successful. Here are the six things I would do, if this were my formula:

- Become an expert in foreclosures. Visit every sale.
- Visit every bank, mortgage company, or credit union in your area and ask to speak to the person in charge of "real estate owned" or the bank repossession department. Ask to study the bank's portfolio of repossessed properties. Perhaps you can look at these properties online on the lender's website. Look for properties in lower price ranges that could be purchased below market with below-market financing offered by the lending institution.
- Make a thorough study of the rental market in your area. Learn what is in demand and what is not. Get a feel for what properties are renting for, what deposits are asked, and so on. The more you know, the easier you will find an opportunity that others may be missing—that area of the market which is in short supply, making the rents higher and the properties easier to rent out.
- Place an ad in the "Real Estate Wanted" classified section of the newspaper; state that you are in the market to buy property at full price on the condition of extremely flexible financing. Don't be disappointed if you have very few calls. You need to advertise. How can you catch fish if you don't have your bait in the water?
- Do a thorough study of prices in your city. How can you know what is wholesale if you don't know what retail is?
- Volume is the key. You may have to sift through a hundred properties before you find one that even comes close to your needs. All sources of properties should be combed. Websites with access to the multiple listing services, real estate agents, ads in the newspaper and driving around the area looking for "for sale by owner" signs.

2. Buy it right and sell it.

Once you have found a bargain property, you may decide not to rent it out for cash flow. You may choose to sell it. And if you sell it, you have two choices. You can sell it for a higher retail price and pocket the cash as your profit. Or you may decide to sell for full price with a small or no down payment and retain your profit in the form of a note with monthly cash flow coming to you over a period of years. There is no secret to this.

If I had decided to make the buying and selling of real estate for cash-flow profit, I would be sure to do the following:

1. Search out five of the top experts in your marketplace who are entrepreneurs in this area. Take them to lunch. Find out the details of their "cookie cutter" strategy.
2. Develop a list of investors to whom you can sell your properties. You may wish to start with real estate agents who deal with investor clients who are looking for good deals. Get in the habit of finding excellent buys that you can tie up for a few dollars (remember the chapter on options) and remarket to these investors for a small cash profit. The better the deal and the lower your markup, the faster you will be able to turn over your properties. And turnover is critical.
3. Advertise online and in the paper. You may even wish to include a clause in your purchase agreements that will give you ample time to market your properties before you close.
4. Set aside a fixed time each week to search for new properties.

A footnote to this approach: Check with your attorney or accountant to make sure your activities are in accord with local regulations and give you the greatest tax benefits.

3. Lease it right and sublet it.

Many beginning investors shun this approach because it doesn't involve ownership. But ownership is not what is critical. *Control* is critical. And when you have a lease on a property, you control it . . . at least partially.

For instance, let's suppose you locate a beautiful three-bedroom home that the owner has leased to a family for $900 per month. You have done your homework and know that the rent would be $1,100 per month on the open market. The seller is a don't-wanter who wants to get out of the rental business and is asking for just enough to cover his mortgage payment of $800. You tell him you will agree to a long-term lease of three years with the right to renew for two extra years at the rate he wants. The owner is thrilled to have the headache taken care of. You proceed to find a new tenant and sublet the property to him—for $1,000 a month. Notice that you don't charge full market rent. You charge less than market to attract a solid tenant who has an incentive to move in and stay there. The positive cash flow accrues to you in exchange for taking over the management of the property.

You can make this even more attractive by asking the seller of the property for a lease with an option to buy. By negotiating a good future purchase price, you can increase your profits. But the key to this formula is the cash flow. In essence, you are in business to find property that is underrented and rerent it for a profit.

If this formula interests you, you would do well to take the following steps:

1. Visit every rental property firm in your area. Establish relationships with these companies. They are looking for good rentals for their customers, who usually pay a fee for the service. You will need a ready source of renters for a fast rental of your units.
2. Become thoroughly familiar with the rental customs of your area. What are the best areas of town? Will people pay more for a furnished apartment? Are one-bedrooms more in demand than three-bedrooms?
3. Join the local Apartment Owners' Association. Learn all you can about tenant laws and rights that may affect your operations.
4. Study carefully the "Houses and Apartment for Rent" columns of the classified section of your local paper or rental website. Call on the new ads daily. If this is going to be your part-time job, you'd better be the best there is.

4. Option it right and sell your option.

In the chapter on options, I talk about a $30,000 profit I made on the sale of an option on a tract of ground. To recap briefly, I found an excellent piece of property that was owned by a major church. The church's board members had been trying to sell but had not generated the kind of offers they wanted. I was informed that for $2,500 option money they would give me the right to buy this four-acre parcel in one year for $200,000. It was in a prime location, I knew the area well, and I felt the price was low. I brought in a partner to put

243

up the $2,500 cash (nothing down to me, of course) and sold the parcel about nine months later to a developer for $275,000. The sellers received a better offer than they were able to generate by themselves, and I was able to split a $75,000 profit among my partners.

What made this profit possible? Of course, my knowledge of the value of property, my decision to act, and my ability to find a suitable buyer. If you want to make money in options, you should be prepared to comb the market for super bargains, have the money to tie up the properties you find, and be prepared to market the property you control up until the final bell. Options are a powerful tool, use them to maximize your investment leverage.

5. Buy discounted paper right and sell it.

To me, the field of discounted mortgages is one of the greatest opportunities for creating wealth in any field of real estate. Billions of dollars of owner-carried-back financing has been created in the past ten years. This means there will always be unwanted mortgages circulating on the discounted paper market.

How do you make money in discounted mortgages? The same way you make it in real estate. You hunt for bargains and don't-wanters. You negotiate for profit. For example, suppose you find the holder of a note with a face value of $100,000 who needs immediate cash instead of this steady income stream. How much cash would you, or your competitors, be willing to pay him for his note? Perhaps $75,000, maybe $60,000 or even $50,000 if the holder of the mortgage is desperate enough.

Study the market until you get a sense of the "going rate" for discounted notes. This can be very time-consuming because mortgages come in a wide variety of rates, terms, and payoff provisions. Some are adjustable, others carry balloon provisions—and you need to consider all these factors. For instance, a fully assumable fixed-rate $100,000 mortgage with twenty-five more years remaining is a very different kind of paper compared with a $100,000 mortgage that has a $50,000 balloon payment due next year.

Once you have a good sense of the market, you may want to find a partner or two who is seeking a higher rate of return. Together, you can make the note holder an offer he can't refuse—and you all walk away happy with the transaction!

Obviously this a complex subject, and you can learn more about it in my book *Creating Wealth* (call 801-852-8711 or visit www.robert allenrealestate.com). I just wanted to give you a taste and tell you how excited I am personally about this area.

As a summary, if your goal was making $10,000 plus an extra $500 a month income within a six-month period of time, how would you go about this now that we have reviewed the many areas of potential cash flow?

I would go immediately to a lease-option formula, placing emphasis on generating cash flow. I would attempt to find two houses in the lower price ranges that I could lease and sublet out for immediate cash flow. This would take two to three months.

Next, and perhaps simultaneously, I would look for bargain properties that could be bought and immediately rented out for cash flow. I would want to buy at a wholesale price to build up an immediate equity position to borrow against later. I would concentrate on finding one such property in a six-month period of time.

I would want to find, purchase, and resell three or four bargain properties purchased at least 20 percent below market and sold within a short period of time thereafter. Two of them would be sold for nothing down at 90 percent of the value, with the profit being carried back in the form of a note with monthly payments. For instance, suppose I found a house valued at $150,000 that could be bought using nothing-down techniques for $120,000. I would resell it for $135,000 (below market) with fantastic terms, retaining my profit in the form of a $15,000 second mortgage or interest in a wraparound. The payments on this note could bring in $150 or more per month. Three more deals like this and you would have $600 a month extra income from the second mortgages—and the ownership of $600,000 in real estate.

I hope this is helpful to those of you who have heretofore kept out of the real estate market because of those negative-cash-flow fears.

Especially for Investors Who Can Get Their Hands on $100,000 or More

Suppose you could get your hands on $100,000, what would you do with it? Let's just dream for a moment. Let's forget about where we are going to get this huge chunk of cash and start thinking about what you could do with it.

First of all, are there not hundreds of bargains in your city right now? You should be nodding your head in the affirmative.

Okay, if there are so many bargains, what should you be doing about it? Answer: If your goal is to create wealth for yourself and your family, you should be buying properties with both hands.

Will these bargains begin to dry up in the next few months? *Yes* and *no.*

There will always be bargains just as there will always be don't-wanters. Even in the best of times there will be bargains. They will just be harder to find and will require faster action.

Let me tell you what I would do with $100,000 if my goal was to triple my money within twelve months.

My first task would be to have a large poster printed up that read:

I will carefully invest my $100,000 so that on _____ , I will have my $100,000 back plus $300,000 equity in several pieces of prime real estate.

Robert G. Allen

Signed this first day of _____ .

I would tape this poster to the ceiling above my bed so that it would be a constant reminder as I went to bed and as I got up in the morning.

Second, I would get my money ready and liquid. Now, this is the hard part for a lot of people. Very few of us have $100,000 sitting in our bank accounts or money market funds. But many more of us have a large amount of equity in our homes that we can borrow against. If you've owned your home for more than a couple of years, you may well be able to get a home equity line of credit for $25,000, $50,000 or even the full $100,000 you want. Another option is to reduce your stock market portfolio—cashing out the "turkeys" and using that money to buy real estate.

Get a current appraisal (as cheaply as possible) on any of your other properties that you intend to use as collateral for obtaining necessary investment funds. I would recommend that you never borrow against any property you own and use the funds for investment purposes unless you do one of two things: either set aside enough money from the borrowing to make the payments on your new loan for at least twelve months, or be sure that you can handle the payment on the new loan from your current sources of income.

You should assume that you might not generate a single dollar of income from your real estate investments for at least twelve months.

And in both cases you had better be prepared to work like heck to make sure you are covered. Many of you have a high net worth, which allows you to borrow against your equities to generate investment capital. Should you refinance your properties with new first mortgages or get a second mortgage instead? If you have a low-rate mortgage, you can visit with your banker and have him set you up on a line of credit using your properties as collateral. The rate will probably be cheaper than other types of loans, and you can structure your line of credit to meet your needs. Those who have not taken the time to build relationships with bankers may have to resort to more expensive alternatives.

If you have followed my advice so far in this book, you should be doing business with at least two or three banks. The managers of each of these banks should be nurtured to a point where they feel comfortable lending you a minimum of $25,000 on your signature alone. Two of these loans could put you halfway to your $100,000 goal. Perhaps you could borrow the balance using your credit cards. These credit card lines should be left open just in case you have a quick need for cash during your twelve-month investment blitz.

For those who have neither cash nor the ability to borrow from conventional sources, the problem of raising $100,000 begins to get a bit sticky. As the old saying goes, you can borrow money only when you don't need it. The obvious alternative is to bring in partners who have the financial strength you need. To a beginning investor, the goal of raising $100,000 from unknown partners may seem both unrealistic and overwhelming. But as someone once said, "There's no such thing as an unrealistic goal. There's only an unrealistic time frame." So don't be discouraged by the task.

Start finding bargain properties while simultaneously looking for partners to help you finance them. After you have proved your bargain-finding ability to a partner or two—and have made them handsome profits—you won't have to worry about partners again. They'll come out of the woodwork to participate in the profit. Lower your sights to buying one or two excellent properties per year until you know what you are doing, and then you can raise your goals and lower your time frames.

The third step is to establish a strategy. With a twelve-month goal to create $300,000 in equity, you're not going to be planning on any appreciation. You're going to have to be buying properties at wholesale prices. The strategy then would consist of buying properties where every $1 you invest buys you $2 in hard equity. For instance, you may want to look for only one property. It could be an eight-unit apartment building worth at least $1.5 million that could be bought for $1.2 million with your $100,000 down and an assumption of the underlying $1.1 million existing loan. In the above case, you would be looking for a property that could be bought for 75 cents on the dollar—a wholesale buy.

It may take you a full year to find such a deal. But if you set your sights on that goal and go for it, I have no doubt you will reach it. You'll notice that I always like to buy such wholesale properties at least 20 to 25 percent below the current market value. Why? Remember our goal? We wanted to turn our $100,000 cash into $300,000 hard equity and still end up at the end of the year with our original investment cash back in our pockets so we can repay our loans to our bankers or partners. If we always buy at 20 to 25 percent below market, we have enough leeway to refinance our properties at the end of the first year so that the new loans will return our original investment funds to us.

For example, a graduate of my seminar recently told me of one of his highly rewarding purchases. He persuaded his father to become a partner with him in his real estate investments. His father's role was to provide the cash or the ability to borrow the cash to buy wholesale properties. The graduate was to provide the time and expertise in finding these wholesale opportunities.

Their first investment was a group of three small houses located in a Sunbelt city. The seller was advertising in the newspaper. He wasn't interested in any creative financing. He wanted all cash but would be flexible in price. The three houses, two two-bedroom units and one one-bedroom unit, were in good condition in an older area of town. The young graduate persisted with this seller, and they finally agreed upon a cash price of $30,000 for all three properties. (I know this sounds like ancient history, but this happened in the 1980s.) The graduate's father arranged for his banker to refinance the properties for $35,000, because the bank appraisal came in at $45,000. Since the three properties had a gross income of $850 per month, there was a positive cash flow of $100 to $150 per month. And the best part was that there really was no need for a cash down payment on the part of the father, only the ability to get a new loan.

In fact, the two happy investors pocketed over $4,000 cash from their first venture, plus $10,000 in hard equity in three positive-cash-flow properties. You can follow exactly the same approach using nothing down techniques in today's market.

Once you get a clear strategy mapped out, the fourth step is to start fishing for the bargains. It would be a good idea to have your hook in several ponds so that you assure yourself of the best selection of bargains. Put an ad in the "Real Estate Wanted" section saying you have $100,000 in cash that is looking for a home in a bargain-priced property. Email a similar note to ten or fifteen real estate offices or stop by and leave them your card. Tell them that you know that such bargains come along rarely, but that you are ready and financially able to close immediately on the right property. A few years ago just such a strategy netted me an excellent bargain property—and guess who the seller was? You guessed it: one of the real estate agents I had talked to that week. Scour the newspapers for those distressed-seller clues. Call the banks and savings and loan associations. Check and see if they have repossessed any properties lately that might fit into your plans.

Once the word gets out, the bargains will start coming to you.

What are you waiting for?

Good luck and God bless.

CHAPTER 28

Creative Self-employment: How to Retire in Five Years on a Tax-Free Income

"Not long ago, my wife and I were planning to retire, but had no income and very little money. We applied Robert Allen's real estate techniques, and now have four residential properties, one commercial foreclosure, seventy-five acres under development, a mortgage and loss mitigation company, and other assets. Our advice is simple: Believe, plan, do it, and simply follow the instructions!

—DON AND GAELLE FERGUSON

Forty-five-minute lunch hours.

Traffic jams in the mornings—and in the afternoons.

Working twice as hard as the guy in the next office for half the pay.

Punching a time clock.

Two measly weeks of vacation in return for fifty weeks of hard labor.

The incessant clang of the alarm clock.

Hand-to-mouth existence.

Shackled.

Aren't you sick of it all?

250

It's time for you to say good-bye to a job you don't enjoy. Use your knowledge of real estate and your creative abilities to become financially independent. The time is right. The opportunities are there. *You* can do it. You have been successful in your real estate investment program even though you were doing it on a part-time basis. Just think what would happen if you could devote yourself full time to it.

Declaring your financial independence by quitting your job is a lot like jumping off the edge of the world. Make sure you look before you leap—and consider the following elements:

Cash Flow

As soon as your last paycheck arrives, you are on your own. Unless you have established a monthly income stream from your investments, it won't be long before you will be in trouble. As a rule, you should not quit your job until you have at least six to twelve months of living-expense money in the bank (or until you have an adequate outside monthly cash flow). Remember, quitting your job is supposed to provide you with more time to cultivate your real estate investments. If you're not financially prepared, you'll waste your time worrying about money—or scrambling for money. Don't leap until you have a parachute of some sort, even if it's only a small umbrella. Can you imagine how embarrassing it would be if you had to come crawling back to your employer—all because you didn't plan your "escape" well enough and weren't prepared to handle cash-flow problems?

We'll never know how many prospectors closed their mines because they ran out of money when they were only days away from discovering a rich vein of gold. Don't let it happen to you. Have a one-year supply of either food or money on hand before you quit.

Office Space

If you have been used to working in an office that your boss provided for you free, you will be shocked to discover just how much it costs to rent and maintain your own commercial office space. You won't need much—perhaps a hundred square feet in a corner somewhere—but you'll need something.

Another, more affordable option is to work out of your home—an increasingly popular solution for solo entrepreneurs and investors in recent years. Chances are you have space in your home that could be devoted to your new business. You will need room for a desk, a computer and accessories, fax machine, and filing cabinet. Be sure to have a separate phone line installed for your investing activities, and get a high-speed Internet connection. Explain to your spouse and children that this is your working space so you can concentrate on business without being interrupted. If you are doing your job, you will be out of the office most days looking at real estate, but there will be times when you'll need a quiet place to concentrate. Do what seems best for you.

Time Management

If you have trouble managing your time, you will find all kinds of excuses not to be out there looking at properties and talking to sellers all day long. It takes tremendous discipline to overcome a streak of laziness or fear. Set rigid goals for yourself on a daily basis: "I'll visit ten homes or apartment buildings today. I'll present five offers today. I'll buy something today. I'll talk to ten real estate agents today. I'll read up and study today." I recently read a story about an investor who woke up one morning and decided to see just how much money he could make that day from dawn to dusk. He began his search, located a property, tied up the property with an option, sold the option to a group of investors—all within the prescribed time limit—and netted for himself over $2 million.

Loss of Company Benefits

When you go out on your own, you will probably leave behind a health insurance program, some kind of retirement benefits, the use of the company car, and all those other goodies that come with the corporate life. These are called "golden handcuffs," and more than one potential investor has not answered the knock of opportunity because of them. These benefits are designed especially to keep the best employees from moving on to other jobs. They are meant to shackle you. You must recognize them for what they are: the bars that invisibly keep you a prisoner in a job that makes you unhappy.

Lack of Borrowing Power

As soon as you quit your secure, steady-paying job, you are also cutting yourself off from the help of the bank. If you are planning any refinancing of properties or borrowing for down payments, you will be wise to do as much of it as you can *before* you quit your job. After you quit you will have to rely on partners with strong financial statements to help you until you are strong enough on your own.

Okay. So there are some disadvantages. You can counter them with adequate planning and conservative judgment if you are aware of the disadvantages and you are determined to overcome them.

There are also some huge pluses.

Time

All day long—every day, if you wish—you can be free to seek your fortune however you wish. That's the biggest plus of them all. No longer will you have to "push someone else's pencil." You will be amazed at how quickly your net worth increases when you work full time at it. A sense of accomplishment will swell inside of you until you feel like bursting. You will be building your own empire instead of building someone else's. You will be leaving a legacy to your loved ones. This sense of freedom was the foundation upon which our great nation was built. Fifty-six brave men signed their own death warrants when they affixed their names to the Declaration of Independence in 1776. Where would we be now if they hadn't? The freedom to spend one's time in whatever manner one wishes is sacred. Don't let someone deprive you of it.

Money

The risks of self-employment are tremendous, but the rewards are well worth the trouble. When the money starts to flow, it will come in larger amounts than you had thought possible. In the meantime, hang on—by your fingernails if necessary. Stay rational. Don't make any hasty decisions.

You must realize that in order to increase your ultimate financial freedom you will have to cut back on your expenditures for a short period of time. As the following chart illustrates, when you become your own boss, your standard of living sometimes has to be adjusted downward in comparison to your neighbors. They keep spending rather than saving or investing. On the other hand, you must learn to sacrifice immediate pleasures for the long-range satisfaction that financial independence provides. There is no other way. You either pay the price now for a short period of time (and live the rest of

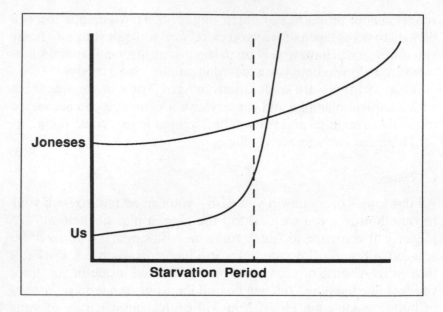

your life in financial independence) or you pay the price later, when you reach retirement age with virtually nothing in the bank. Do you want to rely on a modest social security check for the rest of your days? It's your choice.

Up to where the lines cross on the chart, your lifestyle is lower than the neighbor's because you have chosen to take a gamble and to invest full time in real estate. The "starvation period" won't last long. After the lines cross, you will be financially independent and heading for a secure retirement. Your neighbor will still struggle. You won't.

A ship in a harbor is safe, but that's not what ships were built for. What were *you* built for? Think about it as you drive to work tomorrow morning.

Security

Security? That's right. Security for the future—security that your wise investments of today will afford you a great deal more security than the retirement program you're now paying into. Security that says your income will always keep pace with inflation. It's a solid kind of security, better than the "security" of having a steady, albeit small, income.

What can you do to make your independent experience successful? That means providing enough cash flow to meet your living expenses, and continuing your investment program. Let's look at how you might obtain such a cash flow.

Plan #1. Buy low, sell for nothing down with high price.

This consists of finding an undervalued property that is also available for a small down payment. These kinds of properties are difficult but not impossible to find. They are generally those that require quite a bit of fix-up and cosmetic work. Buy the property, clean it up, and sell it for a nice profit. You might do something like this:

Two-Unit Apartment Building

YOUR PURCHASE PRICE	SALES INFORMATION
Cost: $150,000	Sales price: $220,000
Down payment: $30,000	Down payment: $50,000
Mortgage: $120,000	Mortgage: $170,000
Monthly loan payment: $850	Monthly loan payment: $1,200
Fix-up expenses: $10,000	Net to you: $10,000 cash
Total cash outlay: $40,000	You will also receive the difference between the old and new loans: $350 a month

This $350 cash flow comes in each month and gives you a source to help you with living expenses. You still have $50,000 in capital from the buyer's down payment that you can invest in another project. If you "roll your money over" several times like this, you might be able to generate enough cash flow from your properties to give you the courage to quit your job and devote full time to your real estate ventures. As I mentioned in the chapter on conversions, on one project alone my partner and I were able to create a cash flow for ourselves of almost $1,000 per month by converting a small ten-unit apartment building into condominiums. We bought low and sold high and kept the profit in the form of a steady monthly cash flow.

Plan #2. Triple net lease.

If you are just starting out and you would like to delay buying real estate until you know the ropes, try the triple net lease approach to making a steady monthly cash flow. You simply need to approach owners of apartment buildings or office space in your area who are tired of managing their properties. You tell them that you will pay them a certain guaranteed income from their properties if they will allow you the privilege of operating their building for them.

For instance, suppose you find an elderly gentleman who has owned and operated a twelve-unit building for twenty years, owns it free and clear, and does not have the time or energy to manage his property anymore. He doesn't want to sell it, and he doesn't know management firms exist. Your main selling point would be to relieve him of his headache and give him a guaranteed, steady, hassle-free cash flow each month. If the building rents for $9,000 a month ($750 an apartment) and the expenses are running at 40 percent of the gross income—about $3,600 a month—then he normally receives about $5,400 a month net cash flow before taxes. Offer him a net $5,000 a month for a five-year lease on his apartment building. This would give you $400 a month for your management efforts in the first year. In later years, as rents increase and you are able to keep expenses to a minimum, you might get up to $1,000 a month from your lease contract.

This income will not come without some work on your part. You will have to keep the units rented at all times and take care of maintenance problems. But once you understand the building and how to run it efficiently, you can turn it over to one of the building tenants in exchange for a partial rent reduction. Then you can keep the excess income and spend your precious time on other projects.

The leasing of single-family residences with options to buy (as discussed in the chapter on options) can also provide additional monthly income. I have heard of some investors who have taken the technique seriously and have leased dozens of houses with a small monthly cash flow. A portfolio of nine or ten leased houses could possible generate enough positive cash flow to support a modest living budget for the potential full-time investor.

Plan #3. Buy low, sell high—all cash.

In real estate, a smart investor can make as much money in one transaction as the average American makes working for fifty weeks a year at a job (that he can't stand, I might add). The skill comes in recognizing which property has potential and which property does not. The more you know your real estate marketplace, the easier it will be to recognize the "once-in-a-lifetime deals" that seem to pop up about every other week. In this book I have given examples of buyers who have made tens of thousands of dollars in only *one* transaction in less than a year's time. These are not isolated examples. They are happening every day—around you, in front of your very eyes. On your way to work each morning you are driving by dozens of properties that are crying out for someone with vision and courage to buy them. The next move is yours.

Let's go through a quick example. Suppose you are working nine to five at a job you do not love. You agree with the principle of becoming your own boss but realize that you don't have any money saved up to make the break on your own. You begin studying and researching the real estate market to find out how it operates. At this point, you should be looking for a property that needs some minor cosmetic repair—a "sleeper" that most people have overlooked because of its condition. Suppose you locate a run-down single-family house (the worst house in the best average neighborhood) in a community where home prices are still highly affordable. Let's say the home has a price tag of $130,000 with a down payment of $15,000. With a little work, you determine that it could be placed back on the market for $160,000 with the buyer obtaining a new loan to cash you out. You tie the property up and use one of the techniques outlined in this book to come up with the cash. Then you begin to make the necessary improvements. Since you do a lot of the work yourself, the fix-up job is completed in about three months at a total cost of $5,000. At this point you have $20,000 invested in the property. You place the property back on the market, listed at $160,000. Six months later the building closes and you receive a check for $30,000 for your equity. Subtract the $15,000 for the original down payment and the $5,000 you needed to fix up the home, and you have a net profit of $10,000—that's a 50 percent return on your investments. Plus you have all your original money back ready to go to work for you again. That's not bad for a few extra hours and a part-time effort.

If you look at what you accomplished with only minimal effort, you may begin to ask yourself, "Why don't I do this full time?" Remember, you will need a cushion to start with. It should be adequate to keep you alive for a year until you locate your next property and turn it over for another profit. One cardinal rule to remember is that each time you sell a property for a profit, you should always try to buy a property to keep. Take a portion of your earnings and reinvest it in another property, which you will leave in your portfolio for long-term growth. If you follow this pattern, it won't be long before your money worries will be gone forever.

Plan #4. For property owners only.

If you have property that you've owned for some time, you might be lucky enough to have a cash flow already from your units. If you raise rents regularly on a competitive basis, there will come a time when the building will generate a rather substantial monthly cash flow. There are two other ways to realize cash from properties you already own: refinance the property and reinvest the profit, or sell the property. But why should you sell your property if you don't have to?

Let's look at a really exciting prospect: retirement in five years with a tax-free income, without selling your property.

Of all the formulas mentioned in this book, this one has the most promise, is the easiest to accomplish, and requires the least amount of time.

This plan centers on single-family residences. Why? Because they are in the greatest supply; most people understand the methods of home purchasing because they've gone through the process at least once. And single-family residences are usually easiest to buy for the small investor. (Of course, you can work this same plan with any investment medium, but for our purposes we will discuss only single-family residences. You may apply the principles any way that will benefit you the most.)

Suppose you were able to devote one full day a week—say, Saturdays—to looking for real estate investments. Since you have fifty-two Saturdays a year, you should be able to find and purchase just *one* property, one small home valued at $100,000, from a seller who is anxious to sell and will accept an $85,000 price with a $5,000 down payment. This will take some looking, but remember you have a year to find it. When you find the right property, buy it. If necessary, borrow the down payment using one of the creative methods discussed earlier in this book. Then rent the house.

The next year, do exactly the same thing. Buy just *one* property priced at least 15 percent below market value with a small down payment. Again, rent the house; you'll have to be able to rent the house for enough money to cover mortgage payments, including taxes and insurance. The tenants will pay all utility bills and minor maintenance bills. In the first year or so the rental income will be light, but after several years you will begin to experience a steady positive cash flow.

In the third year, do the same thing. And so on until the fifth year, when you'll own five rental houses, all rented out, with no negative cash flow. If you have chosen the properties well, you should enjoy 5 to 10 percent yearly appreciation on each house.

Let's look at our equity position in five years in these five houses, assuming each was priced at $100,000 and the value has grown by 10 percent a year (all figures are rounded to the nearest thousand):

	HOUSE #1	HOUSE #2	HOUSE #3	HOUSE #4	HOUSE #5
Value	$161,000	$146,000	$133,000	$121,000	$110,000
Loans	$76,000	$77,000	$78,000	$79,000	$80,000
Equity	$85,000	$69,000	$55,000	$42,000	$30,000

In just five years, your total equity in the five properties has grown to $281,000! So, does this mean it's time to sell? No. You refinance. And you attempt to find the highest possible loan on your properties. Help yourself to do just that. Paint the trim on the houses, maintain the yard, or consider new carpeting or draperies. You might even paint the interior throughout the entire house. Do as much as possible with as little money as possible. Your aim is to get the highest appraisal possible for your invested cosmetic dollar.

"Then do your homework. Be prepared to convince the appraiser that the value of the house has increased steadily over the past five years. If you are able to obtain a new loan of 80 percent of the value of the appraisal, you should be able to refinance your first property for at least $129,000.

If your existing loan is $76,000, your net proceeds from the new loan will be $53,000, less any loan fees. That equity belongs to you. Can you now rent the property for enough to make the mortgage payment? A mortgage payment on a $129,000 mortgage at 7 percent interest for thirty years would amount to $858 plus taxes and insurance—perhaps as much as $1,200 a month total. Sound impossible? Remember, you're looking at rents five years down the road; they're bound to be considerably higher.

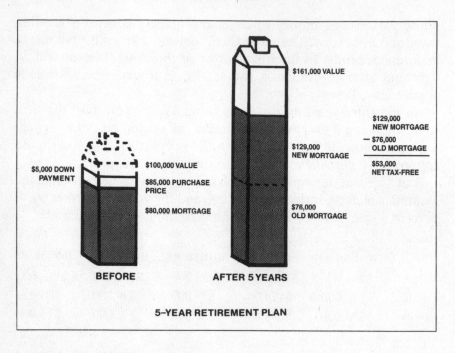

$161,000 VALUE

$129,000
NEW MORTGAGE

— $76,000
OLD MORTGAGE

$53,000
NET TAX-FREE

$129,000
NEW MORTGAGE

$5,000 DOWN
PAYMENT

$100,000 VALUE

$85,000 PURCHASE
PRICE

$80,000 MORTGAGE

$76,000
OLD MORTGAGE

BEFORE

AFTER 5 YEARS

5–YEAR RETIREMENT PLAN

Still uncomfortable? Hold out $8,000 from your refinance profits. That will give you $666 a month for twelve months to apply toward the mortgage payment as you look to raise rents. You'll still have $40,000 left over to spend as you want to, *and it's tax-free.* Kick off your shoes and pursue a full-time real estate investment hobby. In the sixth year of your program, the second investment house is now ready for refinancing after you have experienced five full years of appreciation.

Do this with one house each year. Refinance in January, and you're set for the year.

Is your program finished after you have refinanced the fifth investment house (in the tenth year)? Of course not! Your very first house, which you refinanced (harvested) in the fifth year of your program, has now had five more years to grow a new crop. It's ready to be harvested once more. And so you start all over again. Ad infinitum.

If you want to retire with an even higher income—insurance against inflation—buy *two* houses a year. Then, start refinancing *two* houses a year. It's twice the work, but it will be twice the income. And you'll still have plenty of time for your new hobbies and lifestyle.

Now, what if don't think properties will appreciate at 10 percent a year for the foreseeable future? Change your strategy. Buy properties in foreclosure where you pay sometimes sixty to seventy cents on the dollar. Go the fix-up route. It's up to you. But either way there is a viable way of retiring in just a few years.

Apply these solutions. Commit yourself to a lifestyle that will afford you ultimate freedom and security. Begin planning now for the day you will walk up to your boss with a smile on your face and a letter of resignation in your hand. Dream about it. Plan for it. Make your goal specific; mark the day on your calendar. Do these things faithfully, and you will reach your goal. You're one step closer just by deciding to do it!

Your goal might seem unusual to some, and there will undoubtedly be those who will try to deter you from your course, just as there were those who tried to talk Columbus out of sailing for the New World. Thank heaven he did. And you'll thank heaven you did. Take the road less traveled—it *will* make all the difference!

I'd like to thank Jack Miller and John Schaub for sharing the basic idea for the five-year retirement plan in their nationwide seminar entitled "Making It Big on Little Deals."

CHAPTER 29

Fear: The Ugliest Four-Letter Word

"Fear is our biggest block. Visualize your fear being solved in the other dimension and you will see it's all an illusion!"

—WALTER HOLTSCHI

As you near the end of this book and prepare to begin investing in real estate, there's something you must come to grips with: fear.

In these pages I've stressed the advantages of creating a highly leveraged position: purchasing the most real estate possible with the least amount of cash. I've shown you how to invest in real estate with little or none of your own money. This kind of program works, but it requires that you build a mountain of debt. Unfortunately, that can be scary. It can breed fear. And fear is the ugliest four-letter word in the English language.

Fear can stop you cold. It can clutch at all your good resolves and send you, trembling, to hide from your goals. It can keep you trapped in a job that you hate or in one that is getting you nowhere.

There are eight reasons why people don't achieve success, why they don't reach their goals. And all stem from fear. Let's look at them, and what to do about them.

1. A Confused Mind Always Says No!

If you are confused about how you are going to be able to accomplish your goals, you won't accomplish them. Fear and confusion are the exact opposite of faith and confidence. Without faith and confidence you have a less than one in ten chance of reaching your goals. You can't reach them because you don't think you can.

Get your thinking straight. Think your program through. Reduce your goals to single components that will seem more realistic. Read more, study more, and then get out there and get your feet wet.

2. The Paralysis of Analysis

When a child is afraid of the dark, he usually thinks some scaly monster is hiding under the bed, ready to grab and strangle him. The only solution is to turn on the light and get the child to look under the bed.

There's an adult component, but it doesn't work as well. It says that if you're afraid, read up. A certain amount of reading is good, because it helps eliminate confusion. But don't get paralyzed. In other words, don't read *too* much. Get out and do something.

3. Procrastination

If you keep putting things off, you'll never get anywhere. Don't laugh. Procrastination is not funny. It can get you into hot water. What's worse, it can get you nowhere. Fast.

Ask yourself, "What are the consequences of my inaction?" Every day you are growing poorer—because of inflation—when every day you could be growing richer—because of real estate investments.

Go on, chart it out if you have to. Draw a picture of how much buying power you're losing right now. Then draw a picture of how much money you could be earning through an investment, even a small one, in real estate. Then get your act together; get out and do something.

4. The Conservative Investor

I ran across a friend one day who was lamenting his financial situation. It seems he couldn't quite decide on "the right investment."

"I wish I had your guts," he sighed.

It doesn't take guts. It takes brains. Real estate is a smart investment.

Don't worry about "gambling" on a real estate investment. The worst gamble of all is to be conservative and to talk yourself out of investing. It is foolishness to play a "waiting game," looking only for the one perfect investment.

5. Fear That the Economy Will Fail

When Boeing laid off thousands of employees in Seattle some years ago, someone placed a billboard along a thoroughfare that read, "Will the last person to leave Seattle please turn off the lights?" The banks had such problems with delinquent mortgage payments on homes and apartments that they foreclosed buildings right and left and offered them to any investor who could come along and pick up the mortgage payment with no down payments. Along came Microsoft and dozens of technology companies, and the Seattle area rebounded. Homes and apartments are full again. And those investors became very rich people.

But for the benefit of any pessimists reading this book, I'll say this: What do you lose if there is a crash?

Nothing.

That's all you had when you began. That's all you invested into each building you purchased along the way. You bought with nothing or very little down.

Most important, you gained experience. So what if there's a crash? You've lost nothing. And when things pick up again, you've got the experience, the know-how, to take advantage of low prices and great availability.

Then you've got everything to gain.

So get out there and do it! Don't be like Chicken Little, fretting about the barnyard and announcing "The sky is falling!" You might be right, but you might be wrong. There is always a chance of an economic downturn; if you let fear paralyze you, there's a 100 percent chance that you'll never reach your financial goals. It's simply a matter of placing your bet on the most likely thing.

6. Head-in-the-Sand Syndrome

People who are afraid to do anything do nothing. And so they get nowhere, which is really where they wanted to be in the first place.

They'd rather stand around all day with their heads in the sand. It's more comfortable that way. They don't have to think much. Enough said.

7. Fear of Asking for What You Want

Some people are afraid of asking for a bank loan. Afraid of making an offer on a piece of property. Afraid of buying the unknown. Afraid of talking to sellers. Afraid of asking for what they want.

Try this: Walk up to a friend. Ask him to raise his right hand high into the air. Then ask him to touch the tip of his left ear with the forefinger of his outstretched hand.

He'll do it. It's amazing what people will do if you ask them.

Remember this: You'll never know until you ask. The worst thing that can happen is that someone will say no. That never hurt any-one. The best thing that can happen? The sky is the limit. You've got the world to gain and nothing to lose.

Get out there and do it!

8. Fear of Being Wealthy

Sounds absurd, doesn't it? Replace that fear with a fear of being poor. You can become wealthy with as much or as little effort as it takes to be poor. Remember, financial bondage is *not* fun.

You've got the knowledge. Do your homework: set up your goals, find some good properties, negotiate, buy. Every time you go through that process you come one step closing to financial inde-pendence. You become a little more secure. You've got what it takes. The only thing that can hold you back now is fear. And you're a much better person than that.

I challenge you to quit stalling your financial freedom until it is everlastingly too late. I challenge you to commit yourself to buying at least one property each year until you reach your financial goal. Others have done it. So can you.

Go out and do it!

The Reluctant Investor

I hesitate to make a list.
Of all the countless deals I've missed;
Bonanzas that were in my grip—
I watched them through my fingers slip;

265

The windfalls which I should have bought
Were lost because I overthought;
I thought of this, I thought of that,
I could have sworn I smelled a rat,
And while I thought things over twice
Another grabbed them at the price.
It seems I always hesitate,
Then make my mind up much too late.
A very caution man am I
And that is why I never buy.
When tracks rose high on Sixth and Third,
The prices asked, I felt absurd;
Those blockfronts—bleak and black with soot—
Were priced at thirty bucks a foot!
I wouldn't even make a bid,
But others did—yes, others did!
When Tucson was cheap desert land,
I could have had a heap of sand;
When Phoenix was the place to buy,
I thought the climate was too dry;
"Invest in Dallas—that's the spot!"
My sixth sense warned me I should not.
A very prudent man am I
And that is why I never buy.
How Nassau and how Suffolk grew!
North Jersey! Staten Island, too!
When others culled those sprawling farms
And welcomed deals with open arms . . .
A corner here, ten acres there,
Compounding values year by year,
I chose to think and as I thought,
They bought the deals I should have bought.
The golden chances I had then
Are lost and will not come again.
Today I cannot be enticed
For everything's so overpriced.
The deals of yesteryear are dead;
The market's soft—and so's my head.

Last night I had a fearful dream,
I know I wakened with a scream:
Some Indians approached my bed—
For trinkets on the barrelhead
(In dollar bills worth twenty-four
And nothing less and nothing more)
They'd sell Manhattan Isle to me.
The most I'd go was twenty-three.
The redmen scowled: "Not on a bet!"
And sold to Peter Minuit.

At times a teardrop drowns my eye
For deals I had, but did not buy;
And now life's saddest words I pen—
"IF ONLY I'D INVESTED THEN!"

—DONALD M. WEILL

When he is not writing light verse, Don Weill is a broker and senior vice president of Helmsley-Noyes Company, Inc. The above poem was reprinted from the book *The Reluctant Investor and Other Light Verse,* which can be purchased through the author, c/o Helmsley-Noyes Company, Inc., 20 Broad Street, New York, NY 10005.

CHAPTER 30

Creating Wealth with Real Estate

"To be who we are, and to become who we are capable of becoming, is the only end of life."

—ROBERT LOUIS STEVENSON

Where will you be ten years from today? Will you arrive in style? I know you're hoping for the best. But hope isn't enough, is it? You've got to make a plan, build it upon a solid foundation and stick with it on your way to a brighter, more prosperous future. As my friend Bill Martin says, "In ten years you will have arrived. The question is, where?"

Real estate can be the key to unlocking true success in your life. I firmly believe that the book you now hold in your hand can give you the tools you need . . . my very own, proven strategies for truly Creating Wealth with Real Estate.

Now that you've read this book, there are seven distinct steps you need to take to put all that you've learned into successful action. I call these the seven critical steps.

Step 1. Build on a Solid Foundation

Since you'll be growing rapidly and taking calculated risks in the years ahead, you need to sink your roots deep in preparation for the squalls and storms ahead. Imagine a flat, level site upon which to build your wealth skyscraper. The stronger the foundation, the more enduring your monument. A strong foundation consists of six components—six scarce resources which each of us has to learn how to manage:

Body
Brain
Being
Time
People
Money

In this life, our task is to gain mastery over these six scarce resources. All great failures stem from mismanaging one or more of them. All great successes are the result of wisely mastering them. Let's briefly discuss each of these resources.

Body. Do you have a regular exercise program? A significantly large percentage of the top executives of Fortune 500 companies take time out of their busy schedules for regular, prudent exercise. They can't afford not to. It helps them to think more clearly and creatively, to work longer and more productive hours while keeping themselves healthier and happier. Is this one of the secrets to success? I think so.

Brain. Do you make time for regular intellectual exercise? Do you have a regular study program? Do you set aside a regular time for reviewing your game plan? Are you a positive thinker? Do you monitor your self-talk during the day? Notice how often your internal self-talk is negative. Consciously practice replacing your negative self-talk with a more positive voice. Remember what we discussed in the chapter about Neurobics. Do it daily.

Being. is your character, which is made up of the principles that guide your life. Television has inaccurately stereotyped American businesspeople as greedy, shallow, and unprincipled. In my experience, just the opposite is true. Most businesspeople are decent, hardworking, and motivated by the highest of the traditional American values. Unfortunately, however, there are some who will do almost anything to "get rich quick." They are motivated by a different set of values. In the lists below, I show the distinction between the principles of the get-rich-quick myth and the principles of what I call "Real Wealth." In my opinion, the shortest and safest passage to prosperity is through the principles of Real Wealth.

GET RICH QUICK	REAL WEALTH
Having	Being
Capital	Character
Possessions	Purpose
Power	Love
Fear	Faith
Compromise	Integrity
Obsession	Balance
Mediocrity	Excellence
Imitation	Intuition

In addition to values, Being is also about purpose—who you are as a person and what you hope to achieve. Are you an entrepreneur? Do you love the challenge and risk of business? Do you enjoy controlling your own destiny? Are you willing to put up with the insecurity of being your own boss? Do you have the talent and intuition for business? Do you love to negotiate? Are you enthusiastic about real estate investments? Would you like to eventually be a full-time investor? If not, maybe real estate isn't for you. Think about it.

Time. Are you organized? How well do you control your time? Are you focused enough to withstand the allure of instant gratification? Are you organized enough to find ten extra hours a week to devote to your real estate game plan? Can you consistently do this week in and week out?

People. Real estate is not just a business of numbers and buildings. It's a business of solving people's problems. If people trust you easily, the world is your blank check. The more clearly you understand this, the more powerful you will become. Also, does your family support you? Do you have supportive friends? The stronger your support network, the safer your journey to the top.

Money. An assault up the money mountain will require that you become relatively stable financially. The more stable you are before you mount your assault on the money mountain, the better. Read the following questions and notice which ones hit you in the pit of the stomach. Become determined to strengthen yourself in your areas of weakness:

- Do you have a steady, stable job?
- How good are you at managing your money?
- Are you under severe financial pressure?
- Can you handle more pressure or should you get your financial act together first?
- Are you adequately insured?
- Do you maintain orderly checking and savings accounts?
- Can you save?
- Do you have a "rainy day" account?
- Have you prepared a complete financial statement?
- How is your credit?
- Are you saving your extra cash or spending it immediately?

Where do we learn how to juggle these six resources? Not in school or university. It's just assumed that we'll learn them in the school of hard knocks. If you are strong and balanced in the above six areas of your life, life won't knock you as hard.

This is your foundation. Build it strong.

Step 2. Establish a Long-Term Intention

With a strong foundation in place, you're ready to set your long-term intention. What are you going to want ten years from today? The truth is, most of what you want won't change much in the next ten years. You'll still want a strong foundation—health, personal growth, great relationships, intellectual stimulation, and the satisfaction of being involved in many fulfilling and financially rewarding projects.

As long as you're balanced, fulfilled, generous to people less for-

271

tunate—humble enough to give credit to your Higher Power—then why shouldn't you be making a ton of money? (Have you ever wondered just how much money there is in a ton? How much is two thousand pounds of money? Suppose it takes five hundred one-dollar bills to equal one pound of weight. Then two thousand pounds of dollar bills would equal a cool $1 million!)

Let's get outrageous. Is it unrealistic to expect that you could be earning a "ton of money"—a million dollars or more—in just a few years? Why not? Hundreds of corporate executives earn that now. And what about the thousands of "on purpose" professional athletes, doctors, lawyers, and entrepreneurs? If it's possible for them today, why not for you?

Well, how do you do that? As my friend Zig Ziglar says, "You can have anything you want in life if you'll just help enough *other* people get what *they* want." The only way to earn a ton of money is to provide a ton of excellent professional service. You've got to be good. Darn good. But you've get ten years to accomplish that million-dollar goal.

So with balance, growth, satisfaction, humility, and the ability to earn a ton of money in our long-range sights, what's next?

Step 3. Establish a Short-Term Game Plan

The very next step is to divide your long-term intention into short-term, bite-size morsels. What is realistic for you in the next twelve months? If you're a novice, you'll be lucky to buy one property and profit from it. And that's after many hours of study, market research, and assiduous application.

You could do much better but, as I said, let's be realistic. I don't want to get your hopes so high that you'll be discouraged in the first few months. So set your sights a bit lower. Hunker down for the long haul. Believe me, it will be well worth it. In order to increase the probability of beginner's luck, here is what I expect from you in the first year:

- Twelve months of practical, prudent, profitable practice
- Yielding from one to four completed transactions
- Targeted to existing, small residential properties one to four units in size

- Priced in the bottom quartile of the market
- No more than fifty miles from your own home

In completing these one to four transactions, there are two broad approaches you will choose from: (1) QuickTurn approach, and (2) Portfolio-Builder approach.

With a QuickTurn approach, you focus on rapid turnover of your properties for short-term profit. The key to this strategy is learning how to market properties for maximum profit in the shortest amount of time with a minimum of investment.

With the Portfolio approach, you focus on buying properties wholesale, renting them out, and holding them for cash flow and long-term appreciation. Each year you'll add more properties to your growing portfolio of investments. The key to this strategy is learning how to manage properties for maximum cash flow with minimum hassle.

Either strategy can be excellent, but it depends on your target city, the neighborhood in that city, and your own personal preferences. However, during your first year in this business, no matter where you live, you should focus your attention on the QuickTurn strategy. Even in markets that are declining, the QuickTurn approach can be extremely profitable. Your goal should be to QuickTurn at least one and as many as four properties in order to generate immediate profit.

Thereafter, I would recommend that you broaden out to accumulate select, choice projects for long-term cash flow and appreciation. Eventually you will balance your activities between short-term profit-taking and long-term accumulating. The ratio of QuickTurn versus Portfolio building will depend on you.

All of this now leads us to a discussion of individual cities and where to invest in those cities for maximum profit during good times and bad.

Step 4. Create Your Own Treasure Map

As Diane Ravitch said, "The person who understands 'how' will always have a job. The person who understands 'why' will always be his boss." First, let's understand why your property is going to make you so much money, and then I'll show you exactly how to pull it off.

Within each city, price ranges and rates of growth differ dramatically from neighborhood to neighborhood. Why? Let's take a rough stab at the basics of why properties go up or down, and then you can be clear on why, where, when, and how you're going to buy your next profitable piece of property.

A quick lesson in economics. It all boils down to two words that affect your entire future: supply and demand. Entire books have been written on the subject, but when it's all said and done you have basically three great forces that substantially affect supply and demand:

- Economic forces
- Social forces
- Political forces

How do economic forces affect supply and demand? If jobs are prevalent and interest rates are relatively low, homes are in demand. If unemployment rises and or interest rates rise, demand shuts down. People sit on the sidelines. As soon as the economy picks up and/or interest rates decline, demand also picks up again— and the upward trend continues.

As for political forces that affect supply and demand, I will give you one fine example. In many communities, city governments try to slow growth and limit building permits. This directly affects supply. If the supply doesn't meet growing demand, more and more buyers compete for a dwindling number of properties. This forces prices upward unnaturally, and savvy real estate investors reap huge profits.

What social forces affect supply and demand? Let me give you one example: the rate of divorce. As families split up, the splintering groups each need adequate housing. If more families stayed together, there would be less demand for housing.

With these things in mind, pick a city—any city. Pick a city where you will most likely do the bulk of your investing over the next ten years. Perhaps it's the city where you now reside or a city you are planning to move to. Now, ask yourself these questions:

- What economic, political, and or social forces might affect demand for real estate in my target city?
- How might foreign competition affect local industries and thereby affect the rate of job creation?

- What political forces might cause interest rates to rise thereby lowering demand for housing in my city?
- What worldwide social trends might affect the supply and demand for property in my city?

You can't go on blindly assuming that things will continue forever as they are now. So you had better evaluate the ten-year forecast on industry and business in your target city. Spend some time at the chamber of commerce and other municipal agencies that project future growth.

Obviously, trends will be much more in your favor if you are living in a city with a diversified industrial base, excellent future job-creation potential, and a mild good climate. But even if your city is exactly the opposite, the potential for profit is tremendous depending on your strategy.

So in order to help you fine-tune your individual strategy, I would like you to make a rough, "stab-in-the-dark" guess at the ten-year economic prospects for your target city:

Green light—excellent prospects for solid growth
Yellow light—iffy, could go either way
Red light—most likely declining economic activity

Is your target city red, yellow, or green?

If it's red, there's not much reason to be accumulating property. Property values, because of waning demand, will be stagnant. There are only two reasons to build a portfolio in a red city:

- You're fairly certain that demand will dramatically increase in the foreseeable future, or
- Your strategy is to build solid long-term cash flows by buying larger apartment buildings.

Otherwise, you should stick to QuickTurn projects where you can buy substantially below market and take as long as you need to sell. More on this later.

If you give your target city a yellow rating, this indicates some caution. Sometimes a city experiences a deep economic slump the way Houston did in the late 1980s. Houston civic leaders were forced to attract new industry to broaden their economic base. By

1990, Houston was less dependent on the oil industry, and the prospects for real estate investment grew brighter. Sensing this, many of my seminar graduates moved their investment activities to Houston where between 1988 and 1990 they were able to buy fore-closed single-family homes from banks at unheard-of prices. They stockpiled these properties and are now being handsomely rewarded for their foresight and patience.

If your target city is rated green, you'll probably discover that because of high demand, bargain finding is difficult. At the same time, building a portfolio is also difficult because prices are rapidly escalating and sellers are rarely flexible. Still, the long-term prospects are excellent. Rents will most likely continue to increase, and there will always be a market for your property. Either strat-egy—QuickTurn or Portfolio building—is viable. You'll understand more in a moment when we study WealthTraks.

Now that you've color-coded your target city, I want you to get a map of your city and its outlying suburbs. You're going to begin color coding every area of your target city. For example, on my wall I have an excellent photo of San Diego, taken by satellite from 450 miles above the earth. It shows the growth patterns clearly while giving me the big picture of the neighborhoods in which I'll be investing.

Now, with this map, I want you to do some more in-depth sleuthing. Check with city hall or the local Board of Realtors and try to make growth projections of the various major areas in and around your target city. You might even color various territories in green, yellow, or red, depending on your rough guess about what might happen to property values in those neighborhoods. As you do this, let the following questions roll around in your mind:

- Will anyone want to own a property in this neighborhood in ten years?
- Why would anyone want to rent in this neighborhood?
- Will these become green and yellow zones or red zones?

By the end of this process, you'll be choosing several target neigh-borhoods or territories in your target city. You have created your own TreasureMap. The more informed you are on what is going on in your target territory, the better. Speculators are too lazy to do this kind of homework. They always end up paying too much for property in the wrong areas. You'll build your business on superior information, superior strategy, and superior execution.

With this piece of the puzzle complete, let's choose a WealthTrak.

Step 5. Choose Your WealthTrak

Let's review what you've done so far:

- You've strengthened your wealth foundation
- You've determined your long-term intention
- You've established a one-year, short-term game plan
- You've chosen a target city and created your TreasureMap of the target territory

Now you're ready to choose a specific WealthTrak. Whether you're accumulating or quick turning, each of the following WealthTraks is a way to create rapid equity in property.

Suppose you've found a property worth $250,000. The seller is flexible. How can you profit from it? There are at least five ways to profit from it quickly:

- You can rehab or fix it up
- You can convert it to a higher and better use
- You can creatively remarket it using excellent terms
- You can resell it into a rapidly appreciating marketplace
- You can buy it wholesale and remarket it at retail

Some quick numbers for cxample.

Rehab WealthTrak. You buy a property for $90,000, add $10,000 in cosmetic fix-up, add a bedroom or remodel the kitchen. Then you resell for $150,000, less carrying and closing costs.

Conversion WealthTrak. You buy a property for $150,000 and convert it from a single-family home to offices. Attorneys' fees and rehab come to $25,000. After you rerent to commercial tenants, you remarket the project to an investor for $275,000. The time frame is longer, costs are higher, and there is greater risk and red tape. But the profit makes it worthwhile. Your profit is $100,000, less carrying costs.

Creative Remarketing WealthTrak. Buy a bargain-priced property for $150,000 on good terms and immediately resell it for $160,000 for little or no money down with the buyer paying you your profit in the form of monthly payments on a second mortgage note secured by the property.

Appreciation WealthTrak. Buy a property for $150,000 on the front end of a fast-paced market. Return it to the market after minor cosmetic and landscaping improvements of $5,000. Resell it for $175,000. Your profit is $20,000 less closing and carrying costs.

Whole WealthTrak. Instead of buying properties at full market price, you shop for bargains. The faster the market pace, the fewer the bargains, but cash can always find a good deal. (Use OPM—other people's money—for your purchases so it's always nothing down to you.) You find an excellent buy from a bank's foreclosure portfolio. It hasn't sold to other speculators because of extensive deferred maintenance. You pay $60,000 cash, which you draw from your established bank line of credit. You determine that it will take less than $20,000 to bring the property to pristine perfection. You subcontract out the work and supervise the project while you are looking for other deals. The work takes four months and you put the property back on the market for $135,000. It sells for $125,000 and you pocket $45,000 less carrying costs.

Get the picture?

Review the WealthTraks. Which one strikes you? Which one causes you to say to yourself "That's me"? This is an important clue. Next, get your hands on as much information about your chosen WealthTrak as you can. Read books. Listen to tapes. Visit local investment clubs. Ask questions. Find the people in your city who are using your targeted WealthTrak. Take them to lunch. Pick their brains if possible. If they're tight-lipped, you can do some fairly simple detective work to learn how they're doing it. You can learn what kind of ads they run in the paper to find their deals. You can check at the county courthouse to uncover what they pay for their properties. You can question their employees to learn insider secrets. Research. Research. Research. That brings us to the next step.

Step 6. Closely Monitor Your Target Territory

Now that you've chosen your special WealthTrak, it's time to analyze your target territory even further. Some neighborhoods are more conducive to fix-up, appreciation, or wholesale bargains. The key to a QuickTurn strategy is to sell into a stable or strong market. If the market in your neighborhood is stagnant or weak, you'll have difficulty turning a fast profit. You may be forced to change your strategy to stockpile properties until a spurt of demand forces prices upward. Be careful. If you don't have staying power you'll bleed to death.

Since the localized demand cycle is so critical, I encourage you to do even more homework. Take the pulse of your target area frequently. Note the cycles of real estate demand. Become a regular visitor at your local Board of Realtors. Pore over as much data as it has. Here are some questions for which you should try to find consistent answers:

- How many properties exist in your target price range?
- How many of these properties are currently on the market?
- What is the average number of days these properties remain on the market before selling? (Clue: The longer the selling time, the slower the market.)
- How does this average selling time compare to previous years?
- What are the leading indicators of when the market is beginning to slow down?
- What is the current rate of appreciation of properties in your target price range and target territory?
- How does this compare to recent years? Why the difference?
- During which months do properties sell faster?

The reason you need this information is to be able to anticipate periods of rapid appreciation and to be able to forecast periods of stagnation and slow growth. You wouldn't want to be stockpiling properties at the top of a market. By the same token, you shouldn't try to QuickTurn properties in a severe downturn. Each of these mistakes could cost you precious time and money.

With this input, it's time for the final step.

Step 7. Implement Your WealthCycle

You've laid a firm foundation. You've established a long-term intention and a short-term game plan. In your game plan, you've targeted a city, a territory in that city, and a specific target property. You've

279

chosen a WealthTrak to specialize in. All there is to do now is to implement your WealthCycle. The WealthCycle consists of three skills that you will repeat over and over again in your investments. The three essential skills are:

Finding. You must develop an increasingly sophisticated system for generating leads for the properties you buy. The greater the competition, the more need for a finding system.

Funding. Today, the real estate field is becoming much more sophisticated. If you want to be a player, I recommend that you spend generous amounts of time locating partners to fund your projects. Your nothing-down strategy will be to use OPM. Sooner or later, you're going to have to become a professional fund-raiser.

Farming. This is my term for profiting from your purchases. If you are a Portfolio Builder, your main focus will be on landlording—managing your properties for maximum cash flow and appreciation. If you become a QuickTurn specialist, you'll have to develop special techniques for rapidly marketing your projects during good times and bad.

First you find, then you fund, and finally you farm. Each project requires that you complete each of the three stages of this WealthCycle. Each stage is important. The more times you complete this same WealthCycle, the wealthier you become.

Making a Ton of Money

Complete enough WealthCycles and it's very possible for you to earn literally a ton of money before ten years have passed. Let me show you how.

In your first year, you'll complete the WealthCycle at least once and hopefully four times. If each turn of the WealthCycle generates $10,000 in profit, it's entirely possible to earn between $25,000 and $50,000 in first-year profits.

Not bad for a novice!

As you begin your second year, you can either increase the number of revolutions of your WealthCycle—turn over more properties—or you can try to generate more profit per turn, generating $25,000 or more on each property. This could earn you between $50,000 and $100,000 in your second full year of your real estate investment profession. I have seen this happen many times with those who attend our Creating Wealth classes nationwide (call 801-852-8711 or visit www.robertallenrealestate.com).

In the third year, you can continue to "make it big on little deals," as my friend and colleague John Schaub taught me, or you may choose to challenge yourself with higher-level activities by branching out into development, new construction, larger apartment complexes, industrial or commercial projects, and mobile home parks. Each area will require an entirely different approach and will be accompanied by new risks and rewards. That's the beauty of real estate. It's so varied and exciting, you can literally choose the area that fulfills you the most.

In the fourth and fifth years, you should continue to turn several projects for quick profit while adding several projects to your portfolio for long-term appreciation. Even so, it's not unreasonable for you to be earning $200,000 to $300,000 per year. It's all a function of your superior information, strategy, and hard work.

With current QuickTurn projects providing chunks of cash, and accumulated properties providing increasing cash flow, a million-dollar-a-year income is entirely possible in just ten years.

Whatever path you take, I know you are serious about your financial future and I have a feeling that you and I will meet someday. I'll enjoy hearing about your success. Until then, keep in touch and let me know of any new real estate opportunities you come across.

Robert Allen
Robert Allen Real Estate
5072 North 300 West
Provo, UT 84604
Phone: 801-852-8711
www.robertallenrealestate.com

Have a great life! And happy hunting.

Appendix: Real Estate Information Websites

Here are selected national websites that contain helpful information for the real estate buyer, seller, and investor.

Robert Allen Institute
www.robertallenrealestate.com

National Association of Realtors
www.realtor.com

American Society of Appraisers
www.appraisers.org

Apartment Owners Association
www.apartmentownersassociation.com

Fannie Mae
www.fanniemae.com

Mortgage Bankers Association
www.mbaa.org

National Association of Home Builders
www.nahb.org

National Association of Mortgage Brokers
www.namb.org

National Association of Residential Property Managers
www.narpm.org

Society of Industrial and Office Realtors
www.sior.com

U.S. Federal Housing Authority (FHA)
www.hud.gov

U.S. Veterans Administration (VA)
www.va.gov

Index

Page numbers in *italics* refer to diagrams, charts, and forms.

capitalization rates:
  and determination of value, 93–96
  formula for, 94
  smaller properties and, 96
capital resources:
  overcoming lack of, 225–26
  see also cash-poor investors;
    loans; other people's money
cards, personal, 73
Carrey, Jim, 25
cash, effective nonuse vs. noneffec-
    tive use of, 119
cash deposits:
  defaults and, 118, 121
  not designated as earnest
    money, 121
  size of, 121
cash flow, 87–98
  Annual Property Operating
    Data form and, 76, *79*
  capitalization rate and, 95
  definition of, 88
  in five-unit apartment example, 88
  in five-year retirement plan, 251,
    255–61, *260*
  home equity loans and, 140–41
  investment strategies for, 238–45
  before taxes, 85
  see also negative cash flow
cash-poor investors, 238–45
Certified Commercial Investment
    Member (CCIM) designation,
    for real estate agents, 96
Chaplin, Charlie, 25
city planning departments:
  as source of market information,
    56
  as source of zoning information,
    214
classified ads, 97
  bargain-hunting through, 69–70,
    230
  as information source, 54, 61, 243

taking out your own, 70, 229,
    234–35, 236, 241, 249
closing dates, 121–22
closing officers, title companies
    acting as, 109
Cohen, Oseye, 238
collateral, 132, 135, 158, 246
  substitution of, 168
Columbus, Christopher, 5
commercial banks, *see* banks
commercial properties:
  conversions and, 213–14, *213,*
    215–17, *216*
  disadvantages of, 19
  experience and expertise
    required for, 20
commissions:
  of real estate agents, 57, 89,
    101–2, 127, 175–76, 236
  of real estate brokers, 100
Commitment form, 48, 50, *50–52*
company benefits, loss of, 252
Comparative Market Analysis
    Forms, 97, *98*
concentric circle theory, property
    value and, 56, *57*
condominium conversions, 217–19
Confidential Check List and Survey
    of Investment Objectives,
    38–41
confusion, "no" as result of, 116,
    136, 263
conservative investing, 263–64
Contract for Sale or Purchase, 118,
    126
contracts, 101
  see also Uniform Real Estate
    Contract
control, as more important than
    ownership, 242
conversions:
  of apartment buildings to office
    complexes, 215–17, *216*

conversions (*continued*)
  boom in, 211
  condominium, 217–19
  definition of, 211
  increased land values from,
    211–21, *213, 216*
  profit potential of, 212, 216–21
  reasons for, 212
  types of, 212–21
  WealthTrak through, 277
cosigners, for loans, 129
cost approach, to determination of
    value, 93
Coué, Emile, 48
counteroffers, 121, 124
county courthouses, as sources of
    information, 71–72
county recorder's office, 92
Craft, Nina, 139
cranking, second mortgages and,
    141–47, *143, 144, 146,* 171
Creating Wealth with Real Estate
    seminars, phone number and
    website for, 281
creative acquisition techniques:
  ignorance of, 230
  real estate agents' fear of, 102
creativity, 12–15
  process of, 12–13
  in raising investment capital,
    13–15
credit, home equity lines of, 140
credit losses, 80
credit ratings, 126, 127, 134–35,
    137–38
credit unions, 128, 132, 133
critical skills, 35–36

daily routines, 227
Davis, Erin L., 42
Davis, William C., 22
"deal killers," 107
deal-that-fell-through story, 67–68

debt service, total annual, 85
deep thinking, 14
defaults, cash deposits kept after,
    118, 121
definancing, 168
destiny, 27
Di Carli, Michael, 10
discounted paper, trading down
    payments for, 171
diversification, 232
divorce:
  "don't-wanters" and, 66, 71–72
  social effects of, 274
Dominguez, Kristen, 158
"don't-wanter" seller(s), 47–48,
    61–68, 97, 119, 202, 246
  author's experience as, 62–63
  creating paper and, 169–71, *170*
  deal-that-fell-through story,
    67–68
  definition of, 61
  difficulty in finding of, 229–30
  flyers distributed by, 73–74
  judging the situation, 68
  management problems and,
    62–65, 180, 197
  as necessary for Nothing Down
    deals, 90, 111, 115
  as percentage of all sellers,
    61–62
  personal problems and, 66–68,
    71–72
  shortsightedness of, 63
  small down payments and, 128
  yourself as, 231–37
double escrow, 194–95
down payments, *11,* 121, 126
  balloon, 181–83
  and creation of "alligator" prop-
    erties, 161
  creative sources for, 11–15
  deferring of, 185–86
  for first home purchase, 126–30

finance companies as, 133
mortgage brokers as, 131, 133
mortgage companies as, 131, 132–33
online lenders as, 131, 133–34
hard paper, definition of, 158
head-in-the-sand syndrome, 264–65
Helmsley-Noyes Company, 267
Holtschi, Walter, 262
home equity, 139–47
lines of credit and, 140
mortgage refinancing and, 140
options and, 191–92
second mortgages and, 139–40
home offices, 251–52
home ownership:
as beginning of financial freedom, 8, 125
down payments and, 126–30
mortgages and, 126–27, 129
for your personal use, 125–30
homes:
advantages of, 232
five-year retirement plan and, 258–61
generating cash flow from, 240–42
for lease, 128–29, 240–42
median prices of, 8, 44
rental, 19
using the equity in, 139–47
Hope, Bob, 25
"hot" real estate markets, 93
housing, see rental homes; single-family homes
Housing and Urban Development (HUD) Department, U.S., 129
Houston, Tex., 275–76
"how" and "why," difference between knowing, 273
humor, sense of, 36–37
Humphrey, Ann R., 118

imagination:
sense of, 35
visualization and, 48–50
income, rental:
gross operating, 80
gross scheduled rental, 78
net operating, 84–85
other sources of, 78
total gross, 78
income and expenses analysis, 77–85
income approach, to determination of value, 93–96
income-producing properties:
bargains in, 53–60
definition and types of, 18–19
determining potential income from, 59–60, 87–98
four kinds of financial returns from, 87–88
income and expenses analysis of, 77–85
management problems and, 62–65
physical problems with, 65
as safest investment, 18
income tax:
cash flow before, 85
deductions on, 60
lease/option properties and, 201
options and, 188, 190
professional help with, 226
savings on, 88, 89
inflation, 89, 90, 260
inheritance, 66–67
inspection companies, 97
insurance, property, 81
insurance, title, 108–9
insurance agents, 59
intentions, 42, 43, 44
goals compared with, 23
linking of reasons with, 32–33
long-term, 271–72

About the Author

ROBERT G. ALLEN is one of America's most famous and most influential financial advisors. After graduating with an MBA from Brigham Young University in 1974, Allen began making small rest estate investments, transforming his tiny nest egg into a large, multimillion-dollar net worth in a few short years. He shared his powerful system with the public in the #1 *New York Times* bestseller *Nothing Down,* which has sold more than a million hardcover copies. Following that success, his other bestselling books include *Creating Wealth, Multiple Streams of Income,* and *The One-Minute Millionaire.* For more than twenty years, Allen has been successfully sharing his wealth-building techniques in frequent seminars throughout the fifty states and Canada.